MASS–CUSTOMISED CITIES

Guest-Edited
by TOM VEREBES

ARCHITECTURAL DESIGN
November/December 2015

Profile
No 238

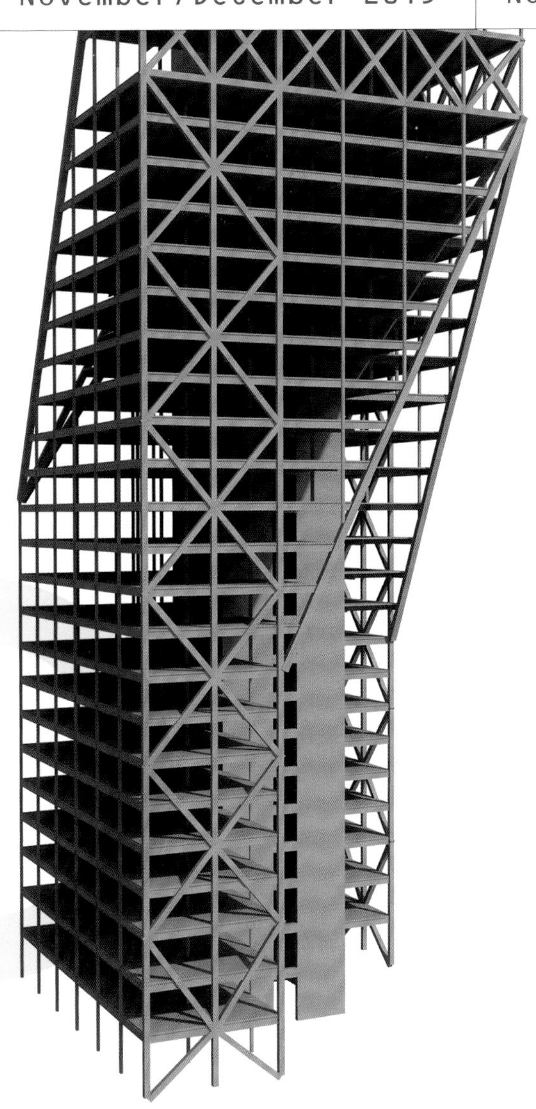

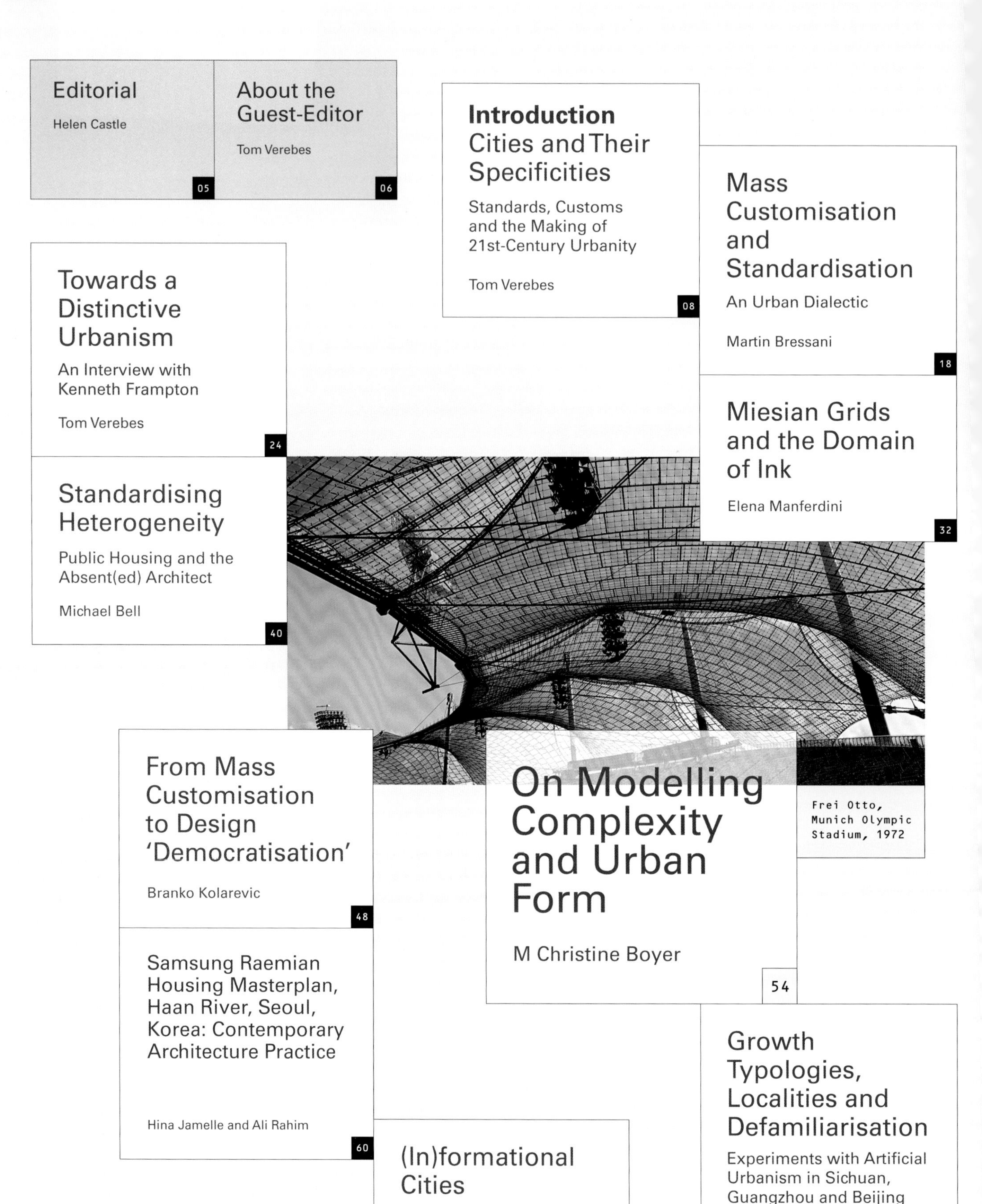

Frei Otto, Munich Olympic Stadium, 1972

ISSN 0003-8504
ISBN 978-1118-915646

Guest-Edited by **Tom Verebes**

Archi-Union Architects, City of Breeze, Shenzhen Bay, Shenzhen, China, 2014

Editorial Offices
John Wiley & Sons
25 John Street
London WC1N 2BS
UK

T +44 (0)20 8326 3800

Editor
Helen Castle

Managing Editor (Freelance)
Caroline Ellerby

Production Editor
Elizabeth Gongde

Prepress
Artmedia, London

Art Direction + Design
CHK Design:
Christian Küsters
Sophie Troppmair
Christos Kontogeorgos

Printed in Italy by Printer Trento Srl

Front and back covers: OCEAN CN Consultancy Network, Masterplan aerial view, Umekita Second Development Area invited competition entry, Osaka, Japan, 2013–14. © OCEAN CN Consultancy Network

Inside front cover: Contemporary Architecture Practice, Samsung Raemian Housing Masterplan, Haan River, Seoul, Korea, 2011–. © Ali Rahim and Hina Jamelle/Contemporary Architecture Practice

06/2015

ARCHITECTURAL DESIGN

November/December 2015

Profile No. 238

Journal Customer Services
For ordering information, claims and any enquiry concerning your journal subscription please go to www.wileycustomerhelp.com/ask or contact your nearest office.

Americas
E: cs-journals@wiley.com
T: +1 781 388 8598 or +1 800 835 6770 (toll free in the USA & Canada)

Europe, Middle East and Africa
E: cs-journals@wiley.com
T: +44 (0) 1865 778315

Asia Pacific
E: cs-journals@wiley.com
T: +65 6511 8000

Japan (for Japanese-speaking support)
E: cs-japan@wiley.com
T: +65 6511 8010 or 005 316 50 480 (toll-free)

Visit our Online Customer Help available in 7 languages at www.wileycustomerhelp.com/ask

Print ISSN: 0003-8504
Online ISSN: 1554-2769

Prices are for six issues and include postage and handling charges. Individual-rate subscriptions must be paid by personal cheque or credit card. Individual-rate subscriptions may not be resold or used as library copies.

All prices are subject to change without notice.

Identification Statement
Periodicals Postage paid at Rahway, NJ 07065. Air freight and mailing in the USA by Mercury Media Processing, 1850 Elizabeth Avenue, Suite C, Rahway, NJ 07065, USA.

USA Postmaster
Please send address changes to *Architectural Design*, c/o Mercury Media Processing, 1634 E. Elizabeth Avenue, Linden, NJ 07036, USA.

Rights and Permissions
Requests to the Publisher should be addressed to:
Permissions Department
John Wiley & Sons Ltd
The Atrium
Southern Gate
Chichester
West Sussex PO19 8SQ
UK

F: +44 (0) 1243 770 620
E: Permissions@wiley.com

Subscribe to AD
AD is published bimonthly and is available to purchase on both a subscription basis and as individual volumes at the following prices.

Prices
Individual copies: £24.99 / US$39.95
Individual issues on AD App for iPad: £9.99 / US$13.99
Mailing fees for print may apply

Annual Subscription Rates
Student: £75 / US$117 print only
Personal: £120 / US$189 print and iPad access
Institutional: £212 / US$398 print or online
Institutional: £244 / US$457 combined print and online
6-issue subscription on AD App for iPad: £44.99 / US$64.99

EDITORIAL

HELEN CASTLE

There is no doubt that cities around the world are at a crisis point, as they fail to keep up with the demand for housing. Globally, the official figure for the number of people who live in slums is 863 million, but this is more likely to be 1.3 billion and, if current trends continue, by 2050 the world's slum population will reach well over 2 billion.[1] This is a problem no longer confined to the poorer sections of society; as global cities such as London and New York become investment magnets for the internationally wealthy, the full force of the impact of the shortage of affordable housing is being experienced by middle-income earners whose salaries have not kept up with property values and rents.[2] There is the very real danger that in the endeavour to provide basic provision, which in itself seems to be an increasingly ungraspable challenge, the quality of the built environment – whether individual buildings or urban spaces – will get pushed further and further down the agenda. It seems almost inevitable that by default highly standardised housing is rolled out with mass-production methods at an industrial scale.

Whereas mass-produced standardisation is most commonly associated with postwar public housing, speculative development has also defaulted to a dangerous level of uniformity in its bid to be ever more cost effective and profitable. Michael Bell (pp 40–47) vividly describes how in the US federal decentralisation and the introduction of voucher systems and private-public partnerships since the 1980s and 1990s has led not to the anticipated entrepreneurial emancipation of housing provision, but to an impoverishment in the design and planning qualities of schemes. In Seoul, construction companies have had such a grip on development that it has resulted in profoundly repetitive housing towers; in 2009, the mayor of the city interceded, requiring variation (see p 62). For uniformity is bad not only for the individual and society, but also for the economic and political life of the city.

This issue is a call for arms by Guest-Editor Tom Verebes for architects to embrace the possibilities of engaging new technologies to create differentiation at the urban scale. As Verebes states in his introduction, 'advances in computational design and fabrication technologies ... have largely been limited to the scale of discrete buildings, pavilions, interiors, furniture and products, and remain largely untested in urbanism'. This can be a differentiation that incorporates the required density of rapidly urbanised cities, like those in Southeast Asia, as described in Rocker-Lange Architects's ingenious Shanghai Lilong Tower Urbanism project (pp 76-9), which uses computational adaptable systems to recreate the urban qualities of the traditional low-rise city of access lanes and workshops in its stepped podium. The possibilities of emerging computer-aided fabrication and robotic techniques are also explored at the end of the issue in a feature on specialist material fabricator E-Grow and an article on the work of Gramazio Kohler Research.

But are formal differentiation and technological innovation sufficient for a city to thrive and ultimately survive? In the Counterpoint to the issue, Colin Fournier puts forward an argument for a different type of variation – as dependent on social and political forces as material input. ⅅ

Notes

1. John Perry, 'There's a Global Housing Crisis and Politicians Must do More to Tackle it', The Guardian, 10 June 2015: www.theguardian.com/global-development-professionals-network/2015/jun/10/from-beds-in-sheds-to-super-slums-theres-a-global-housing-crisis-and-politicians-must-do-more-to-tackle-it.
2. Clive Coleman, 'Buddy Can You Spare $2m? New York's Housing Crisis', BBC News, 8 September 2015: www.bbc.co.uk/news/world-us-canada-34172282.

OCEAN CN Consultancy Network, dotA Architects and the Hong Kong Parametric Design Association

Liantang/Heung Yuen Wai Boundary Control Point Terminal Building

Hong Kong–Shenzhen, China

2011

Proposal for an iconic border-crossing facility between Hong Kong and Shenzhen. The project confronts the dichotomous characteristics of a border and aims to correlate the categories of the artificial and the natural. A singular building straddles the border and channels the vast flows of people, cars and coaches.

OCEAN CN Consultancy Network and SED Landscape Architects

Xiangmi Park

Shenzhen, Guangdong Province, China

2014

Proposal for an urban park, in which the specificities of the site – its topography, hydrological organisation, surrounding urban perimeter and other parameters – help to generate a highly distinctive scheme.

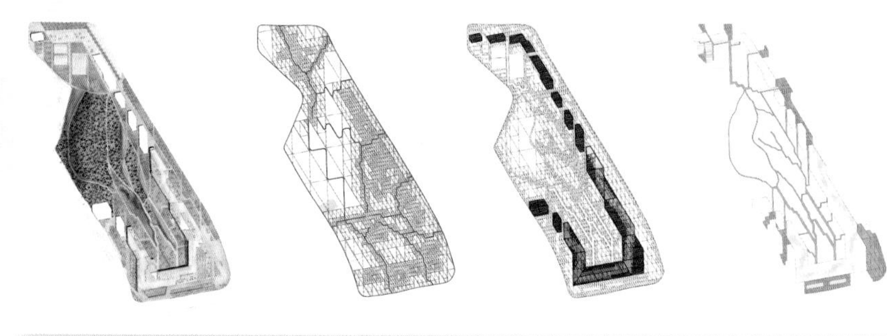

OCEAN CN Consultancy Network and dotA Architects

Yan Jiao Hua Run 4D City Masterplan

Hebei, China

2012

This proposal for a 25-square-kilometre (10-square-mile) masterplan extension aims to create a new heterogeneous form of urbanism through the differentiation of orientation and sizes of plots, blocks and lots, the mixing of uses with coherent identities, and the regulation of heights across the entire area.

ABOUT THE

GUEST-EDITOR

TOM VEREBES

Tom Verebes's extensive and longstanding engagement with urbanism spans an academic career as well as professional experience in Asia, Europe, North America and the Middle East. His sustained research on the implications of computational design and production technologies for urbanism has distinguished his work from a generation of computational designers whose output ranges between smaller-scale experiments and larger iconic architecture. His experimental design approach has been applied to increasingly more complex and larger-scale design issues and endeavours.

He is the Creative Director of OCEAN CN Consultancy Network, a Hong Kong-based specialist design consultancy practice that he established out of OCEAN UK Design Ltd, the London node of OCEAN, which he co-founded in 1995. At the University of Hong Kong, he served as Associate Dean for Teaching & Learning (2011–14), and has been Associate Professor in the Department of Architecture since 2009. He was formerly Co-Director of the post-professional Master's (Architecture & Urbanism) programme at the Design Research Lab (DRL) at the Architectural Association (AA) in London, where he taught from 1996 to 2009. He has been the Director of the AA Shanghai Visiting School for ten consecutive years, and was previously Director and founder of the AA DLab (2006–7) and an AA Diploma Unit Master. Between 2004 and 2006, he was a Guest Professor at the Staatliche Akademie der Bildenden Künste Stuttgart. He studied architecture at McGill University in Montreal, the Laboratory of Primary Studies in Architecture (LoPSiA) in Paris and Briey in northeastern France, as well as at the AA, and is currently working on his PhD at the Vietnam campus of RMIT University, Melbourne.

His practice-based design research work with OCEAN D and OCEAN CN has been widely published, and exhibited in over 50 venues worldwide, including the Venice, Beijing, Hong Kong, Shenzhen and Seville biennales, the 'Zoomorphic' exhibition at the Victoria & Albert Museum, London (2003–4), 'Latent Utopias' (Landesmuseum Joanneum, Graz, Austria, 2003), 'Experimental Architecture' (FRAC Centre, Orléans, France, 2003) and 'Sign as Surface' (Artists Space, New York, 2003).

He has lectured extensively in Europe, North America, Asia, Africa, Australia and the Middle East, and contributed to over 140 publications, including authored books, book chapters, articles and project features. His recent books include *Masterplanning the Adaptive City: Computational Urbanism in the Twenty-First Century* (Routledge, 2013) and *New Computational Paradigms in Architecture* (Tsinghua University Press, 2012). ⅅ

INTRODUCTION

TOM VEREBES

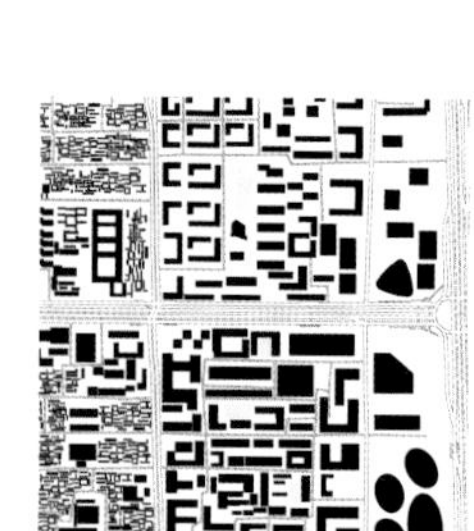

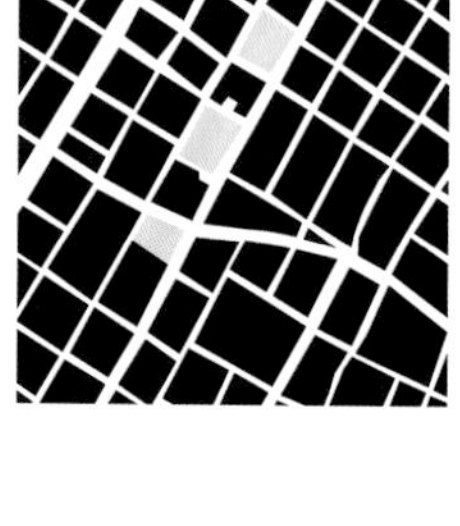

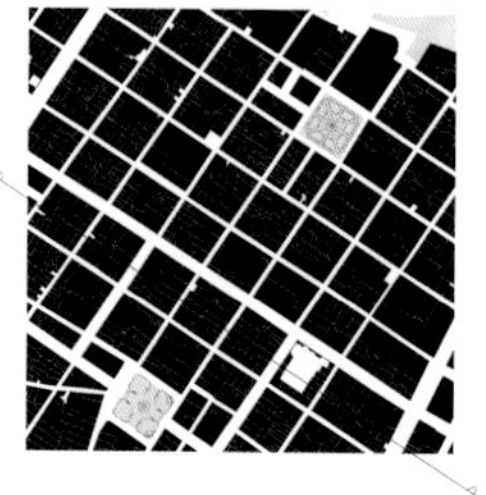

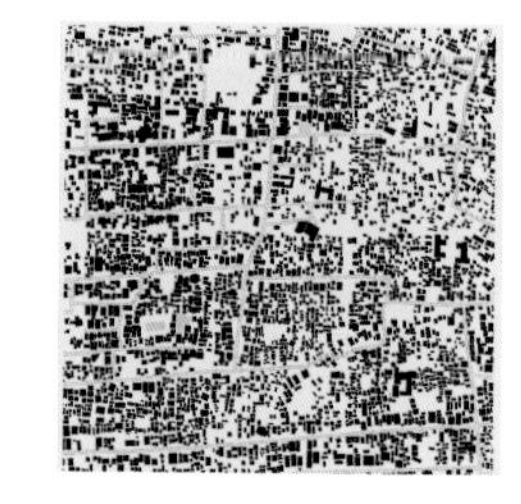

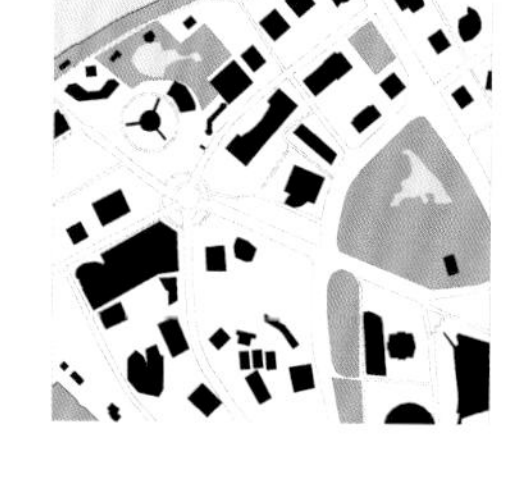

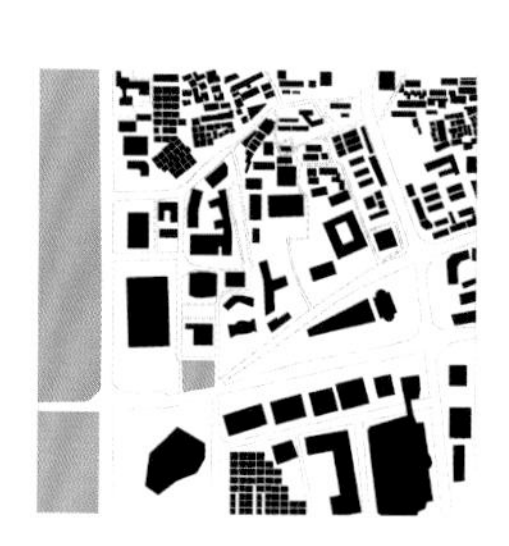

Tom Verebes

Cities and Specificities

MArch Elective Seminar

University of Hong Kong

2015

Array of 25 city plans, demonstrating the inherent specificities of cities worldwide. MArch seminar professor: Tom Verebes. Students: Chow Tung Tiffany, Katarina Camacho Ednalaguim, Jiang Hejia, Lau Man Wai Vivian and Lau Yik Tung.

Cities and Their Specificities

Modern Industry had therefore itself to take in hand the machine, its characteristic instrument of production, and to construct machines by machines.

— Karl Marx, *Capital*, vol I, 1887, p 384[1]

This title of AD, *Mass-Customised Cities*, locates two interrelated contemporary problematics at the intersection of the ubiquitous uniformity of cities with the causal legacy of the 20th-century industrial paradigm of standardised mass production. Given the unprecedented speed and seemingly unstoppable pace of city building in the 21st century, a paramount challenge to overcome is the convergence of sameness among cities worldwide. Despite the past five decades of postmodernity, and the disciplinary promiscuity and posturing with architectural complexity and diversity, there is today a critical lack of any substantive theories of difference across the design disciplines of the built environment with which to guide cities towards the greater coherence of heterogeneous and individuated attributes. At the core of this problem lie questions as to the ways in which the qualities of cities can be amplified and differentiated to become identifiable rather than indistinguishable, during the most prolific era of urbanisation ever to occur.

This issue speculates on a research gap in the urban implications of emerging technologies indicative of a significant transition in production paradigms that has revolutionised how architecture is conceived, practised, built and experienced. In the past two decades, advances in computational design and fabrication technologies, the methods and applications of which are well rehearsed in architectural design, practice, teaching and research, have largely been limited to the scale of discrete buildings, pavilions, interiors, furniture and products, and remain largely untested in urbanism. This AD issue forgoes yet another exposé of a niche thematic area of algorithmic architecture or numerically controlled fabrication, and as such is less concerned with the leading edge of architecture than it is with the future of cities. Through a survey of disciplinary design research approaches, the aim is to hazard timely insights concerning the latent potentials and repercussions of computational design and production processes when ramped up to the vast scale of 21st-century cities.

Standards, Customs and Old Habits

Confronting the apparent problem of urban homogenisation, the issue intentionally provokes the urban equivalent of the ideation of choice and identity for a mass populace in late capitalism. This novel territory is the domain of the consumer, the end user and the hacker, rather than that of political authorities, investors or designers. Perhaps less focused on the personalisation of standardised cars, clothes and other mass-produced products, the term 'mass customisation', despite more than a hint of an overtone of crass commercialism, challenges the legacy of uniformity as the hallmark of Fordist standardisation. This AD questions how new technologies are enabling an important shift away from mass production to increasingly bespoke and custom-designed production. Whereas the introduction of standardisation and mass-production processes in the 20th century saw the industrial city take on repetitious and homogeneous qualities through the replication of architectural components, non-standard bespoke production systems hold out the promise of realising buildings with distinctive attributes through the differentiation of serial production and the variation of simple parts leading to larger and more complex architectural assemblages. In the transition from standardised production, in which universalised, uniform and repetitious spaces are by-products, the consequences of numerically controlled prototypical practices for the scale and complexity of urbanism are addressed.

Throughout the 20th century, mechanised standardisation pervaded nearly all industries, driven by efficiencies of minimising cost and time, and reducing complexity. Evidence of how 20th-century mass production failed to achieve sufficient variation and differentiation to express the world's diversity and heterogeneity can be found in the pervasive Corbusian architecture of mass housing, or the ubiquity of office towers in central business districts worldwide. At the core of the ambition of non-standard design lies a critique of universality and monotony of the Modernist industrial paradigm. Cities are inextricably tied to a society's model of production, and the prevalence of generic urbanism comes out of the legacy of globalised, standardised mass production. Capitalism's perpetual paradox, as both Marxists and Libertarians may agree, lies between unpredictability and, hence, instability, and attenuated eras of productivity. So-called 'late capitalism' has spawned innovative trajectories, driven by technologies targeting variation over reproduction.

Searching for Cities with Qualities

The indistinguishable and featureless facsimile is a longstanding quandary in urbanism. Modernism was initiated and sustained by the paradigm of mass production, by easily reproducible architecture and reductive urban planning. The Modernists, as Lewis Mumford lamented, in their will to install mechanical order, 'confuse mere formalism and regularity with purposefulness, and irregularity with intellectual confusion or technical incompetence'.[2] Functionalism, or the economic law of utility, depended upon the mechanised decomposition of repetitive tasks. Le Corbusier wrote in 1923: 'Standardisation is imposed by the law of selection and is an economic and social necessity.'[3] His Ville Radieuse (Radiant City) model for Paris had been reproduced ad infinitum for nearly a century. An even more extreme modernist historical moment is the repetitive unitary spatiality inherent to Ludwig Hilberseimer's High-Rise City project of 1924. Since the demise of International Modernism, research on the city has given rise to a plethora of post-Fordist neologisms with which to redefine the paradigm of the city more precisely to what it has evolved to become. From the Metropolis of the early 20th century we have taxonomies such as the Megalopolis, the Global City,

Greg Lynn FORM
Embryological House
1999

Greg Lynn, an 'early adopter' of computational design technologies, designed this prototypical series of houses as a differentiated set of spaces and systems, demonstrating some of the conceptual ideas of customisation in relation to the notion of a repetitive housing configuration.

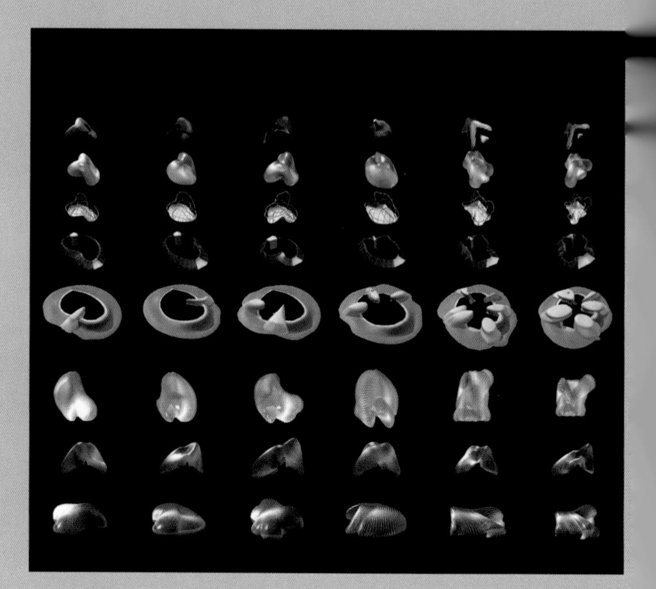

Archizoom
No-Stop City
1968

In this polemical 'paper project' by the Italian Radical Architecture group Archizoom, a typewriter was used to display mechanical inscriptions, indicating the notion of a 'city without qualities'.

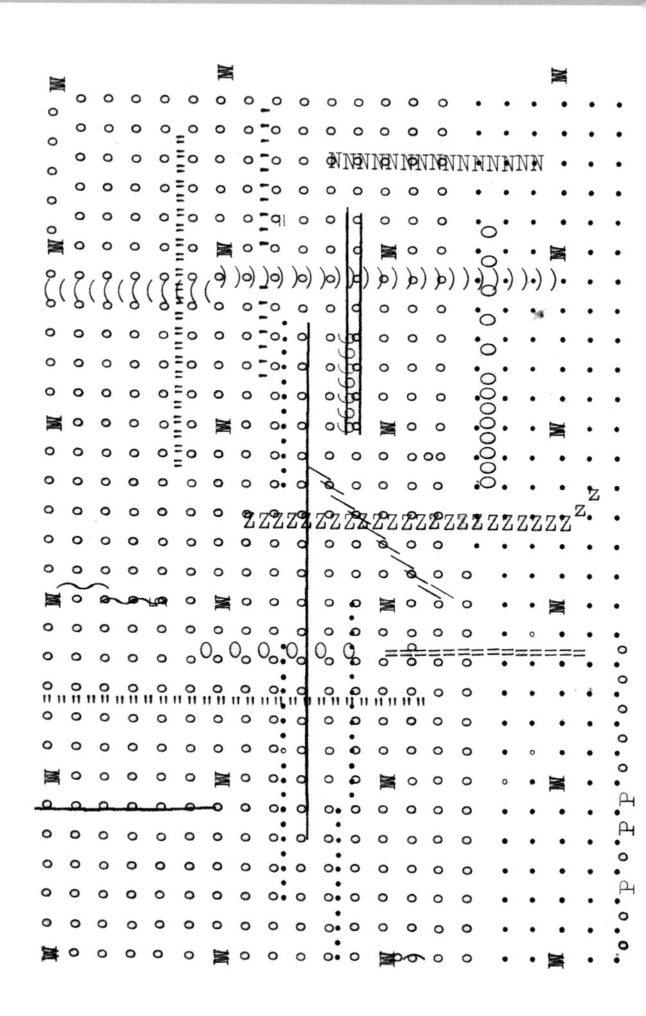

Madelon Vriesendorp

The City of the Captive Globe

Delirious New York

1978

below: Painting by Vriesendorp, published in Rem Koolhaas's book *Delirious New York*, depicting the inherent architectural heterogeneity of the urban grid of Manhattan. The urbanism of this painting is expressed as the collaged aggregation of the radical differences in the architecture of each block.

Ford Motor Company

Highland Park

Detroit, Michigan

1914

bottom: A seminal monument to assembly-line standardisation, as the first and largest of the Ford Motor Company's factories to mass-produce the Model T car from 1909.

the Network City, the Megacity, the Generic City, the Smart City, the Eco City and the Adaptive City, each suggesting that in order to study the status of urbanity and to be projective towards its future, one must first rename it. This issue of Ꭰ aims to locate alternatives to the many early postmodern guiding theorisations of cities rooted in Collage (Colin Rowe and Fred Koetter), Memory (Aldo Rossi) and Events (Bernard Tschumi), or the learnings from Las Vegas, the delirium of New York, or any number of other local models. Even among the other recent Ꭰ titles on urbanism, '*Cities*' are nominated with prefixes such as '*Digital*', or '*Typological*', or chart out the '*New Urban China*'. There is ample evidence of a call for postmodern fragmentation to be theorised, again, as a call for the *Specificity of Cities* in response to the failure of Modernism to universalise. The Futurists declared over 100 years ago how 'each generation will have to build its own city'.[4] In Archizoom's No-Stop City project of 1968, the mechanical reproduction of characterless objects and spaces is literally imprinted onto paper by a primitive typewriter, describing 'a city without qualities', non-figural and void of substantive design criteria:

... a city without qualities for a man (finally) without qualities – that is, without compromise – a freed society (freed even from architecture) similar to the great monochrome surfaces of Mark Rothko; vast velvet, open oceans in which the sweet drowning of man within the immense dimensions of mass society is represented.'[5]

A thousand cars—one day's output at the great Ford factory. The line is nearly eight hundred feet long

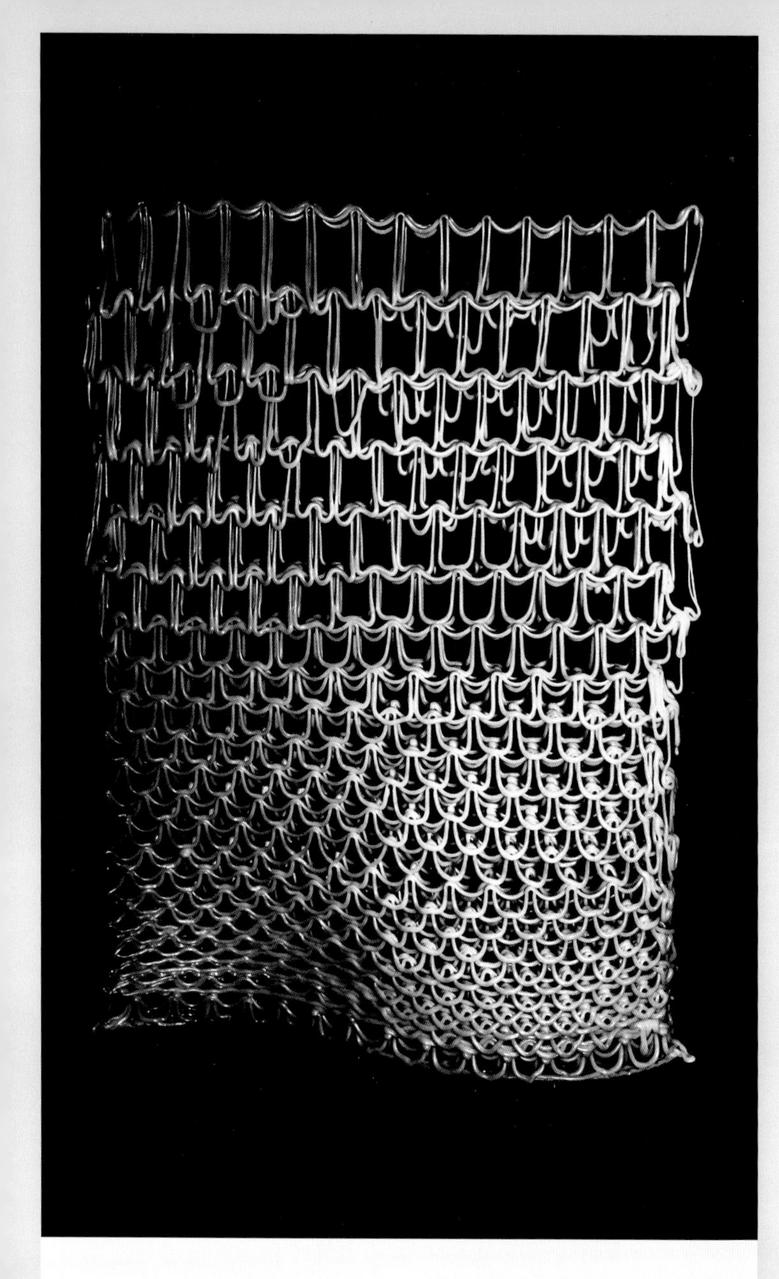

Ellen Duff, Jordan Lutren and Ryan Scanlan

Continuous Line

Studio Manninger-del Campo

Taubman College of Architecture and Urban Planning

University of Michigan

2015

Material prototype produced with a robotic arm deploying soft polyethylene which cures to acquire rigid material properties.

As a result of the inception of the digital into the city, William J Mitchell insisted some 20 years ago how 'the very idea of the city is challenged and must be reconceived'.[6] The attributes of the taxonomy here announced, a Distinctive Urbanism, stands in opposition to generic and ubiquitous urbanism, biasing the specific and unique over the general and reproducible.[7] This AD seeks to expose the transformative cultural effects instigated by contemporary industrial change.

Globalisation, Urbanisation and the Asian Century

The 21st century is known as the 'Urban Century' as well as the 'Asian Century', a durational increment at the confluence of the forces of globalisation and the unprecedented extent and rate of urbanisation in Asia. Amid mass urbanisation in China and the declared imperative to house 300 million new urbanites in the coming two decades, there is both an exceptional opportunity and a huge responsibility presented by rapidly urbanising contexts. The sheer volume of construction and quantity of new cities being built, in the middle of nowhere, out of nothing, and in effect without history, begs the questions of how to derail the effacing force of blankness, to install an invigorated sense of contemporary character and identity in the countless new cities being built in Asia. Contemporary Chinese urbanism is not so far off from Branzi's articulation of the qualities, or rather lack of them, in Archizoom's No-Stop City, which he brands as a 'city without architecture'.[8] The by-products of the haste to urbanise include widespread erasure and lateral urban expansion, in Chinese a phenomenon colloquially called '*tan da bing*', or 'making a big pancake'.[9] Lewis Mumford lamented the wastefulness of rapid urbanisation, in which he saw cities as becoming consumable and indeed expendable. The themes and arguments presented in this issue are rooted in longstanding yet unresolved problematics, and together with their associated paradigmatic crises will have imminent practical consequences for the rest of the developing and developed world.

The Legacies of Henry Ford and Frederick Taylor

Two important historical paradigms emerged as a result of the Industrial Revolution – Taylorism and Fordism – which, in turn, contributed immeasurably to the standardisation and mechanisation of cities. Taylorism arose as the scientific management of rationalised industrial work tasks into discrete, measurable, simpler segmented components, and was coupled with Henry Ford's appropriation of the assembly line from the food industry towards a new application of routinised and standardised production of the Model T car from 1909 onwards. These enabled repetitive production, routinisation and standardisation to take command.[10] Sigfried Giedion, in *Mechanisation Takes Command: A Contribution to an Anonymous History* (1948), consolidates his heralding of the industrialisation of a mechanised construction industry, earlier in the century, through demonstrations of mechanised slaughterhouses, bakeries and other industrialised processes.[11] Transiting

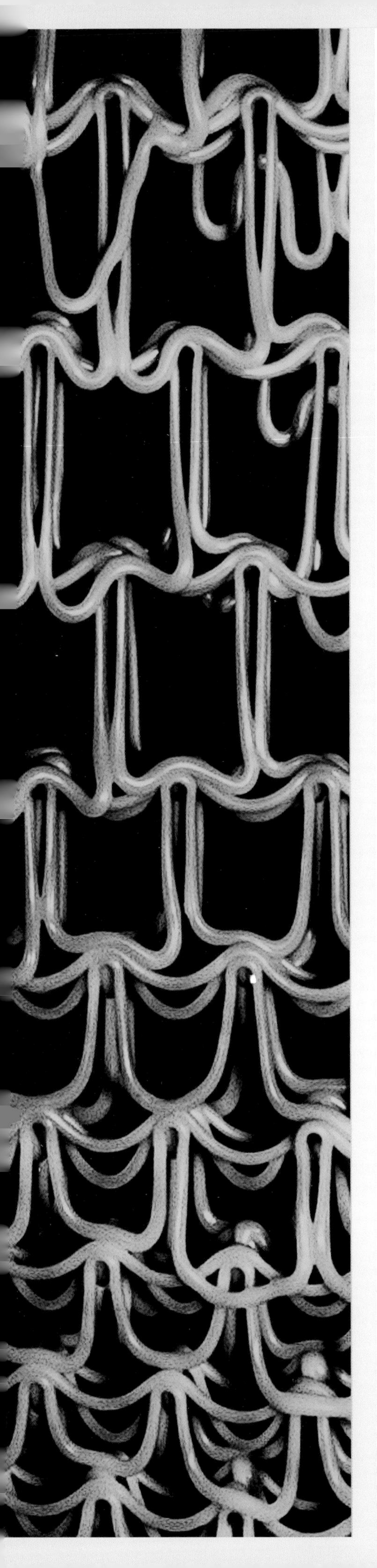

from the 'batch production' workshop, the mechanised factory, with the new affordances of its division of labour, reigned supreme over the industrial workshop with its limited capacity to produce smaller, more distinct and bespoke batches of production.[12] Just over a century ago, the Deutscher Werkbund introduced a new potential to standardise and repeat components of products through mass production made for mass consumption, relegating to history the notion of the bespoke on-off product made by a single craftsman for a single consumer. Modernism relied on the inherent mechanisation and standardisation of Fordist mass-production assembly-line processes and Taylorist rationalisation and routinisation.

The transition from the workshop to the mechanised factory resulted in the deskilling of workers and the diminishing of craft. In the midst of this current industrial and informational evolution, Branko Kolarevic (who is also a contributor to this issue – see pp 48–53) summarises the paradox of new techniques and methods of 'digital making' that he claims 'are reaffirming the long forgotten notions of craft'.[13] The contemporary fabrication workshop is indicative of the re-emergence of the bespoke, articulated by dialectics such as repetition versus differentiation, or stability versus flexibility. Technology transfer, interdisciplinarity, and developments in specialisation are products of postmodern fragmentation. Along with its new methods, machines and techniques, the information era represents a new industrial revolution, despite being an unevenly distributed paradigm shift, and one that has not achieved mass integration, nor fully uprooted earlier production models. Dedlef Mertins warned about the constraints of current technologies and epistemes in the recurrent pursuit of paradigm shifts, and the planning of cities is still hounded by standardisation and mechanisation in the name of efficiency and profit.[14] The Fordist and Taylorist legacies of standardisation and bureaucratic routinisation have prevailed, to a greater extent, within the practices of urban planning rather than in architecture, especially in east Asia. In the absence of definitive turning points and adequate and accepted universal 'theories of transition' in industry, an evolutionary interpretation of transitions features a 'mixture of continuity and change' from one dominant phase to the next.[15] The post-Fordist debate of the early digital era often heralded epoch-making transformations in how architecture was conceived and made. Of the many theories of technological transition from Fordist to post-Fordist production, the age of 'flexible accumulation' is defined by flexibility of labour patterns and greater adaptability to market demands and instabilities, and to disparate geographies, through networking and outsourcing.[16] The ongoing evolution of consumption patterns in terms of increasing variation stands in opposition to standardisation and its relation to economies of scale, both of which can no longer be fulfilled through mass-production methods.[17]

As early as 1969, Nicholas Negroponte forecasted automated 'machines to assist the design process' with the capacity to work with evolutionary processes to generate unique and optimal outcomes.[18] And Lars Spuybroek heralded the coming of 'variable modulation' over a decade ago, echoing Gilbert Simondon's second-order cybernetic discourse of interactive, intelligent variegation, and thereby liberating moulding processes from 'the doom of identical copies'.[19] This new material culture points towards more specific and, hence, non-generic architecture, to serial rather than singular design outcomes, and the mass customisation of products.

This issue of AD features a series of essays, interviews and projects, with contributions by leading theorists, historians, architects, engineers and fabricators, which collectively seek alternatives to the legacy of standardised, repetitive modes of spatial and material production. The projects and essays speculate upon the implications and relationships between the cumulative tasks of planners, architects, engineers and other building professionals, the economic and political system, and material modes of production, manufacturing and assembly, which altogether contribute towards the production of cities.

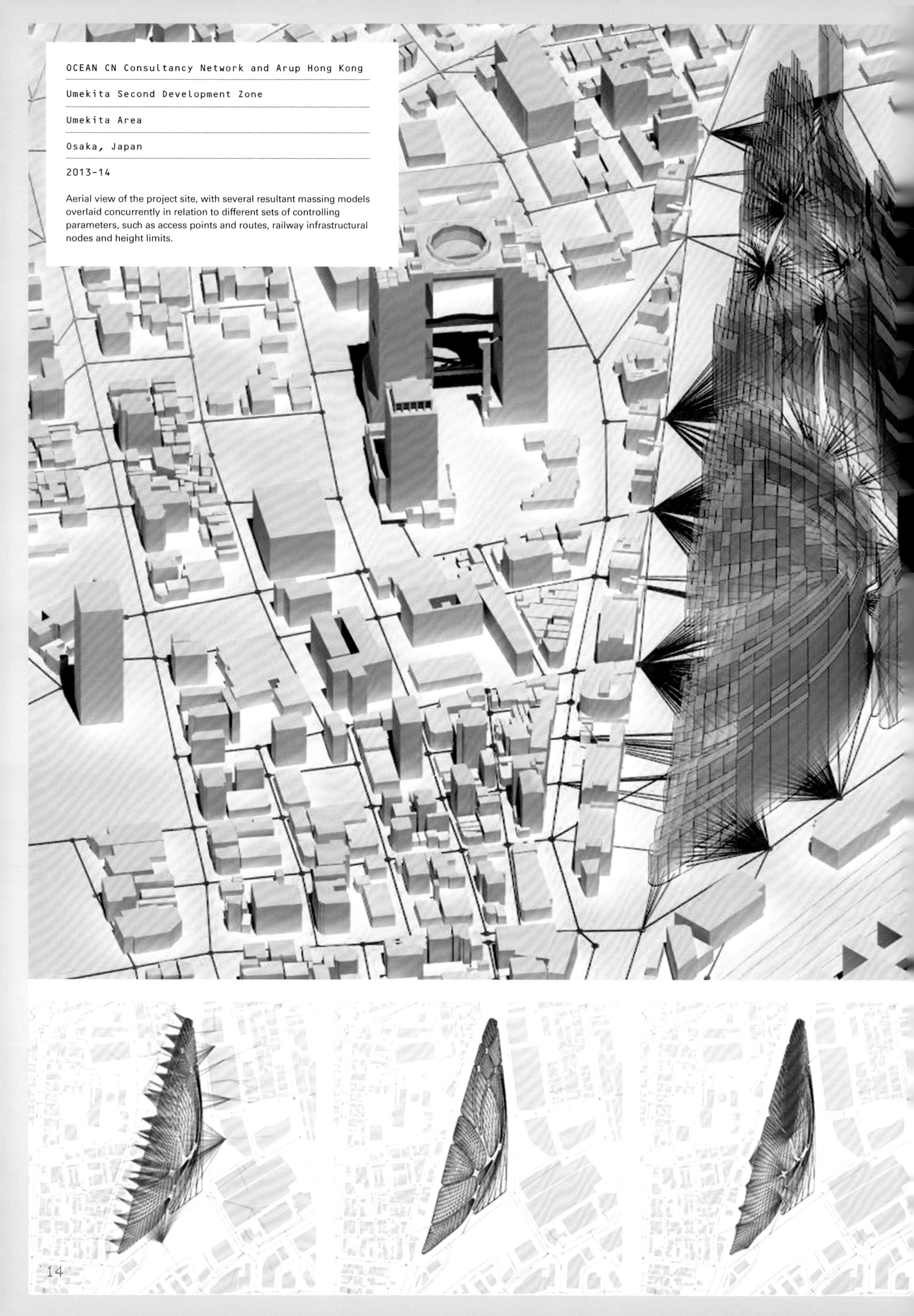

OCEAN CN Consultancy Network and Arup Hong Kong

Umekita Second Development Zone

Umekita Area

Osaka, Japan

2013-14

Aerial view of the project site, with several resultant massing models overlaid concurrently in relation to different sets of controlling parameters, such as access points and routes, railway infrastructural nodes and height limits.

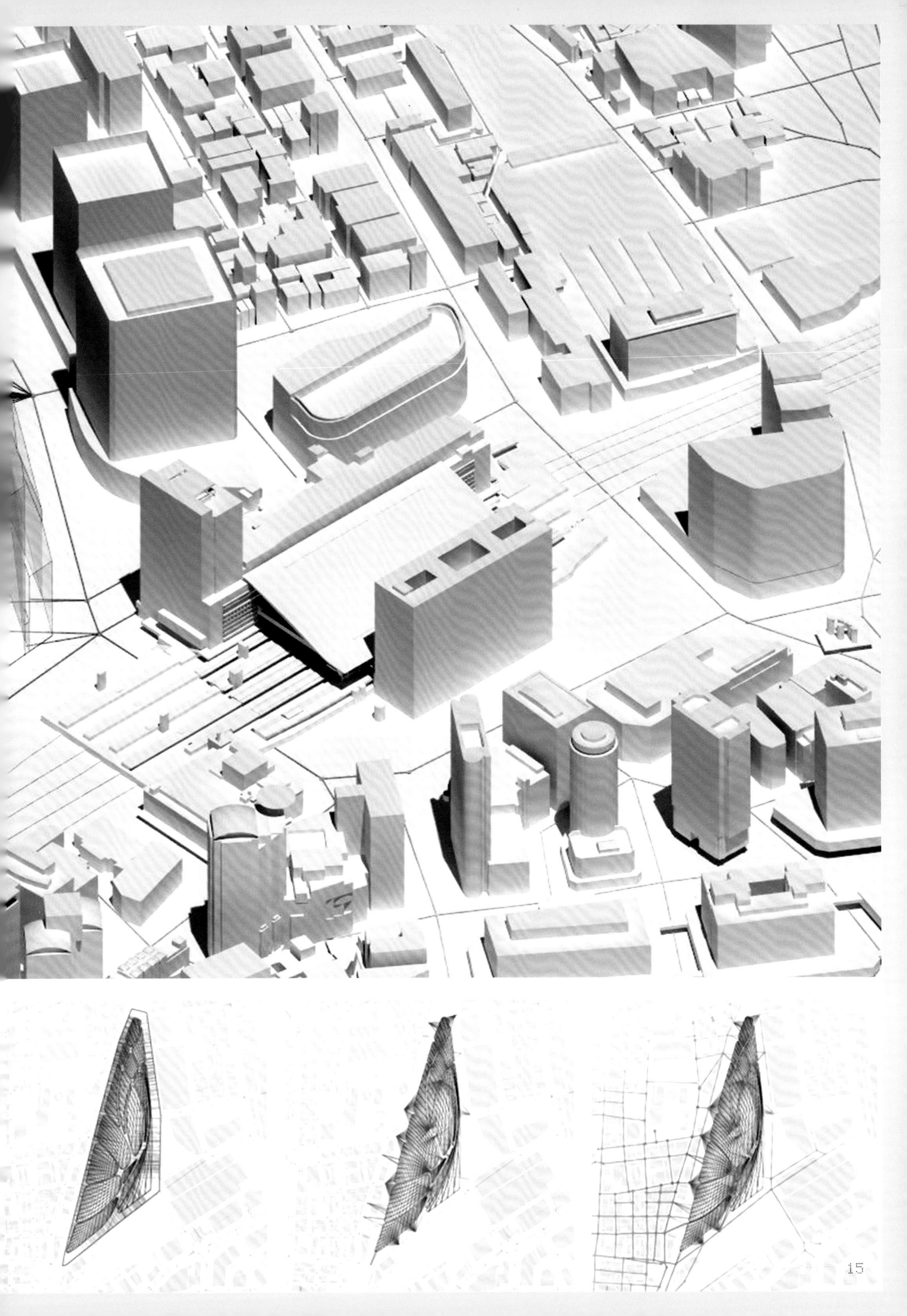

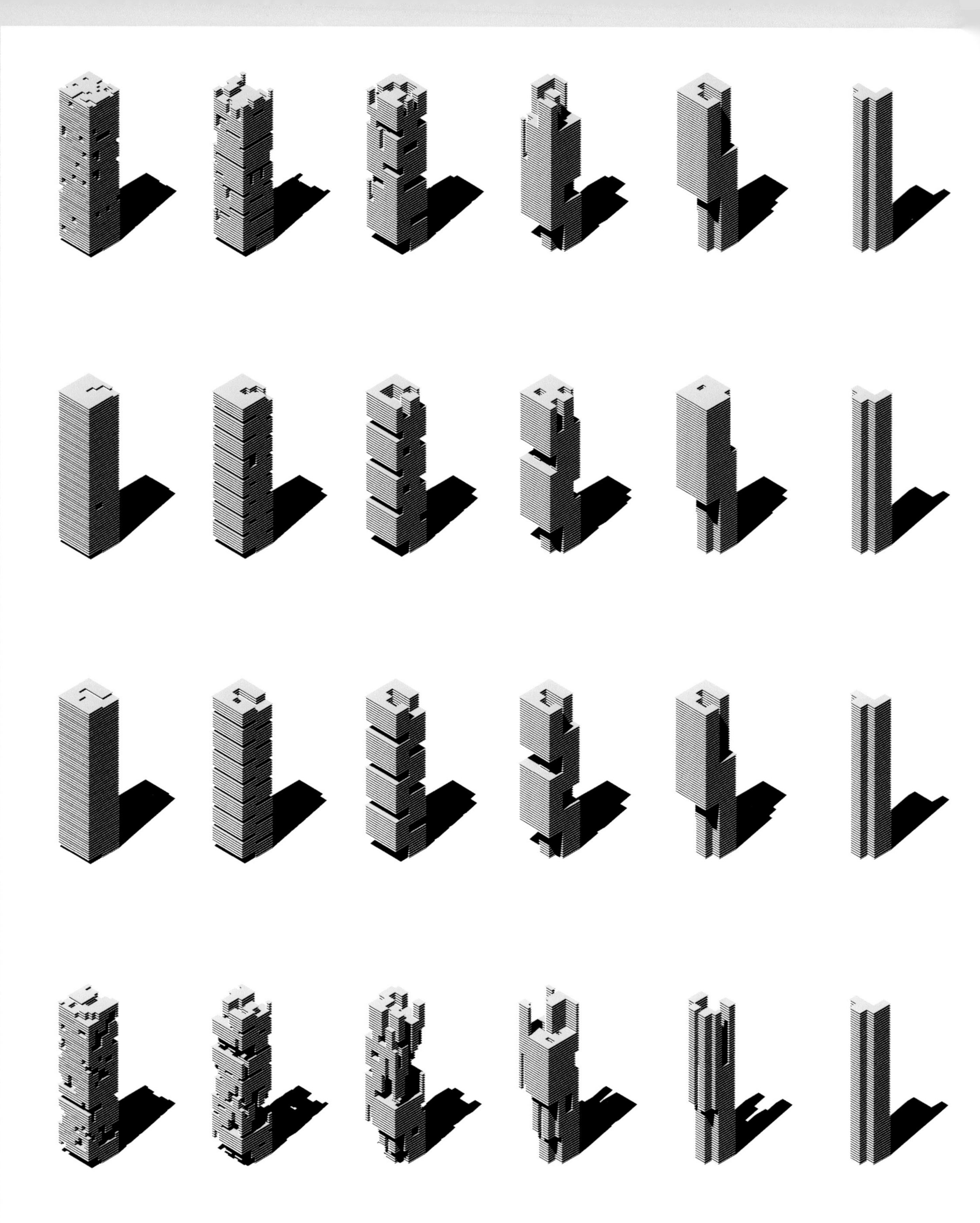

Rocker-Lange Architects

Differentiated series of towers

Hong Kong Architecture Biennale

2012

A differentiated series of towers, indicating variations in solid interior spaces and exterior void green spaces, designed as an exhibition research project.

Navigating Histories and Theories of Industry and the City

Taking a speculative position towards architecture and cities in the future, the issue dissects the histories and theories of standardised mass production to speculate on the emerging potential of associative design systems linked to an increasingly large scale of automated manufacturing. Customs are equivalent to manners, but more pejoratively can be understood to be accepted habits and traditions, and in time they make history. Martin Bressani posits how the city, both in medieval times and in the potentiality of today and the future, has the capacity to 'self-generate' (see pp 18–23). The pre-standardised model of custom urban spaces is returning, he argues, through the application of evolutionary computation and democratic participatory processes. In an interview with Kenneth Frampton (see pp 24–31), the self-proclaimed rear-guard position of his formulation of Critical Regionalism more than 30 years ago is queried in the search for clues as to how distinctive forms of urbanity can be generated today.

Industrial Paradigms: Drivers of Change

If this AD is less about architecture than it is about cities, it is also less about the leading edge of computational design and more about its link to engineering, industrial production methods, specialist knowledge and expertise in material fabrication, and the potential of these workflows to impact on the design of cities. The contributors to this issue of AD in various ways collectively theorise computational urbanism through the instrumentality of computational interfaces for their capacity to regulate design variation, and highlight the material possibilities of a new paradigm of participatory design inputs directly from the end users. The material fabric of cities will no doubt be influenced by the radical inception of massive databases, information systems and interfaces with which to search, navigate and personalise the space of the contemporary city. The algorithmic codes that underlie contemporary design processes are analogous to genetic processes, embedding computational coding as a basis upon which to generate, analyse, provide feedback and hence build in the capacity for intelligence in the resulting form of an artefact.[20] M Christine Boyer's essay (pp 54–9) investigates the historical roots of the accelerating capacity to model complex urban behaviour through simulation models with iterative feedback loops; and the practical ramifications of the theoretical postulations are explicated by the design projects featured throughout the issue. This body of work explores variable material fabrication at various scales and applications. In his essay (pp 48–53), Branko Kolarevic confronts consumer culture, individuality and sameness by surveying the 'democratisation of design' through mass customisation, from products to furniture and architectural components, to the differentiation of mass housing. In the interview with Jerry Ku and Philip Vernon of E-Grow (pp 114–21), a specialist in non-standard fabrication and construction delivery, we find clear indications of current transitions in industrial production paradigms, and the re-emergence of a 'workshop model' capable of producing large quantities, or batches, of non-standard variable production.

Scaling-Up Architectural Urbanism

Given the substantial changes both in the scope and kind of technology associated with architecture and cities since the Industrial Revolution, and especially in the last 20 years of the so-called Information Revolution, we are witnessing an unprecedented use and application of technology in the design and management of our urban environments. The projects featured in this AD range from 'blue sky' design research to commissions and competition entries for architectural urbanism. Algorithmic computation is applied in the projects in response to variations in performative criteria. Importantly, the projects emphasise non-standard approaches to materialisation, and the scaling-up of prototyping practices and sensibilities of the last decade or more, which are beginning to chart the potential for the heightened customisation of our urban environment.

At the leading edge, and increasingly in the mainstream of these design disciplines, today's design technologies link more directly to engineering, manufacturing and construction delivery systems, opening new possibilities to create increasingly heterogeneous and differentiated urban environments. The implications of the new paradigm of non-standard variable production for the 21st-century city has yet to be consolidated, but in time it may be articulated as a Distinctive Urbanism. AD

Notes

1. Karl Marx, *Capital*, vol. I, Progress Publishers (Moscow), 1887, p.384.
2. Lewis Mumford, *The City in History*, Harcourt Brace Jovanovitch (San Diego, New York and London), 1961, p 302.
3. Le Corbusier, *Towards a New Architecture*, trans Frederick Etchells, Dover Publications (New York), 1986, pp 129–48 (first published in 1923, and in English in 1927).
4. Tommaso Marinetti, 'The Futurist Manifesto', in Ulrich Conrads, *Programs and Manifestoes on 20th-Century Architecture*, MIT Press (Cambridge, MA), 1970, p 38.
5. Andrea Branzi, *Weak and Diffuse Modernity: The World of Projects at the Beginning of the 21st Century*, Skira (Milan), 2006, p 71.
6. William J Mitchell, 'Soft Cities', *City of Bits: Space, Place and the Infobahn*, MIT Press (Cambridge, MA), 1994, p 107.
7. Tom Verebes, 'The Adaptive City: Urban Change, Resilience, and the Trajectory Towards a Distinctive Urbanism', in Huang Weixin, Liu Yanchuan and Xu Weiguo (eds), *DADA2013: Digital Infiltration and Parametricism*, Tsinghua University Press (Beijing), 2013, pp 477–87.
8. Andrea Branzi, *op cit*, p 70.
9. Thomas Campanella, *The Concrete Dragon: China's Urban Revolution and What it Means for the World*, Princeton Architectural Press (New York), 2008, p 190.
10. David Gartman, 'Introduction', *Autos to Architecture: Fordism and Architectural Aesthetics in the Twentieth Century*, Princeton University Press (New York), 2009, pp 7–11.
11. Sigfried Giedion, *Mechanization Takes Command: A Contribution to Anonymous History*, Oxford University Press (Oxford), 1948.
12. Bryn Jones, 'Past Production Paradigms: the Workshop, Taylorism and Fordism', *Forcing the Factory of the Future: Cybernation and Societal Institutions*, Cambridge University Press (Cambridge), 1997, pp 23–50.
13. Branko Kolarevic and Kevin R Klinger, 'Manufacturing/Material/Effects', *Manufacturing Material Effects: Rethinking Design and Making in Architecture*, Routledge (New York), 2008, p 7.
14. Dedlef Mertins, 'Variability, Variety and Evolution in Early 20th Century Bioconstructivism', in Lars Spuybroek (ed), *The Architecture of Variation*, Thames & Hudson (London), 2009, p 55.
15. Ash Amin, 'Post-Fordism: Models, Fantasies and Phantoms of Transition', *Post-Fordism: A Reader*, Blackwell (Oxford), 1994, p 3.
16. David Harvey and Allen J Scott, 'The Practice of Human Geography: Theory and Empirical Specificity in the Transition from Fordism to Flexible Accumulation', in WD Macmillan (ed), *Remodelling Geography*, Blackwell (Oxford), 1988–9, pp 217–29.
17. Klaus Neilsen, 'Towards a Flexible Future: Theories and Politics', in Bob Jessop *et al*, *The Politics of Flexibility*, Edward Elgar (Aldershot), 1991, p 24.
18. Nicholas Negroponte, 'Towards a Humanism Through Machines', in *Architectural Design*, no 7/6, September 1969, p 511.
19. Lars Spuybroek, *The Sympathy of Things: Ruskin and the Ecology of Design*. V2 Publishing (Rotterdam), 2011, p 56.
20. Tom Verebes, *Masterplanning the Adaptive City: Computational Urbanism in the Twenty-First Century*, Routledge (New York), 2013, p 171.

Martin Bressani

An Urban Dialectic

Mass Customisation and Standardisation

How has the impetus to standardise diverged and interacted with the impulse to customise over time? Architect and architectural historian **Martin Bressani**, who is Professor and Director at the School of Architecture at McGill University in Montreal, describes how until the late Medieval period the fabric of Western towns remained highly customised. This was a situation that was only overturned with the consolidation of absolute monarchy and the desire to create ceremonial backdrops, which demonstrated 'classical regularity' on a grand scale. The path towards standardisation and Modernism, though, remained in no way linear; Modernism being at least in part a response to the monumental, but overtly bourgeois ornamental forms of Baron Hausmann's Second Empire Paris.

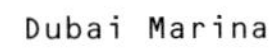

Dubai Marina

Dubai Municipality

United Arab Emirates

2013

The new Dubai Municipality provides one of the most effective images of a mass-customised city: mass-production at the service of distinction and branding.

Since their medieval origins, Western cities were 'mass-customised' in the sense that they formed a concentration of organised processes of production and distribution of goods and services producing 'custom' outputs. The first upsurge of urbanisation in early-modern Europe in the 12th and 13th centuries was controlled by an upper-class oligarchy of wealthy merchants and urban nobility who tailored their cities according to a complex system of symbols related to princely, religious and bourgeois competition. The idea of standardisation played no part in this first urban accumulation of wealth and prestige. The celebrated medieval plaza – the coherent form of which has been brandished as a model of legibility and stability by generations of architects – was in fact in constant flux, prey to the contrasting forces of public and private interests.

> The celebrated medieval plaza was in fact in constant flux, prey to the contrasting forces of public and private interests.

Even if we turn to such a prominent icon of the so-called 'ideal city' painted by Luciano Laurana in the early Renaissance, we are still confronted with a phenomenon of mass customisation. If the overall spatial layout follows a strict geometrical order and the 'temple' at its centre reflects the Albertian ideal of absolute regularity, the surrounding city is a surprising medley of differences, acknowledging the role of architecture in establishing distinction rather than homogenisation within the semantic universe of the early bourgeois city. The 'ideal' rational form may well triumph in the middle of the composition, but it does not erase the logic of the 'real' city encroaching on both sides.

It was not until the consolidation of absolute monarchies in the 17th century that standardisation entered into the fabric of Western cities, when classical regularity became a symbol of court privilege. One of the most representative examples is the Place Royale (now Place des Vosges) in Paris. Begun by Henri IV around 1605, it was the first planned square built as a royal embellishment and part of the larger transformation of the medieval city into a capital for a modern centralised state.[1] But of course the king never envisaged regularising his city as a whole. The rhetorical power of the Place Royale lay precisely in its being a static (royal) model embedded within the larger dynamic of a city that grew through spatial diffusion following a complex network of interests. Henri IV's royal building programme for the city of Paris was itself harnessed to the burgeoning real-estate market and the need to make the French capital a centre of European manufacturing and commerce. The standardised urban square was merely a ceremonial sign of royal authority: in no way was it conceived as a means of controlling the multifarious processes and elements that combined to form the organic whole of the kingdom's capital. If anything, the French king wanted to encourage and accelerate these processes by providing them a royal sanction.

In some of its aspects – such as the rebuilding of bridges, quays, ports and gates – Henri IV's plan for Paris anticipated Baron Haussmann's large boulevards of 250 years later. Like his royal predecessor, but at a much larger scale, Haussmann sought to transform Paris into a monumental capital, consolidating its title as a global centre of commerce, luxury and pleasure. But even if the latter was carried out during the Second Empire as mechanised industrialisation (and globalisation) took command of the West, the transformation did not imply homogenisation, as is too often assumed, or the creation of a single standardised space – an urban form too much associated with the Ancien Régime. Instead, a picturesque sinuosity prevailed, for instance in the Haussmannian parks and gardens, starting with the Buttes-Chaumont inaugurated during the 1867 Exposition Universelle.[2]

Haussmann's engineers also rejected the orthogonal grid in their plans for the expansion of Paris. To be sure, the 'alignment' of boulevards conformed to strict zoning ordinances, which assumed a certain regularisation and standardisation. But when considered at the micro level of surface and ornament – in other words, as experienced by a pedestrian – a sense of individual agency, disaggregation and heterogeneity remained palpable. Except for a few exceptional ensembles, such as the avenue de l'Opéra, facades were designed separately, the masonry being of course always carved by hand. Seen in this light, 19th-century Paris exemplifies mass customisation at the monumental scale of a modern metropolis – form and pattern emerging from the dynamics of a modern capitalist city in never-ending gradations and variations.

The 19th century thus brought us far from the sort of urban ceremonial developed by Henri IV, in which economic institutions were subordinated to, or at least curbed by, the moral norms of court

Luciano Laurana, *View of an Ideal City*, c 1470

One of the most celebrated representations of the so-called 'ideal city' of the Renaissance keeps nonetheless a sense of customisation: the surrounding dwellings, despite their classical language, remain clearly individualised.

Claude Chastillon, Royal Ceremonies, Place Royale (now Place des Vosges), Paris, April 1612

The Place Royale built under Henri IV's patronage is among the first examples of a totally regularised urban square in a Western city. Standardisation was to remain for many centuries the prerogative of court society and privilege.

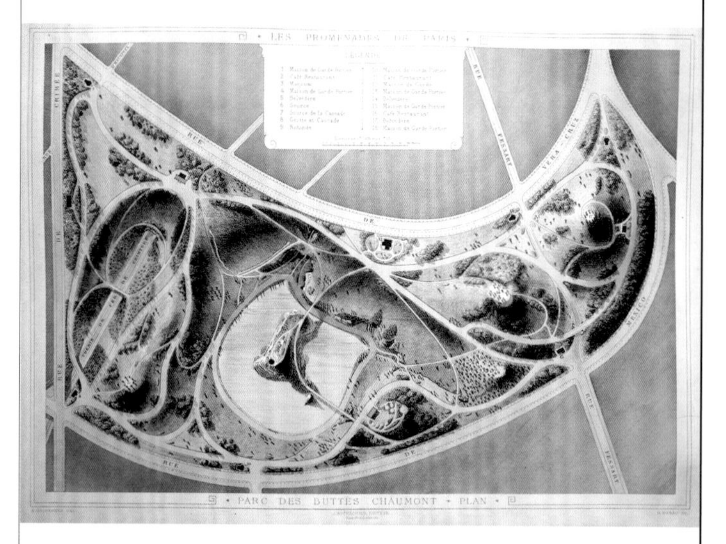

Jean-Charles Alphand, Plan of the Buttes-Chaumont Park, Paris, 1867

In many of its aspects, Baron Haussmann's transformation of Paris was more committed to a picturesque sensibility than to standardisation and regularity.

Ludwig Karl Hilberseimer, High-Rise City (Hochhausstadt), East-West Street, 1924

Hilberseimer's haunting view of a high-rise city represents one of the most extreme yet stillborn attempts at regularising urban form.

society. At the time of Haussmann's transformation, Paris had become a fully autonomous and self-regulating market system, a city of entrepreneurs following the expediential norms appropriate to a technological society. Haussmann sought to transform the huge consumer market and the immense workshop of the Parisian agglomerate into an operative whole.[3] Such advanced liberalism required mass customisation at a new scale: individualism at its basis assumed the right to one's idiosyncratic desires outside any obligation to the community. Everything must indeed be customised to satisfy the illusion of commodity fetishism.

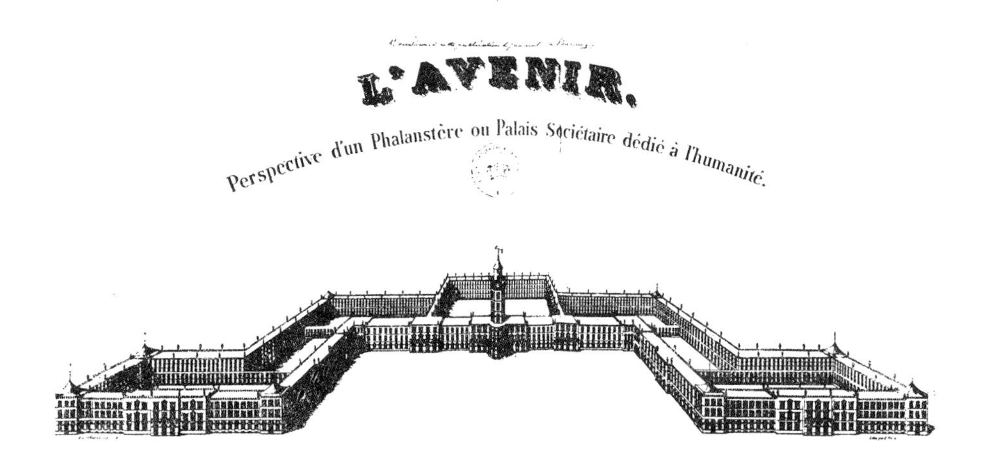

Victor Considérant, Perspective view of the urban area of Charles Fourier's Phalanstery, 1834

After the fall of court society, standardised urban form was often recuperated by utopian reformers such as the Fourierists.

Utopia and Standardisation

It is for this reason that, from the 19th century onwards, truly standardised urban forms emerged almost always from radical discourse – transforming in some perverse ways the aristocratic privilege of regularity into utopia. Often drawing from precedents such as Versailles, Charles Fourier's Phalanstery (1834), Robert Owen's New Harmony community in Indiana (1824) or Jean-Baptiste's *Familistère* (social palace) in Guise, northern France (1859–84) were the radical speculations of social and political thinkers who wished for the complete restructuring of society. Le Corbusier's Plan Voisin, Paris (1925), which sought to 'regularise' capitalism through architectural metaphors, is not so distinct from these earlier utopias. Far from reflecting the logic of capitalism, the standardisation of urban spaces sought to limit technology's self-moving, ends-transforming circular process: 'architecture or revolution' as Le Corbusier liked to warn.

The most rigorous architectural effort at self-restraint (or self-annihilation in this case) is Ludwig Hilberseimer's *Grossstadt Architektur* (c 1927), described by Michael Hays in terms of the dissolution of the object and the renunciation of humanist subjectivity.[4] By turning towards the objective effects of modern industrial capitalism, to its structures and processes understood as factors of form-making – by forcefully rejecting the logic of 'mass customisation' and commodity fetishism of the metropolis – Hilberseimer kept to only the technical principles in his architectural configuration: in other words, absolute standardisation. As he himself would later describe it: 'it is an architecture that is direct and free from all romantic reminiscences, in agreement with present daily life, not subjective and individualistic but objective and universal.'[5]

The formal mechanism Hilberseimer set in place, virtually unauthored, was conceived as an agent to pull the modern city dweller away from the urban phantasmagoria – what he simply called 'urban chaos'. By letting the productive attributes of capitalism – Fordism, Taylorism, planification – generate their own city, art and life could finally merge to achieve collective form. Paradoxically, however, Hilberseimer's matter-of-factness, his new ascetic and disenchanted vision, fascinates us precisely because of its lack of reality. Gazing at his spectral city, the urban order never appeared less natural and less rational, and never more uncanny. His representation of regularised urban blocks extending to infinity is ghostly, something that we contemplate at a distance, and through an act of mourning.[6] Perhaps standardisation will never be able to return to the contemporary city except through such spectral effect, as a simulated, prosthetic image. It becomes itself a phantasmagoria within the production of continual newness that begets technology.

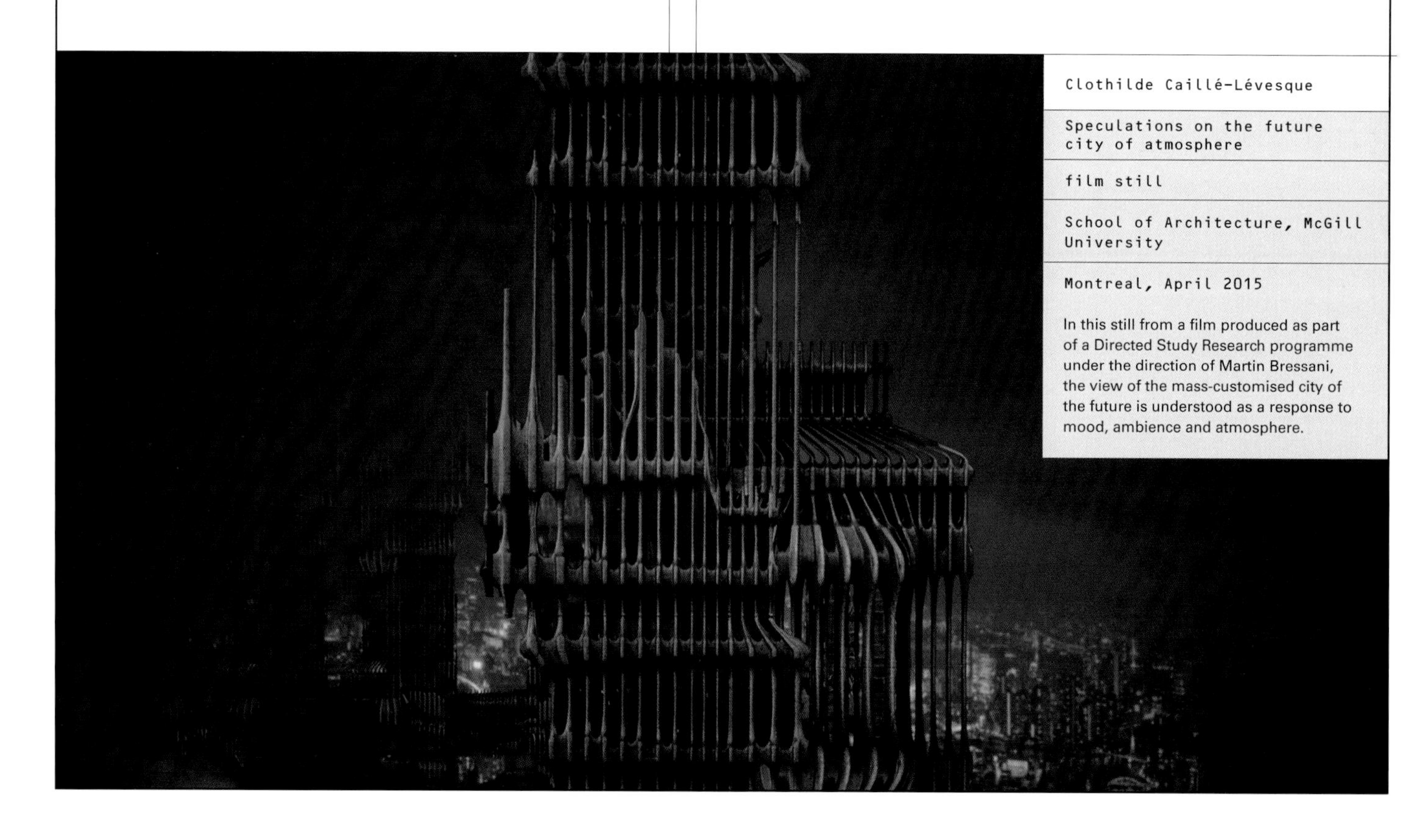

Clothilde Caillé-Lévesque

Speculations on the future city of atmosphere

film still

School of Architecture, McGill University

Montreal, April 2015

In this still from a film produced as part of a Directed Study Research programme under the direction of Martin Bressani, the view of the mass-customised city of the future is understood as a response to mood, ambience and atmosphere.

Mass Customisation and the City of Affective Alliances

Mass customisation meanwhile continues to run unhindered. Lately the question has been how to comprehend the myriad processes of urbanisation in terms of complexity theory and computation through evolutionary algorithms.[7] For the first time, efforts are being made to capture and visualise generative models at the very heart of the formation of advanced capitalist cities. But to what end? If urbanisation does indeed possess a formative logic, why not simply let it run its course? If it is (still) a question of finding ways for urban dwellers to identify themselves with their 'agglomeration', then urban planners and architects will be in dire need of theories of popular culture. As Lawrence Grossberg recently affirmed, 'everyone is constantly located within the field of the popular, for one cannot exist in a world where nothing matters'.[8]

What could be an 'evolutionary' map of affective relations? It is indeed affect that anchors people in particular experiences, practices and spaces, and thus directs their investment in their world. The substance of daily life is always disjointed and manifold, always positioned in the convolutions and layers of the structures of social power. Affect is itself articulated in the relations between practices. It is thus through affective alliances that people know where and with what intensities they can become absorbed in the urbanised globe. The true challenge for both architects and urban planners may lie in understanding the new ways in which today's urban dwellers 'care' about the spaces in which they conduct their lives. The ceremonial or utopian city with its well-ordered spaces may be a thing of the past, but affective empowerment remains the only resource for the construction of possibility in the modern city. ⌂

Notes

1. Hilary Ballon, *The Paris of Henri IV: Architecture and Urbanism*, MIT Press and the Architectural History Foundation (Cambridge, MA), 1991.
2. See Antoine Picon, 'Universal Expositions, Utopia and Architecture', in Martin Bressani and Christina Contandriopoulos (eds), *The Blackwell Companion to Architecture: Nineteenth-Century Volume*, Wiley-Blackwell (New York), 2016.
3. As Baron Haussmann himself famously described in his *Mémoires*. Quoted by Françoise Choay, *The Modern City: Planning in the 19th Century*, George Braziller (New York), 1969, p 16.
4. Michael Hays, *Modernism and the Posthumanist Subject: The Architecture of Hannes Meyer and Ludwig Hilberseimer*, MIT Press (Cambridge, MA), 1992.
5. Ludwig Hilberseimer, 'The Berlin School of Architecture', manuscript of 1967, Ludwig Karl Hilberseimer Archives, Art Institute of Chicago, series 8/1, box 7/10, 49–51, quoted in Hays, *op cit*, p 203.
6. The theme of spectrality has been explored in the work of Hilberseimer, but from a different perspective by Daniela Fabricius in 'Who's Afraid of Ludwig Hilberseimer? Spectrality and Space in the Groszstadt', *Journal of Architectural Education*, 67 (1), March 2013, pp 39–51.
7. See, for instance, Michael Batty, *Cities and Complexitity: Understanding Cities with Cellular Automata, Agent-Based Models, and Fractals*, MIT Press (Cambridge, MA), 2005, and Tom Verebes (ed), *Masterplanning the Adaptive City: Computational Urbanism in the Twenty-First Century*, Routledge (New York), 2014.
8. Lawrence Grossberg, *We Gotta Get Out of this Place: Popular Conservatism and Postmodern Culture*, Routledge (New York), 1992, p 84.

Zhongyuan Dai and Lu Wan

Community centre project

Rosemont, Montreal

Feeling Orange Studio

School of Architecture, McGill University

Montreal, 2012

In this project for the working-class neighbourhood of Rosemont, produced in a third-year studio under the joint direction of Martin Bressani and Aaron Sprecher, the space of moods is the source of 'customised' urban architectural expression.

An Interview with **Kenneth Frampton**

Tom Verebes

Towards a Distinctive Urbanism

When renowned professor, architectural historian and critic **Kenneth Frampton** wrote his seminal essay 'Towards a Critical Regionalism: Six Points for an Architecture of Resistance' (1983), he shot a sharp arrow into the side of the Modernist corpse. He argued against the ubiquity and uniformity of International Modernism in favour of an architecture that was distinct in its local character and identity. Over 30 years later, Guest-Editor **Tom Verebes** went to interview Frampton in his office at Columbia University to see if he could convince him that contemporary design and production technologies might be the means of realising a new distinctive urbanism.

This issue of AD, *Mass-Customised Cities*, raises questions concerning ways in which to generate, guide and grow distinctive forms of urbanism. Does Kenneth Frampton's influence on received ideas around the local specificities of architecture and cities qualify him today as indeed a pre-eminent theoretical kingpin for this AD issue? Frampton's seminal essay 'Towards a Critical Regionalism: Six Points for an Architecture of Resistance' (1983) was rooted in a deep critique of the ubiquity, and the apparent inappropriateness, of International Modernism, seeking rather the specificities of differentiated architectural identity and character, in and through locales.[1] Some 30 years on, it is pertinent and timely to interrogate ways in which to conceive, articulate and produce specific and distinct attributes in the design and planning of unprecedented city building. Although Frampton agrees, generally, how cities have become overly repetitious and homogeneous, he remains unconvinced that design and production technologies could be used to realise a 'Distinctive Urbanism', projecting towards the vast scale of contemporary urbanisation, the specific and unique, over the general and reproducible.[2]

CULTURE AND CITIES IN THE AGE OF GLOBALISATION

Cities today vary greatly across the world, and are largely defined by post-colonialism in Europe, and the legacy of the mythologies and metaphors of the melting pot and the mosaic in the Americas and the New World. Cities are comprised of people of mixed identities, ranging from the mobile global transnational elite, to economic and political migrants. Globalisation provokes much debate. Driven largely by expansive networks fuelling market economies, architecture, in the age of globalisation,[3] oscillates between paradoxes of memory versus amnesia, and lingering nostalgia amidst an anxious culture of innovation. As the cultural force we call 'cities' is more universalised than ever, how can the specificities of cities be nurtured?

Cities, along with their dynamic cultures, histories, traditions and identities, are no longer synonymous with the nation state. Through global connectivity, cities have even gained unprecedented autonomy from their host nations. National identity also no longer provides a comprehensive and adequate impetus for architecture to innovate itself in this century, and for the specificity of new cities yet to be built, to be articulated. Frampton agrees: 'You are right to imply, as I believe you do, that the city state is of more consequence today than the nation state, even though decentralised power is more vulnerable to legal pressure.'

I also ask Frampton whether the design agenda inherent to his essay on Critical Regionalism – ostensibly against ubiquity and uniformity – has been renovated to address the differentiation of cities, based on the uprootedness and mobility of an increasingly globalised world. 'I am not sure how the Critical Regionalist strategy might be modified so as to be of pertinence to the current urban predicament,' he replies. Frampton, like so many other architects and urbanists, values metropolitan density over what he calls 'low-density suburban detritus spreading across countries'. Despite the homogenising sameness and insidious complicity with commodity culture, Frampton prefers not to engage with the extensive urbanisation that planet Earth is facing, and seems to be distracted with resistance to the 'universal non-place' of the megalopolis.

ASIAN URBANISATION: CITIES WITHOUT HISTORY

According to Fredric Jameson's critique of it in his 1994 volume *The Seeds of Time*, Critical Regionalism shared with Postmodernism a disillusionment with the avant-garde, a utopianism and the anxiety

Office for Metropolitan Architecture (OMA)

Dubai Renaissance Business Bay

Dubai

United Arab Emirates

2008

Above: Icons can at times, in a meaningful way, define their identity through its difference from, rather than its deference to, its context. OMA's proposal for the centrepiece of Business Bay in Dubai sets a theoretical backdrop of 'iconic architecture', rather proposing blank, generic, standardised Modernism against the tendency of complex gymnastics of contemporary design.

Caracas
Venezuela

Left: Emergent urbanism, as apparent with informal slums, embraces the complex correlations between the forces which shape cities. As a relational approach to conceiving cities and their adaptive capacities, computational urbanism targets a parallel to grown and evolved urbanism, in which the structure of systems such as building massing, topography, routing, hydrology etc are deeply associated.

Plasma Studio
Xi'an Horticultural Expo
Xi'an, China, 2010

Previous spread: Professor Frampton proposes the discipline of Landscape Urbanism as a 'stratagem with which to mitigate the universal non-place of the megalopolis', perhaps also an endorsement of the associative logic of architecture and urbanism as being part and parcel of ecological systems. Here 'universal technique' is applied towards the generation and formation of a locally specific integration of systems.

of universal homogenising and effacing of local identity.[4] Given the unprecedented extent and rate of urbanisation in the last 30 years, especially in Asia, Frampton is one of the most pre-eminent living historians who has strong views on the making of cities built, in effect, without history. This notion of 'cities without history' evokes the effacing vacuity of urbanisation today, and is perhaps, polemically, the converse of Bernard Rudofsky's *Architecture without Architects*, which sought the deep valorisation of 'non-pedigreed' traditional vernacular architecture.[5] Turning to Heidegger, Frampton calls for a 'bounded domain' as a precondition for an architecture of resistance.[6] Undeniably, Asian urbanism installs not only Jean Gottman's unbounded 'megalopolis', but also other paradigmatic theoretical positions, including Manuel Castells's 'megacity' and 'network city', Rem Koolhaas's 'generic city', and even Saskia Sassen's 'global city', in locales.[7] Frampton describes the vast scale of urbanisation in Asia, 'a project which makes Lenin's NEP [New Economic Policy] compromise seem tame', yet he still calls for resistance to 'the myth of inevitable progress' which he claims we have inherited from the 19th century. Often citing Hannah Arendt's 'space of public appearance', he argues that the resonance of this concept may be difficult to locate in the context of city building in this century.[8] Ironically, the ultimate *u-topos* is found in Marc Augé's description of 'non-places': they appear out of nowhere, in the middle of nowhere, with no urban history in their particular locality.[9]

Las Vegas
Nevada
USA

Las Vegas is, today, the ultimate late capitalist city as theme park, and has its roots in the strip of postwar America, celebrated by Robert Venturi and Denise Scott-Brown in *Learning from Las Vegas* (1972). Professors Scott-Brown and Frampton famously debated their respective distinctions of 'popular taste', in which Venturi's vernacular pop scenography bantered with Frampton's well-mannered moral rejection of both the modern and the postmodern.

(NEO-)TRADITIONAL CULTURES AND VERNACULARISM

Critical Regionalism turned to peripheral traditions and their associated vernacular architecture persisting in residual localities, as its mode of resistance to universal civilisation, in a world which is increasingly globalising in its acceleration further away from traditions of the past and the social cohesion they foster. In Critical Regionalism, the avant-garde was indeed discredited for its obsession with positivism, and a self-proclaimed *arrière-garde* (rearguard) position was promoted. The formation of new cultures and hence new traditions are based on social, demographic and professional demimondes in cities – for example, the international finance culture of cities; art culture; culture of leisure and entertainment, etc. – or what we call, in the World-Wide Web parlance of today, 'communities'. Cities, through their critical mass, and via the links forged by the Internet, persist to be the locus of innovation, most evident in today's culture of collaboration, in which cities have the capacity to create shared platforms.

In Critical Regionalism, 'civilisation' was assumed to be the adversary of traditional culture. In an era in which cities have been globalised more than ever and 'universal civilisation' is more universal than ever, the paradox now lies in how cities are the main producers of culture. Might Frampton believe there to be a contemporary equivalent to traditional vernacular which may help to shape specific and unique new vernacular forms of urbanism in the 21st century? He responds to recall how 'the vernacular and its Latin root *verna* meaning rustic is only possible where the pattern of land settlement is intimately integrated with agriculture'. The vernacularism inherent to Critical Regionalism, according to Fredric Jameson, was founded on remoteness and peripherality, rather than centrality. Assuming vernacularism's deep connection to rural traditions, the possibility of a contemporary urban vernacular is in abeyance, especially in the current urbanisation of China, where cities are generally segregated from rural and agricultural land.

Frampton seems to share a view that culture, when thriving as well as when waning, is never static. How, then, does culture evolve in order for innovation to take place? In Frampton's words, 'Zygmunt Bauman

bil
rdistan
aq

e coherence of regional vernacular is rooted in purity, continuity
d the absence of contamination by colonialism and other forms
global influence. Erbil is an evolved, rather than designed, city, in
ich the emergent growth of the city is seeded by the domestic unit
d the strong figure of the ancient Citadel. If Bernard Rudofsky's
chitecture Without Architects valorised 'non-pedigreed architecture',
sk: What is a city without planners?

'our overall challenge to Critical Regionalism recalls he words of Jürgen Habermas as to the way in which technology and science may be an *a priori* ideology; that which Tomas Maldonado once characterised as technoidolatry.'

has argued in his book *Culture as Praxis*,[10] tradition and innovation are mutually interdependent and while one cannot have a *living tradition* without innovation, one also cannot have *significant innovation* without tradition. The ruthless maximisation of profit under the indifferent abstract logic of globalised capitalism makes this balance between tradition and innovation difficult to sustain.'

Frampton then refers, albeit paradoxically, to Arnold Gehlen, who suggested 'once invention becomes routine we are in the epoch of post-histoire'.[11] As a counterpoint, the reliance on tradition limits Critical Regionalism's projective capacity. In the absence of an authoritative arbiter of what may be meaningful, culture cannot be arrested, and nor is it enduring and unchanging. Given today's complex composition of urbanity, which single tradition do neo-traditionalists defend, so dearly, against time? Installing 'civilisation' as the enemy of instantiated local heritage is tantamount to valorisation of the past over the future.

UNIVERSAL TECHNIQUES AND TECHNOLOGIES

Industrialisation has always been a catalyst for urbanisation. Perhaps the greatest technological revolution to occur since the Industrial Revolution is the digital information revolution, which has pervaded the ways in which architecture and cities are conceived, made, inhabited and used. Frampton, in promoting an *arrière-garde* position of resistance in architecture, claims an ambiguous middle ground as the only route which has 'the capacity to cultivate a resistant, identity-giving culture', while concurrently having 'discrete recourse to universal technique'. 'Universal technique' is assumed to be at odds with specific regional and local practices. As a contradistinction to Critical Regionalism, the power of design technology today is its potency to create architectural differentiation. Computational design and fabrication is possibly the most effective means with which to specify a design to its contingencies, and to establish associations between spaces, material systems, programmes and people. Given the material logic of post-Fordism, and its emphasis on difference and specificity, Frampton seems to represent a significant voice on today's technological context, and perhaps also the potential for computational design and production technologies to open new possibilities to create varied and highly specific, unique design outcomes. Despite the global interconnectedness of the digital world, people of diverse cultural heritage apply technology in different ways, as he believes 'applied technique has been and should be capable of cultural inflection'. Frampton however seems unconvinced that emerging non-standard manufacturing is representative of a paradigm shift from mass-produced urbanism towards increasingly diverse and unique characteristics of cities.

Frampton's thesis on tectonics has been debated through Greg Lynn's 'groovy topology' and Reiser + Umemoto's force-driven approach to the formation of matter, among others.[12] To pitch in to a next-generational debate on the discourses of tectonics, speculations are needed upon the ways in which computational design and production has affected, or will do in the future, how cities are designed, built, managed and experienced. During our interview, Frampton dismisses any enthusiasm for the creative capacity of technology as a 'recurrent dream', and only recounts his perception of the enduring pitfalls of architectural experimentation with technology: 'Your overall challenge to Critical Regionalism recalls the words of Jürgen Habermas as to the way in which technology and science may be an *a priori* ideology; that which Tomas Maldonado once characterised as technoidolatry.'

In 'Towards a Critical Regionalism', Frampton writes that 'Modern building' had become 'so universally conditioned by optimising technology that the possibility of creating significant urban form [had] become extremely limited'.[13] Given the changes in technology which have occurred since the 1980s, and the ways they have effectively

'You are right, of course, to insist on the importance of the image and on the key role that the image played in the so-called heroic modern movement from 1923 to 1939. However, I would maintain that this is quite different from the caricature of the brand image as this has been promulgated by 'star architects'.'

Shenzhen
Guangdong Province
China

Shenzhen was a fishing village of 25,000 in 1980. Today, boasting a population of some 21 million, it stands emblematic of the countless 'instant cities' which have mushroomed all over Asia, yet unimaginably more quickly than Manchester or Chicago had emerged in the 19th century. Its evolution from a manufacturing industrial city to a burgeoning global hub for financial services and creative industries has occurred in less than three decades. Shenzhen is an 'instant city', largely without history, and produced through standardisation and mechanisation of bureaucratic planning processes and homogeneous generic architecture, yet it has unique residues of its own short-lived urban vernacular – its urban villages.

revolutionised architecture, the potential of creating significant urban form, I would argue, has never been greater. Frampton, however, bemoans how the 'maximising drives of late capitalism reflect our technological capacity' and how the use of what he calls 'algorithmic digital drafting techniques' are being applied universally, 'to produce totally gratuitous parametric form'.

URBAN IDENTITY IN THE 21ST CENTURY

There has been much debate over so-called iconic architecture. Although the prevalent critiques against iconicity base their arguments in the commodification of architecture as branding, scenographic sensationalism, we may consider another view of the icon. The history of architecture chronicles its seminal moments, or the exemplar icons of a particular era. Postmodern morality most often expected architecture to be polite, well-mannered and 'in keeping with' its context. Paradoxically, the highlights of architectural history often have alien and incongruous relationships to their existing contexts, leading to the fundamental and radical change of a context. Frampton responds to questions about the drivers of the projective imagination capable of shaping multifarious characters and identities of cities in this century: 'You are right, of course, to insist on the importance of the image and on the key role that the image played in the so-called heroic modern movement from 1923 to 1939. However, I would maintain that this is quite different from the caricature of the brand image as this has been promulgated by "star architects".'

Frampton's essay on Critical Regionalism resounds with some of the ambitions of *Mass-Customised Cities*, to chart ways in which the specific character and identity of cities can be nurtured. In the 1980s, fiery debates raged between various Postmodernists and their postulations on popular culture, universality and the instrumentality of history.

Jameson's critique of Critical Regionalism questioned the marginality of resistance being rooted in peripheral cultural attributes and the claims they represent the entirety of national identities. Despite the apolitical and moralistic pitch of 'Towards a Critical Regionalism', Frampton's anti-capitalist rejection of the 'scenographic brand image' is argued through mildly Marxist rhetoric against commodity culture. Jameson locates a gaping paradox in the legacy of postmodern urban contextualism which had championed pluralism and difference. Although Frampton asserts that 'capitalism is mostly an ideology of waste', he eludes the question as to whether he believes his essay on Critical Regionalism has been misused as the nostalgic commodification of history within late capitalist culture. In retrospect, this brand of contextual urbanism was themed and aestheticised, then fabricated, packaged and sold as a branded commodity, flogging the myth of cultural continuity.

Frampton still hopes to cohere the fragments of modernism's failed unity. In the ongoing age of globalisation, an entire generation is searching for the theoretical basis for projecting how cities in this century can escape the routinised monotony of Modernist city planning and the legacies of repetitious standardisation of architecture. Today's progressive discourses on urbanisation privilege cities, not regions nor the nation state, yet perhaps without nostalgia for any loss, in a world which is increasingly connected yet distributed, inhabited by nomadic actors flowing in networks. In the Asian century of urbanisation, we ought to approach universality in how specificities are sought over generalities, and to value civilisation as the foundation, rather than the adversary, of culture. Technology, or 'universal technique' as Frampton calls it, will no doubt continue to contribute to the making of distinct memorable cities, and has become a catalyst for design innovation and the evolutionary motor of tradition. A 'Distinctive Urbanism' targets the creation of radical differences within and between cities, rather than deference to what we assume to be culture, and its repetition. AD

This article is based on an interview by Guest-Editor Tom Verebes with Kenneth Frampton on 5 February 2015 at Columbia University, New York.

NOTES

1. Kenneth Frampton, 'Towards a Critical Regionalism: Six Points for an Architecture of Resistance', in Hal Foster (ed), *The Anti-Aesthetic: Essays on Postmodern Culture*, Bay Press (Seattle), 1983, pp 16–30. See also Kenneth Frampton, 'Critical Regionalism: Modern Architecture and Cultural Identity', in *Modern Architecture: A Critical History*, Thames and Hudson (London), second edition, 1985, pp 313–27.
2. Tom Verebes, 'The Adaptive City: Urban Change, Resilience, and the Trajectory Towards a Distinctive Urbanism', in Huang Weixin, Liu Yanchuan and Weiguo Xu (eds), *DADA2013: Digital Infiltration and Parametricism*, Tsinghua University Press (Beijing), 2013, pp 477–87.
3. See Kenneth Frampton, 'NEW Architecture in the Age of Globalization: Topography, Morphology, Sustainability, Materiality, Habitat and Civic Form 1975–2007', in *Modern Architecture: A Critical History*, Thames and Hudson (London), 4th edition, 2014, pp 328–424.
4. Fredric Jameson, 'The Constraints of Postmodernism', *The Seeds of Time*, Columbia University Press (New York) 1994, pp 129–205 (pp 188–205).
5. Bernard Rudofsky, *Architecture Without Architects: A Short Introduction to Non-Pedigreed Architecture*, Museum of Modern Art (New York), 1964.
6. Martin Heidegger, 'Building, Dwelling and Thinking' ['Bauen, Wohnen, Denken', 1954], *Poetry, Language, Thought*, trans Albert Hofstadter, Harper Colophon Books (New York), 1971.
7. Jean Gottmann, *Megalopolis: The Urbanized Northeastern Seaboard of the United States*, The Twentieth Century Fund (New York), 1961; Manuel Castells, *The Rise of the Network Society*, Blackwell (Oxford), 1996; Saskia Sassens, 'The Global City: Introducing a Concept and its History', in Rem Koolhaas *et al* (eds), *Mutations*, Actar (Barcelona), 2001; Rem Koolhaas, 'The Generic City', in Rem Koolhaas and Bruce Mau, *S,M,L,XL*, Monacelli Press (New York), 1998, pp 1248–64.
8. Hannah Arendt, *The Human Condition*, University of Chicago Press (London and Chicago), 1958.
9. Marc Augé, *Non-Places: An Introduction to Supermodernity*, Verso (London), 1995.
10. Zygmunt Bauman, *Culture as Praxis*, Sage (London), 1973.
11. Arnold Gehlen, *The Role of Standards of Living in Today's Society*, Lehnen (Munich), 1952.
12. Greg Lynn, 'Blobs, or Why Tectonics Is Square and Topology Is Groovy', *ANY* 14 (1996), pp 58–62; Jesse Reiser and Nanako Umemoto, *Atlas of Novel Tectonics*, Princeton Architectural Press (New York), 2006.
13. Frampton, 'Towards a Critical Regionalism', *op cit*, p 17.

Elena Manferdini

Miesian Grids and the Domain of Ink

Atelier Manferdini

Building the Picture

The Art Institute of Chicago

2015

Drawing of a fictional skyline, printed at full scale for the exhibition.

Using pictures of Mies van der Rohe's building facades as a point of departure, the *Building the Picture* suite of drawings attempts to address how a city (and thus its architecture) can be conceived and designed with greater specificity. The suite was commissioned by the Art Institute of Chicago for a show entitled 'Elena Manferdini: Building the Picture', which ran at the museum from 7 March to 20 September 2015. The drawings subvert the mechanical repetition of the grid and the relation of that to modular systems in building construction, instead using optical effects and saturated visual fields as a confrontation to Mies's modular and mass-producible systems. They explore a new role for the contemporary grid; that of 'picturing' the idea of fenestration and building facades. Through a contemporary use of the grid, deploying colours, woven patterns and apertures, the project offers an alternative identity to the generic building.

A Sense of Order

To those outside of the discipline, it might appear that architecture has an unlimited faith in the power of geometry.

What happens when you subvert the standardised repetition of the Modernist grid? In *Building the Picture*, a series of drawings that architect **Elena Manferdini** produced for an exhibition at the Art Institute of Chicago that ran during the spring and summer of 2015, visual effects and colour were applied to counteract Mies's highly uniform and modular mass-producible systems.

Architects consider these formal techniques almost as a professional trade secret that informs their ability to comprehend, represent and instruct the complexity of a built environment. One such geometry, yet perhaps the most diffused one, is the grid: an overall mastering system that has been able to lock into place a good portion of our surroundings. It could be argued that the success of the grid lies in its ability to simultaneously respond to a fundamental aesthetic attraction to order and a logical need for intellectual comprehension. In other words, the grid delivers a sense of order. Silent, minimal and optimal, grids are able to host the complexities of our realities. As a consequence, the city has always occupied a privileged spot in the dreams of architects; it is a place where this tendency to organise large data finds its physical manifestation. The urban scale embodies an abstract disciplinary place where a myriad of different patterns can be projected in an unlimited repository of ruled aesthetic principles and where that desire for overall geometrical rigour finds a possible ground to exist.

Modern Generic Grids and Multifaceted Contemporary Subjectivities

For centuries, gridded systems have proven their efficacy as graphic tools for urbanisation and the management of the multitudinous networks of relationships that constitute the essence of a metropolis. Grids have slowly been sprawling not only across the ground plane, but have been visual and analytical protagonists of building facades, created by the rhythm of their fenestrations, ornamentations and structural systems. The geometry of the modules, their degree of variation, as well as the pattern and nature of joints, has assumed the task of architectural expression.

When confronted with the scale of the city and its pragmatic realities and physical manifestations, grids inevitably lost their neutral abstraction and assumed strong social connotations. Throughout history the architectural grid became a political project in addition to being an aesthetic one. However, it is only in the case of modern American cities that architecture tested at a large urban scale how

below and opposite:
Scripted coloured drawing representing the elevation of a mid-rise typology.

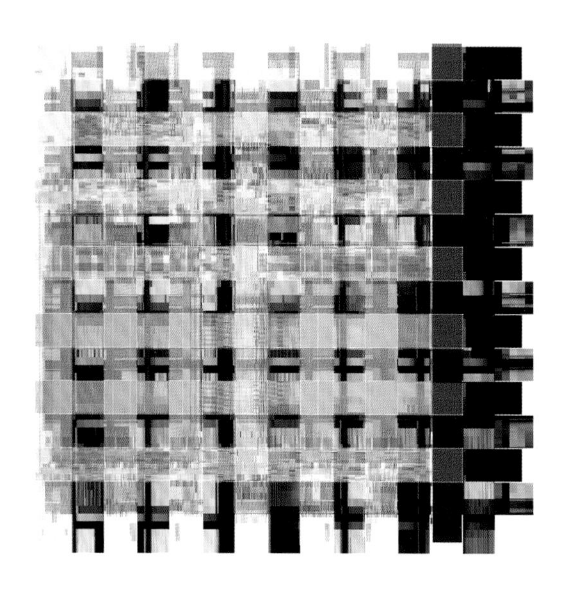

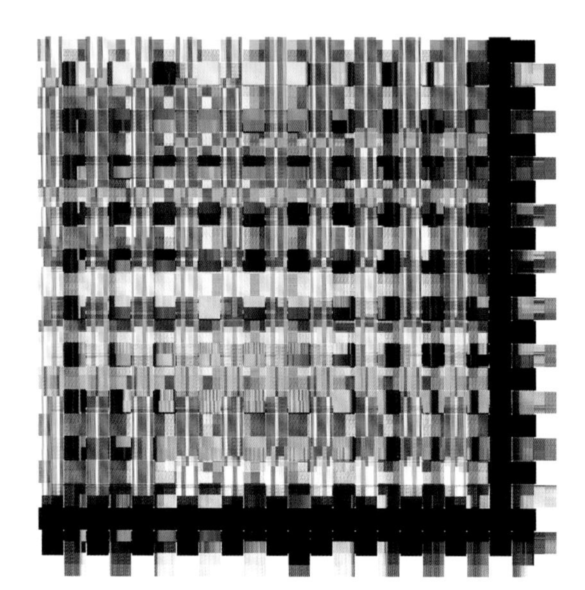

the primary trait of the grid – its compulsion to repeat – could embody the essential traits of capitalist civilisations: democracy and mass production.

If it is true that European modern architects laid down the theoretical principles connecting geometrical modularity with industrial production and social politics, it is in the American cities – the most apolitical and corporate ones – that the tension between the wilful Jeffersonian grid and its political implications can be witnessed in its purest and most controversial state. Among these, it is in Chicago that the modern grid as both a project at work and a project in decline can be clearly understood.

In Europe, modernisation – as a large-scale phenomenon – took place mainly in the peripheries and outside the historical city walls. With few exceptions, the European city centre was often too dense with historical residues, and its urban section was, in the majority of cases, already in place and immutable. In these settings the overall ruling modern grid had to face a

top left: Drawing of woven facade using a picture of a Mies van der Rohe facade as a point of departure, for the 'Elena Manferdini: Building the Picture' exhibition at the Art Institute of Chicago.

top right: Scripted drawings weaving threads of coloured lines into a Mies facade image.

above: Scripted coloured drawing intertwined with an image of an existing Mies building facade.

right: Diagram of a Miesian grid applied to various building typologies.

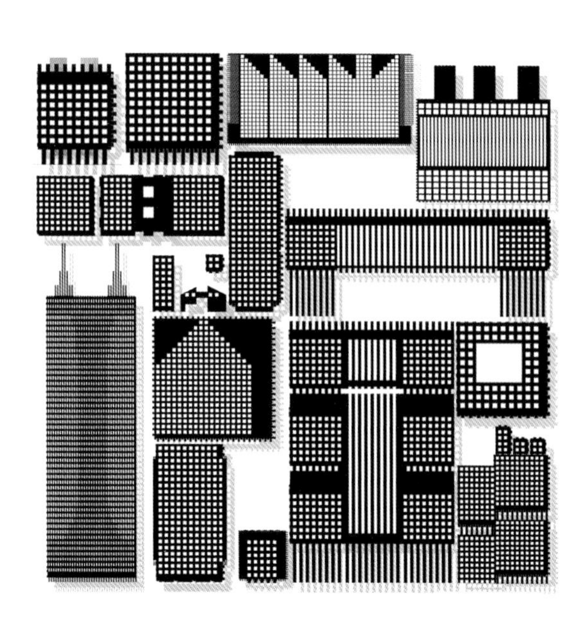

complex reality that would not allow for its full deployment, both on the urban ground and on building facades. In most circumstances European Modernism manifested itself as set of exceptions. Whereas in the US (traditionally a place where politics and city governments tend to operate at a much larger geographic scale on vast, relatively low-density territory) the tabula rasa point of departure and more recent city growth timeline made it possible to deploy the powerful abstraction of the grid at the urban and building scale at the core of the city.

In this context, it becomes interesting to pay closer attention to some of the late modern work by Mies van der Rohe in Chicago. In particular, the *Building the City* suite of drawings uses some of the most iconic pictures of Mies facades to develop contemporary applications for the grid. Like many other examples of modern architecture, Mies's buildings assume the generic attributes of production, such as the adoption of ready-made steel members as mullion systems for the facade. In contrast to Europe, where early modern architecture construction was centred on the use of concrete, Mies embraces the economic reality of an American corporate scale that relies on industrial prefabricated, off-the-rack, modular products rather than on-site construction technology. If one takes a closer look at Mies's facades, the effect achieved by these big, mute black buildings in the city is all but generic: the steel mullions, along with the dark glass curtain wall, are able to create vibrant optical effects that dynamically reflect one building on the facades of those surrounding it. The tectonic qualities of the grid facade are able to create unique architectural experiences without resorting to formal iconicity. Similarly, the orchestrated placement of multiple recessed lobbies on a generic plinth within a Jeffersonian city block is able to frame a public space that moves precisely from open plazas to private buildings: over the course of the day, the silence of Mies's minimalist buildings allow for the cacophony of the city to enter his architecture. And if the task of architecture is to reify the political organisation of space, in the case of Mies the application of the grid to his facades was able to propel the ethos of the city of Chicago.

Like many other examples of modern architecture, Mies's buildings assume the generic attributes of production, such as the adoption of ready-made steel members as mullion systems for the facade.

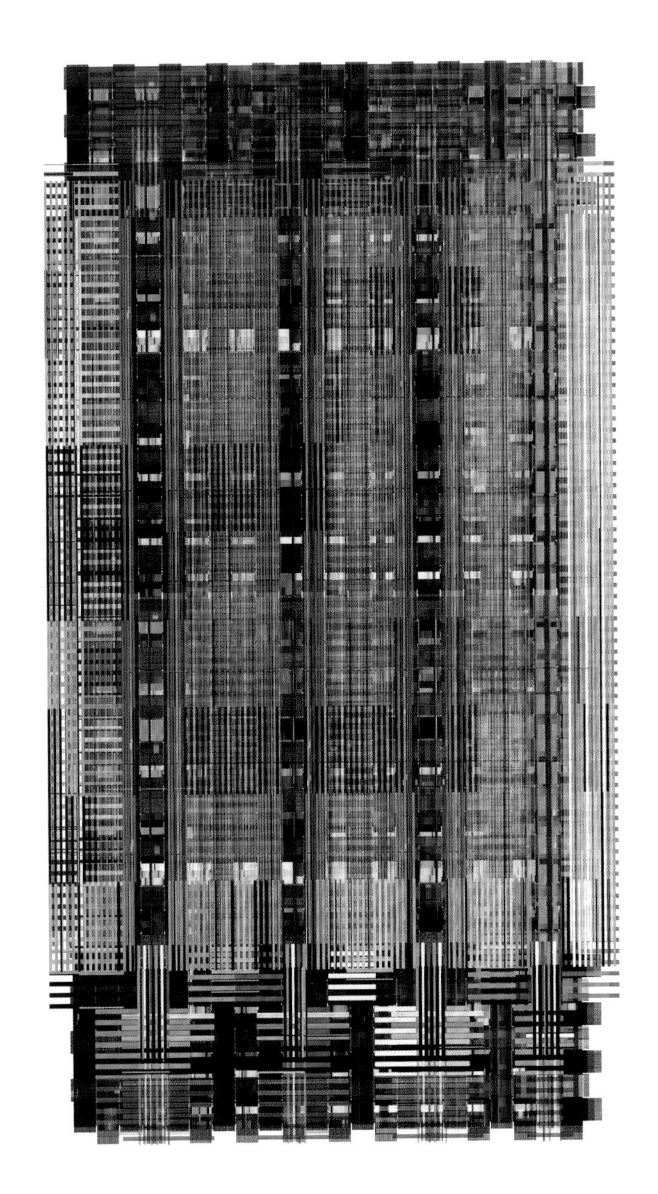

Scripted coloured drawing intertwined with the picture of an existing Mies facade to create a new mid-rise typology.

On the downside, there are also too many examples of American buildings – even cities – where the grid became synonymous with repetition; where the sprawl of the ubiquitous copies replaced the wilful strength of the original. Buildings became universal versions of the minimal mute box. The generic was no longer a framework able to embrace the complexity and ambiguity of the urban politics, but an ever-growing blanket, a corporate recipe for economic efficiency and palatable aesthetic. In many cases this monotonous mass-production of repeated buildings represented a difficult heritage for architects. With time it became clear that modern architecture fell short of expressing the complexity of current sensibilities where heterogeneity increasingly defines contemporary culture. In response to this changed landscape, over the past 20 years we have seen the emergence of iconic buildings whose figures stand alone in city skylines, striving to project a new identity through their formal effigy. The proliferation of stylistically idiosyncratic constructions around the globe is the result of our current anxiety with the generic. In the age of globalisation, where multifaceted political subjectivity is constantly reformulated, contemporary architecture has still to find a flexible and original response to the generic. Instead, iconic formalism has crystallised its superficial antithesis to the ordinary with a set of uncommon geometric figures.

Building the Picture attempts to find an alternative to such iconic formalism, to update the political project of the grid in the age of computation and globalisation. Underlying the research is the belief that, reapplied to urban facades but now with a revised, contemporary materiality and computational geometry, the grid is once again able to distance these buildings from the ordinary and render them unique architectural experiences without resorting to a facile formal fluidity. Each drawing uses a picture of Mies's building facades in Chicago or New York. The original images are transformed via computer script in a series of cyclical operations that construct and deconstruct each picture into a set of vector lines. By changing the scale of the grid, each picture variously gains and loses abstraction. The monochromatic originals are then weaved with a second, colourful image at a different resolution.

Physical model of a fictional building integrating graphic coloration and projected fenestration techniques with a typical Miesian grid.

The decision to start a set of autonomous drawings on modular facades came from a personal fascination with the work of Mies van der Rohe and its significance for interpreting the politics of the grid. Mies's buildings can be read as part of the modern movement that was invested in making the traditional hierarchy of a facade (bottom, centre, top) disappear in favour of an egalitarian image of the built environment. The envelope of a modern building was supposed to be a by-product of its constructive technology, and the modularity of its assembly system reinforced by the idea of technical efficiency and social democracy. Following this tradition, Mies's facades revealed the load-bearing structure, and its construction methodologies became its primary expression, but at the same time he corrupted the functionality of his envelopes with ornamental fine-grain mullions that had no use other than to create optical effect.

Building upon Mies's facade discrepancy between superfluous features of the modules and building functionality, the *Building the Picture* drawings disrupt the mechanical use of the grid and its relationship to the modular systems in building construction. The scripted animation that produced them is able to subvert the static nature of the neutral grid, replacing it with the dynamic character of a multi-directional grid. The scales of the weave and fenestrations have no fixed relationship to one another and do not correspond to the location of the slabs behind them. This misalignment of the windows follows the general tendency of contemporary buildings towards air-tight curtain walls that replaced an outdated way of thinking of the grid as a structure for fenestration, and promoted instead the contemporary proliferation of a grid as a series of custom patterns and joints. The role of the grid in the drawings is instead one of 'picturing' ideas of fenestrations on a curtain wall; often out of scale or with misaligned edges, the windows pattern suggests a familiarity that at times reveals instead a radical departure from what we know as being generic; their optical effects manage in fact to surprise us.

Modular rigour is also applied to the chromatic finish of the facades: a relatively small selection of colours is able to create a wide variety of shades because of the intricate digital juxtapositions and overlay of threads next to each other. A small range of CMYK colours replace the monochrome black of Mies's buildings and produce infinite chromatic combinations for the contemporary facade. The computational process of overlaying pictures on top of drawings and finely weaving them together merges the sterile lines of the computer with the fecund lines of the pictures: computational abstraction and photorealistic figuration woven together to simultaneously occupy the viewers' perception. In addition, the weaves present a set of discrepancies and fringes as they reach the borders of the buildings. And while fraying, they dismantle any canonical understanding of boundaries as symbols of hierarchy and traditional typology.

Computational Grids and New Collective Imaginations

The conceptual basis for the *Building the Picture* suite of drawings is rooted in the belief that contemporary architecture has been able to produce new models of computational geometries, effect-driven political forms that can no longer be structured on the traditional opposition between front and back, private and public. These new envelopes rely on a highly choreographed experience of the skin; their building mass is often a multidirectional, faceted volume that resists traditional representational mechanisms and cannot be precisely oriented. The aim of the research is to test the suitability of this work as a design process and its applicability to current architectural practice. The work is not based on a historical-interpretive methodology or logical argumentation; its goal is to provide a working methodology for a contemporary aesthetic of computational, directional, dynamic grids. The drawings remain marginally unrealistic on purpose; their domain is that of ink, while their genesis is one of vectors and pixels. They elucidate forms that are immanent in the existing grid, while guiding new collective imaginations.

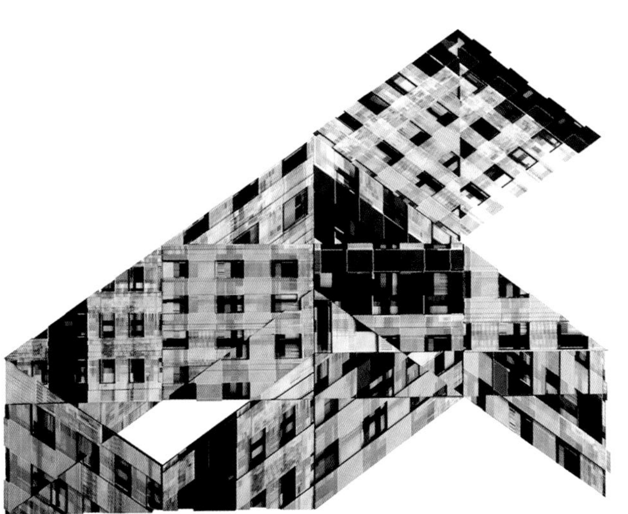

Unfolding of the physical model, demonstrating how flatness and tri-dimensionality are able to coexist using various parallel projections of a typical Miesian grid.

At the urban scale, the work suggests that grids can still be at the centre of contemporary urbanisation, but they cannot be generic; on the contrary, they need to be able to simultaneously respond to the current demand for fast production and greater request for customisation now characteristic of our culture. The new grid must be able to respond to a hybrid, polychromic, multifaceted, globalised society. It needs to adapt to a new norm, where standard is no longer synonymous with the modular and generic, but ubiquitous and specific. ⌂

Standardising Heterogeneity

Bell/Seong:
Visible Weather
Simultaneous City
Temple Terrace
Florida
2012

Utilising underdeveloped property and zoning setbacks, a 5.6-hectare (14-acre) site becomes a newly hybridised city hall, incubator office, retail and housing development.

Michael Bell

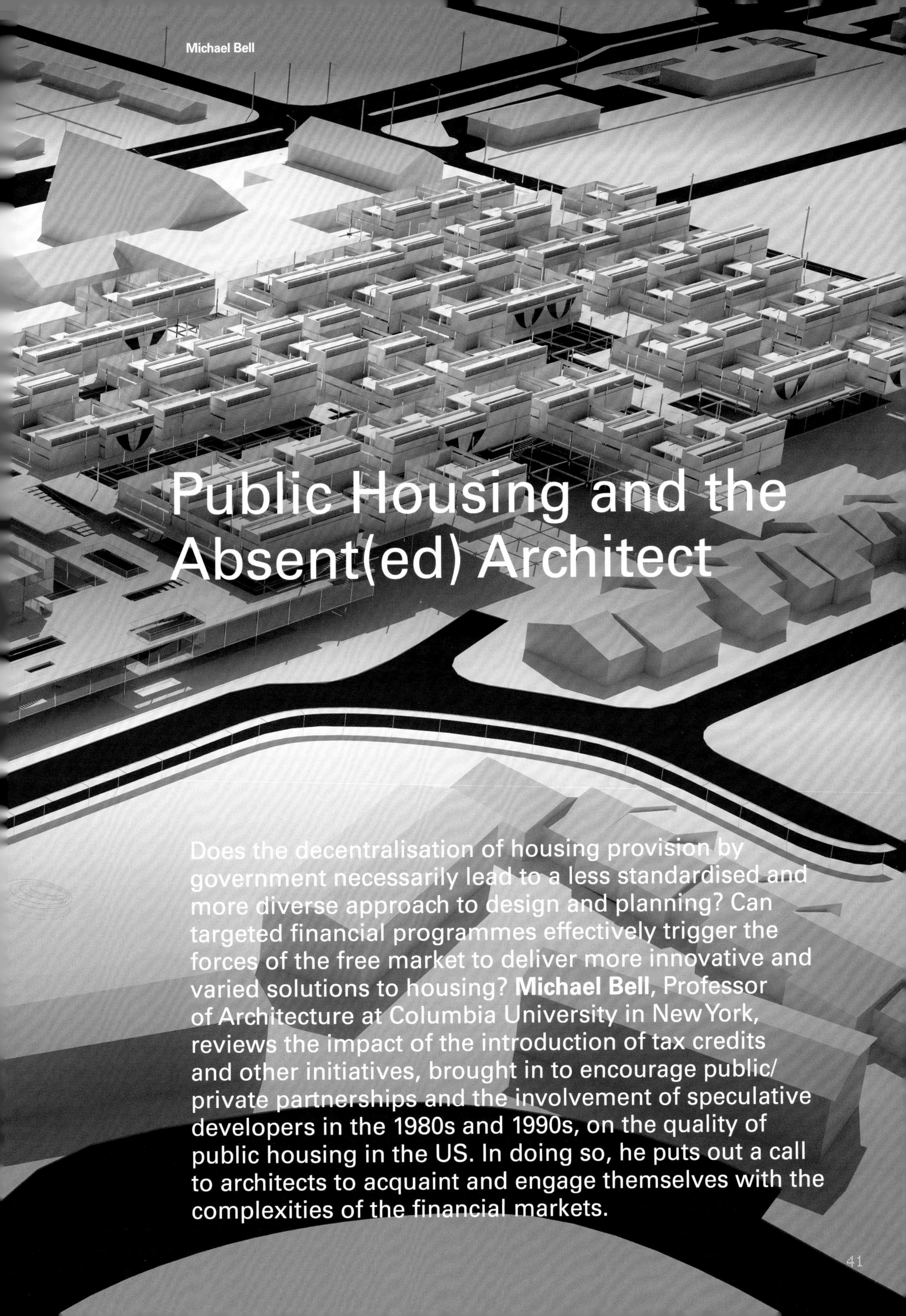

Public Housing and the Absent(ed) Architect

Does the decentralisation of housing provision by government necessarily lead to a less standardised and more diverse approach to design and planning? Can targeted financial programmes effectively trigger the forces of the free market to deliver more innovative and varied solutions to housing? **Michael Bell**, Professor of Architecture at Columbia University in New York, reviews the impact of the introduction of tax credits and other initiatives, brought in to encourage public/private partnerships and the involvement of speculative developers in the 1980s and 1990s, on the quality of public housing in the US. In doing so, he puts out a call to architects to acquaint and engage themselves with the complexities of the financial markets.

In the early 1990s, as the US federal government was increasingly incentivising the development of low-income, affordable and public housing within public/private partnerships, architectural discussion of these changes centred on design and planning initiatives instead of on financial or economic transformations of the development means. A goal was to break down the standardised housing blocks emblematic of the early decades of public housing and engage the entrepreneurial logic of the market as a driver of new housing solutions. At the root of the changes was an architecturally formless instrument – the Low Income Housing Tax Credit (LIHTC) – created by Congress in 1986 and intended to fund subsidised housing by deferred revenue rather than direct expenditure. It was also intended to shift ownership of affordable and public housing to investors who theoretically could deliver an antidote to the monolithic housing blocks and essentially customise subsidised housing development to local contexts and needs.

The shifts were monumental in scope, but were barely registered in architectural discourse: the formerly centrally funded, planned, developed, owned and managed public housing schemes that emerged since the 1937 Housing Act would over time be reborn as products of smaller-scale non-profit developers seeded by the sale of tax credits against profits they did not have. The actual credit, sold to a for-profit company that makes use of the credit, provides the initial equity to start a project. The changes have had an inverse effect on architecture, leading to a new mass standardisation of market housing construction techniques; an architectural heterogeneity applied atop a very uniform set of financial practices. This has also dramatically altered how and when architects engage with the design and social questions central to housing.

Bell/Seong: Visible Weather, Simultaneous City, Temple Terrace, Florida, 2012

Courtyard housing units made of fibre-reinforced concrete provide the ballast that instigates tension in a cable-stay/tensegrity structure. Private dwellings are grouped tightly, but with private outdoor spaces. The living space harvests the prevailing winds for dehumidification as bedrooms are seated low in the courtyard and protected from direct heat gain.

Deconcentrating Poverty: Topological Housing Policies

At the federal level the creation of LIHTC and an array of subsequent programmes to reduce direct federal ownership of public and low-income housing were in large part taken as a step to diminish concentrations of poverty in public housing developments and were instigated under two left-to-centre Clinton-era federal programmes. Funds made available by the Department of Housing and Urban Development (HUD) for Public Housing Administrations (PHAs) during this period were also designed to address decades of deferred maintenance in PHA developments. Unable to take on debt, ageing public housing sites in the US long suffered a deficit in funding maintenance from rent rolls. Under HUD's new HOPE VI programme, funding streams were targeted for renovation and repair, but the policies also required the demolition of a portion of each development's 'hard units', and the funding was only available if the PHA also agreed to remove actual ageing apartments developed and managed since the PHA's inception by the New Deal legislation introduced in 1937.

New housing built to replace these hard units, beginning in the 1990s and only recently abated, was intended for those on a higher income (not the original tenants) and paralleled a wider move by HUD towards using vouchers and other subsidies to alleviate rent – as 'soft units', these new dwellings (or now subsidised quasi-market apartments) have an attached yet portable subsidy (a voucher), but outwardly they were intended to appear as part of the wider and generalised housing market. Similarly, the Quality Housing and Work Responsibility Act (QHWRA) of 1998 offered means to 'deconcentrate' poverty concentrations that had become endemic in much public housing by allowing PHAs to more actively distribute their populations, but also to effectively become participating public owners within a non-profit corporation created to realise the new public/private housing within HOPE VI redevelopments.

Changes in the development mechanism meant that public housing, centrally funded, planned and managed since its origins 60 years earlier has increasingly been built since the 1990s within the same building logics – labour, material, financial means – as speculative housing. The often referenced and broad declaration of a decline in welfare-state funding was actually more accurately a shift of that funding from direct expenditures to a myriad of deferred-income instruments (such as LIHTC programmes) intended to instigate diversity or heterogeneity in public housing developments. At the architectural level, this included a mandate to create a more heterogeneous building design – a veil of difference in the building facades to mask the otherwise large scale of the new housing. New quasi-public housing developments were realised within the same means of building that speculative housing in the US has long relied on – a market that has long been broadly acknowledged as inadequate at serving lower-income communities, and also lacking any capacity for innovation.

Programme types are layered and form thermal as well as economic support: private housing units sit atop a second-level incubator office and a ground-level city hall. The energy requirements of each programme sustain each other during the daily cycle. Housing forms thermal barriers over offices that harvest their heat gain in the evenings.

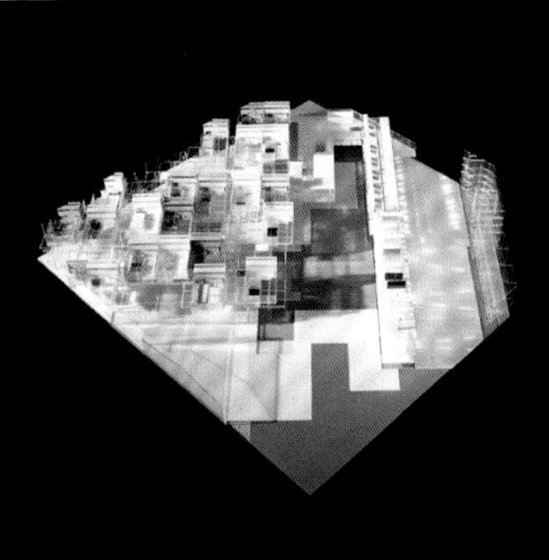

Core sample model: the diamond cropping of the model vertically and horizontally reveals the extension of space.

The narrow building wing to the right offers two types of floor-through apartments. All building types fuse structural, environmental and material engineering in a wider network of systems that make up the overall development.

Architect: Removed

Tax credits and the entrepreneurial mechanisms they were intended to incentivise would ideally carry a reflexive capacity, tipping this market into an innovative milieu. Yet in many ways the opposite has been true. A case study of Houston, Texas, in 1998, as HOPE VI programmes were taking hold, found speculative houses (in this instance, single-family homes typical for the area) were built with virtually no architectural engagement. In one case of several hundred standardised houses, it was found that the overall design fee paid for architectural services was less than US$5,000, or an average cost for design services per single-family house of $12. Architects in the US routinely seek 15 per cent of construction costs as a design and architectural service fee; in this case the market had provided a professional fee of 0.028 per cent.[1]

In US housing markets, mass-standardisation has of course meant low, if not nonexistent, design fees, but also little, if any, investment in research and development. While the debate of New Urbanism's relation to the transformation of public housing drew major attention in a range of ideological stances, it ultimately deflected the more urgent question of architecture's role in housing when the market is the denominator, and how the federal government, in seeking to disaggregate concentrations of poverty and incentivise the entrepreneurial aspects of capital markets, had also diminished architects' part in the deeply social and material aspects of housing.[2]

Tax credits and the myriad of financial instruments invented in the US since the early 1980s created a new strata of affordable and low-income housing development, but when coupled with a somewhat normative building industry and a latter-day form of syndication and distribution of the credit allocations (a narrow market), a new, generally non-innovative genre resulted that essentially sought to occlude the presence of these funding streams – the past modelled on the mode of neo-vernacular architecture here makes it difficult to see the actual financial, social and, ultimately, economic history of what is being worked on.

Standardising Mass-Heterogeneity

During this same period, other genres of architectural inquiry were often focused on dismantling the modes of mass-standardisation that were at the root of public housing. From conceptual work on the calculus of continual change to new fabrication methods and their capacity for individuation, a double project was at hand in the 1990s. Increasingly focused on reflexive behaviour and unique and one-off final products, this sprung from technical innovations that required large aggregate sums of money for research and development and the factories capable of complex production. If the conditions (the building industry in speculative housing) are not optimal or the example of public versus private housing seems unfair, the question remains: at what point does the drive for customisation that today is often seen as a game changer alter the role of the designer in the development market? Is mass customisation a way to allow deep market logic and yet sustain innovation – originality? New Urbanism has in many

ways been a mandated form of heterogeneity; certainly not mass customisation, but intended to provide difference and often mask the monolithic aspects of housing development (formally and financially). But today new computational control in design (even low-cost software) provides new levels of digital coordination with development practices, and a more precise way to define and stage risk and its management (of all types). These means often constitute the basis for a move towards an individuated landscape – a mass-customised environment. The normative way to discuss the transformation is to invoke a post-Taylorist or post-Fordist economy, to describe a new way to build or fabricate as an attribute of a new economic paradigm. In this realm, the reflexive capacity of a new architectural posture and a customised product has advocates, but what has been missing in this debate is a drift away from the social aspects of economics in production, and what could be seen as a shift towards more immediate forms of finance as a localised practice and the generative basis for a more local and therefore customised product (a building, a car, clothing).

Has the faith in mass customisation unwittingly made it difficult to discuss the wider project of economics, and more so to address the deeper strains of inequity that are enabled by enriched computational capacity in finance and banking regimes – capacity coupled with a lack of regulatory means to address a new milieu of transactions and their effects? In public and low-income housing, the customisation of financial practices has found a new means of standardisation – one that architectural heterogeneity leaves less evident or transparent to the public, but also the design world who sought change. In short, could mass customisation somehow short-circuit a critical engagement with the mass modes of economics and social capacities that are only possible if one seeks to understand that scale of collective wealth and capacity? Here, the architectural or urban focus on specific forms of reflexive or customised works often has the effect of diminishing a compensatory knowledge of the wider environment. A real-estate developer need not be an economist to be successful at housing (or office buildings), but they do need to enter and exit a market with some control over their investment – the 'return on investment'.

Decapitalising Innovation

During the past 20 years, low-income affordable and public housing policies have sought to diversify and disaggregate the funding streams that originate at the federal level. One goal has been to reinforce housing as a local territory, but also to create layers of financial innovation and market-like entrepreneurial development that (ideally) serve lower-income housing. Such efforts are still dependent on immense sums of money, and wide as well as deep federal resources, but the distribution means are now state- and city based by way of block grants, and often break down to the grain of a single voucher that in the hands of

left: The 'tensegrity deck' forms a network of public passages and gathering places above the city hall. Access to the deck is by way of elevators to parking below, but residents can walk in shaded areas to the retail or other housing types in the development, or along a wider zoning area in the city.

opposite: Courtyards visually fuse the diverse programmes and allow an immediate conflation of experiences – working at home is in immediate proximity to offices and government bodies. The Florida sky is seen through the tensegrity cables laced through the collective. Each house is an individuated form of mass and ballast in the wider network.

a homebuyer or renter is then attributed to a market house/apartment. This means that innovation in housing has to rely on less direct funding, but more so that it has to be realised within the same markets that produce housing for the whole of the US. The effect has been a dramatic loss of access to the deeper changes in housing economics; from the bundling of mortgages and tranches of debt to the widespread use of collateralised debt obligations and credit default swaps. A market fuelled by complex and time-based financial derivatives bet against a very normative and rudimentary building construction process. Perhaps more critical is a dramatic shift in the way in which architects, planners and engineers engage with the social questions that lie at the root of their work. On one hand it seems that mass customisation and other forms of coordinated or parametric control in design can indeed assist in creating a more advanced building industry (and surely will), but not necessarily in the reflexive aspects – the ergonometric zone of immediate need – that they often display an affinity for. Instead, the parametric capabilities in design by way of computation could bring architects into a more comprehensive relationship with the reflexivity of the market, in terms of the range of specific markets – from the pricing of materials to the orchestration of labour. But also in terms of the wider economic ability and capacity to envision new means of research and development or how a project is capitalised, altering the scope of parametric imagination and thereby the social potential of work.

Simultaneous City

Bell/Seong's Simultaneous City, commissioned for the 'Foreclosed: Rehousing the American Dream' exhibition at New York's Museum of Modern Art (MoMA) in 2012, followed the curators Barry Bergdoll and Reinhold Martin's mandate to seek a new form of public housing in the post-foreclosure US landscape. Exploring the potential of a public role in housing development, the project avoided (as untenable) direct government expenditure on housing, and instead focused on steering the small city of Temple Terrace, Florida towards using its local and immediate economic capacity to hold the land it had begun to assemble with tax revenue. The land purchased by the city was originally intended for release into a public/private partnership. However, instead of subsidising the private market (a developer), the project proposed the city re-zone property setbacks as well as purchase under-utilised private property and then reorganise these areas into a unique zoning and land use for the development of new housing types for previously underserved communities. The architecture in this zone would be realised

right: Working with Transsolar, Bell/Seong developed the 'Cool-Core' concept. The conditioning of the dwelling units was carried out in stages, from no air conditioning at the upper levels to a fully dehumidified and air-conditioned lower-level bedroom area. The programmatic layers reinforce each other financially and thermally to form a coordinated overall development.

opposite: Development plan. The site adjacent to North 56th Street serves as a model for a scale of engagement that could sustain housing, offices, retail and governmental uses. If realised as a unified structure, the aggregate funding could sustain a high level of structural and environmental engineering, and innovation.

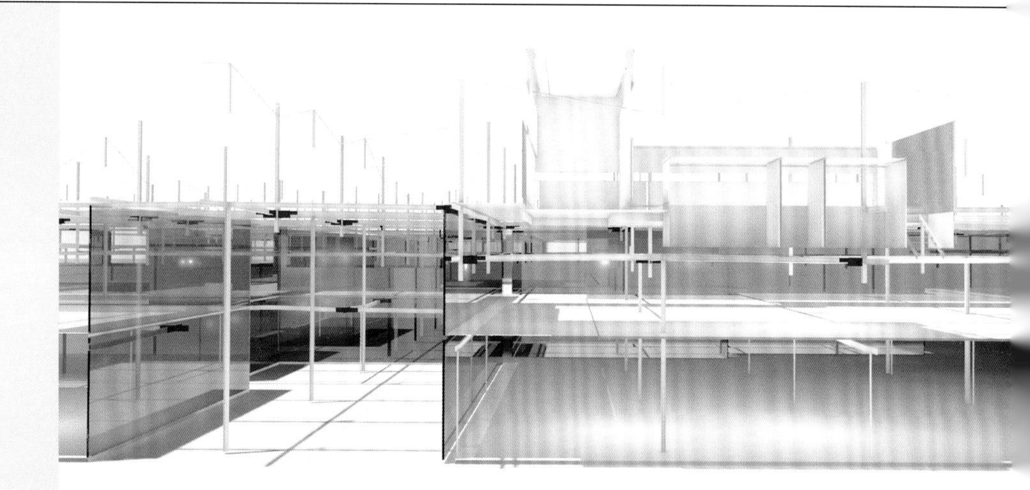

at a scale that sustains high levels of capital investment, but more so is imagined within the wider economic capacity of the citizens. A 90-hectare (225-acre) redevelopment zone that would have been subsidised for a private developer is instead held by the city, creating a new urban density that takes as its economic basis the collective capacity of the aggregate income of the households. Within this scheme, the architecture is reverse engineered, adding as many as 10,000 new residents to a city of 24,000 and seeking a development model that optimises the aggregate financial resources of those residents (approximately 4,000 new households).

Building to the collective income of the households meant that innovative material, structural and environmental engineering resources could be engaged, and also gave access to advanced building technologies and better quality control. The privacy and other aspects of suburban living could thus be sustained in a much deeper well of experimentation, modelling and coordination than suburban housing has historically provided. In effect, Simultaneous City is a new form of public housing on publicly held land, but it also relies on the aggregate private wealth of its inhabitants to generate the buying capacity necessary to fund a highly capitalised, R&D-laden and centrally conceived yet spatially distributed new architectural work.[3] It would not be possible to build with this level of engineering or material innovation without such capitalisation.

Much of the mass customisation we see today seems focused on immediate circumstance. Instead of analysing the breadth of financial resources as a long-term economic project, an immediate form or (micro) equity is granted (or sought after), paid by way of an ergonometric or responsive product (be this architecture, a TiVo-like experience, programmatic exchange). There is no doubt that customisation is powerful and has been so for some time, but it seems a crisis is brewing in the form of an amnesia of mass, standardised means of didactic value. In the US, the drive towards vouchers as a disaggregated and individuated type of former monolithic state support for low-income housing has had an inverse effect on architecture, leading to a mass-standardisation of market techniques and the dis-admission of architects within the social equation. Side effects and unintended consequences aside, one could be wary of a world so customised it masks real and necessary conflict, or worse keeps it from occurring. This has long seemed to have become a kind of anti-ideology – a way to avoid taking a stance.

Custom Finance, Social Economy

As housing and urban planning in the US continue to operate under the tremendous pressure of a prolonged process of foreclosure, the immense scale of federal subsidy that has underpinned a deeply uneven recovery has left one thing clear: speculative housing development as we know it and have allowed it to be realised for half a century is unstable, and has undergone wrenching forms of transformation that leave the idea of a responsive market under extreme duress (and without an alibi). In raw numbers, the foreclosure crisis that has unfolded since 2007 remains staggering. More than 15 million homes in the US have entered foreclosure proceedings since 2007, with more than 6 million having been completed and/or repossessed. This is approximately 11 times the number of public housing 'hard units' built since 1937. Discrepancies in the foreclosure market are regional, and also based on who has made new investments; that is, purchased houses out of foreclosure. Private equity funds account for as much as US$25 billion invested in foreclosed houses (with more than 200,000 homes purchased and re-securitised as rental income streams). Can architectural and manufacturing customisation techniques alter the economics and delivery of housing in the future? So far we have seen a wildly complex customisation of markets by way of financial instruments, and it could be said that architects have done little to acquaint themselves with, yet alone challenge, this strata of authority. The mathematics of customisation and the use of time in so much of the experimental architectural work today constituted under these auspices promise a new sophistication and entrée to the time-based scene of money. ⌂

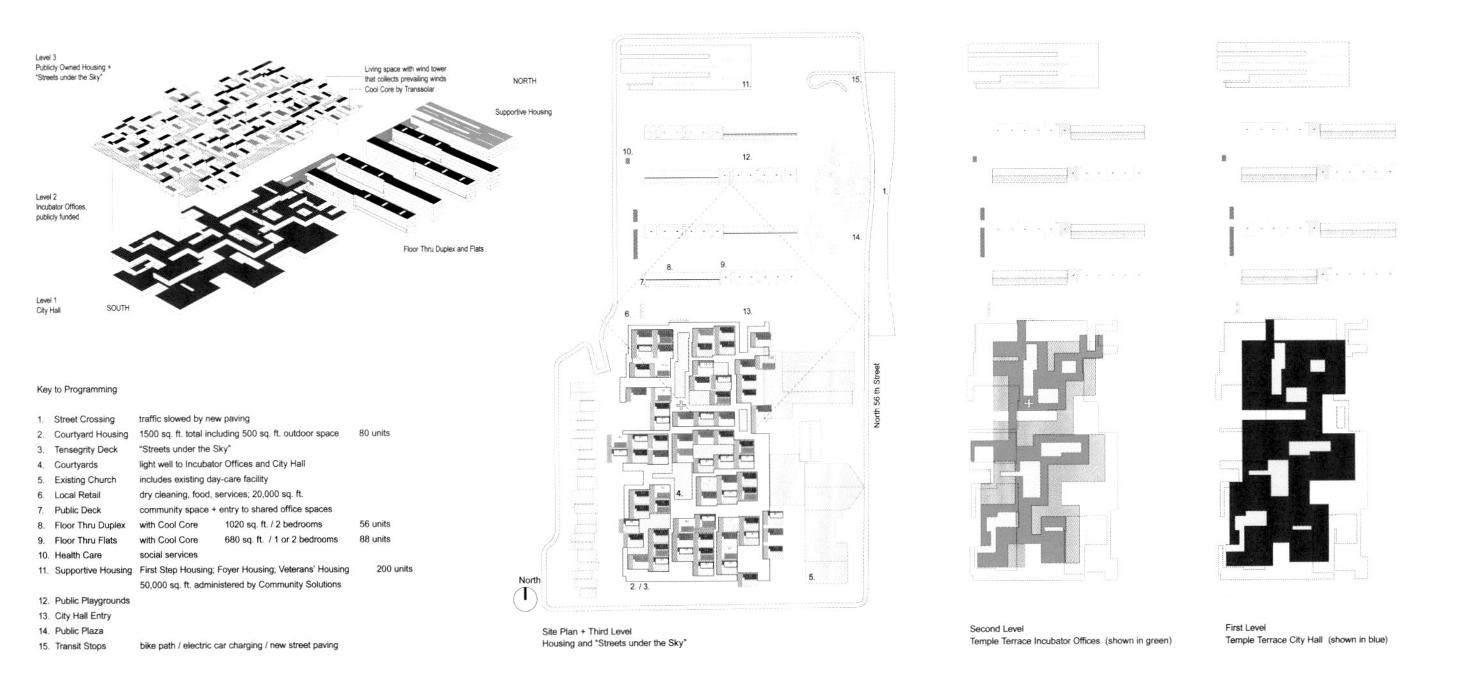

Site Plan + Third Level
Housing and "Streets under the Sky"

Second Level
Temple Terrace Incubator Offices (shown in green)

First Level
Temple Terrace City Hall (shown in blue)

Notes

1. For an analysis of quasi-market aspects of affordable and public housing development and federal shifts in housing policy during the 1990s, see Michael Bell, *16 Houses: Designing the Public's Private House*, Monacelli Press (New York), 2004.
2. For analysis of the geographic transformations in federal funding streams for housing, affordable housing and public housing development during the rise of tax credit programmes, voucher and other forms of localised public/private redevelopment, see Pascale Joassart-Marcelli, Juliet Musso and Jennifer Wolch, 'Federal Expenditures, Intrametropolitan Poverty, and Fiscal Disparities Between Cities', in Jennifer Wolch, Manuel Pastor and Peter Dreier (eds) (with a foreword by Michael Dear), *Up Against the Sprawl: Public Policy and the Making of Southern California*, University of Minnesota Press (Minneapolis, MN), 2004, pp 195–224.
3. For context on MoMA's 'Foreclosed: Rehousing the American Dream' exhibition and the Simultaneous City, see Barry Bergdoll and Reinhold Martin, *Foreclosed: Rehousing the American Dream*, The Museum of Modern Art (New York), 2012.

Branko Kolarevic

Centuries of capitalism and democracy in North America have led to a landscape that can be characterised by an unrelenting normalcy and uniformity, whether it is rows of family houses behind picket fences in suburbia or clusters of glazed towers in downtown districts. Here, **Branko Kolarevic**, Professor and Chair in Integrated Design at the University of Calgary Faculty of Environmental Design, questions why at a time that the production of consumer goods has been revolutionised by mass customisation, buildings and cities have remained largely resistant to its forces.

From Mass Customisation to Design 'Democratisation'

Housing development near Markham

Ontario

Canada

2005

Aerial view of a typical suburban development in North America.

The relative cultural homogeneity that pervades North American cities is in large part conditioned and perpetuated as such through the sameness of the physical environments in which the lives of middle-class Americans (and Canadians) unfold, from the suburban homes in which they live, to the glass-clad high-rise office buildings in which they work, and the endless low-rise strip malls where they shop. Karl Ove Knausgård, a contemporary Norwegian writer, vividly captured in a recent essay this synergetic relationship between the physical fabric of a typical North American city and its culture:

> The identical cars are followed by identical gas stations, identical restaurants, identical motels and, as an extension of these, by identical TV screens ... broadcasting identical entertainment and identical dreams. Not even the Soviet Union at the height of its power had succeeded in creating such a unified, collective identity. [1]

Knausgård is not the first to attribute such sameness – or, more precisely, lack of difference – to a modern system of mass production. Large-scale repetition was recognised early on in the 20th century as necessary for economic, low-cost production, whether of cars, houses or 25-storey glass towers. All of that, however, was supposed to change with the emergence of mass customisation in the 1990s as a post-Fordian paradigm for the economy of the 21st century. Mass customisation, defined by Joseph Pine as the mass production of individually customised goods and services,[2] offered the promise of a tremendous increase in variety and customisation without a corresponding increase in costs.

Over the past two decades, almost every segment of the economy, from services and consumer products to industrial production, has been affected by mass customisation. For example, today's consumers can create their own unique, non-standard, industrially produced shoes and jackets, choosing materials, colours and finishes as they please, at the same or marginally higher cost as the standard products made by the same manufacturer. Such 'material' or 'surface' customisation by customers is now an option in a range of industries, including commercial housing; 'dimensional' or 'geometric' customisation, however, is rather rare.

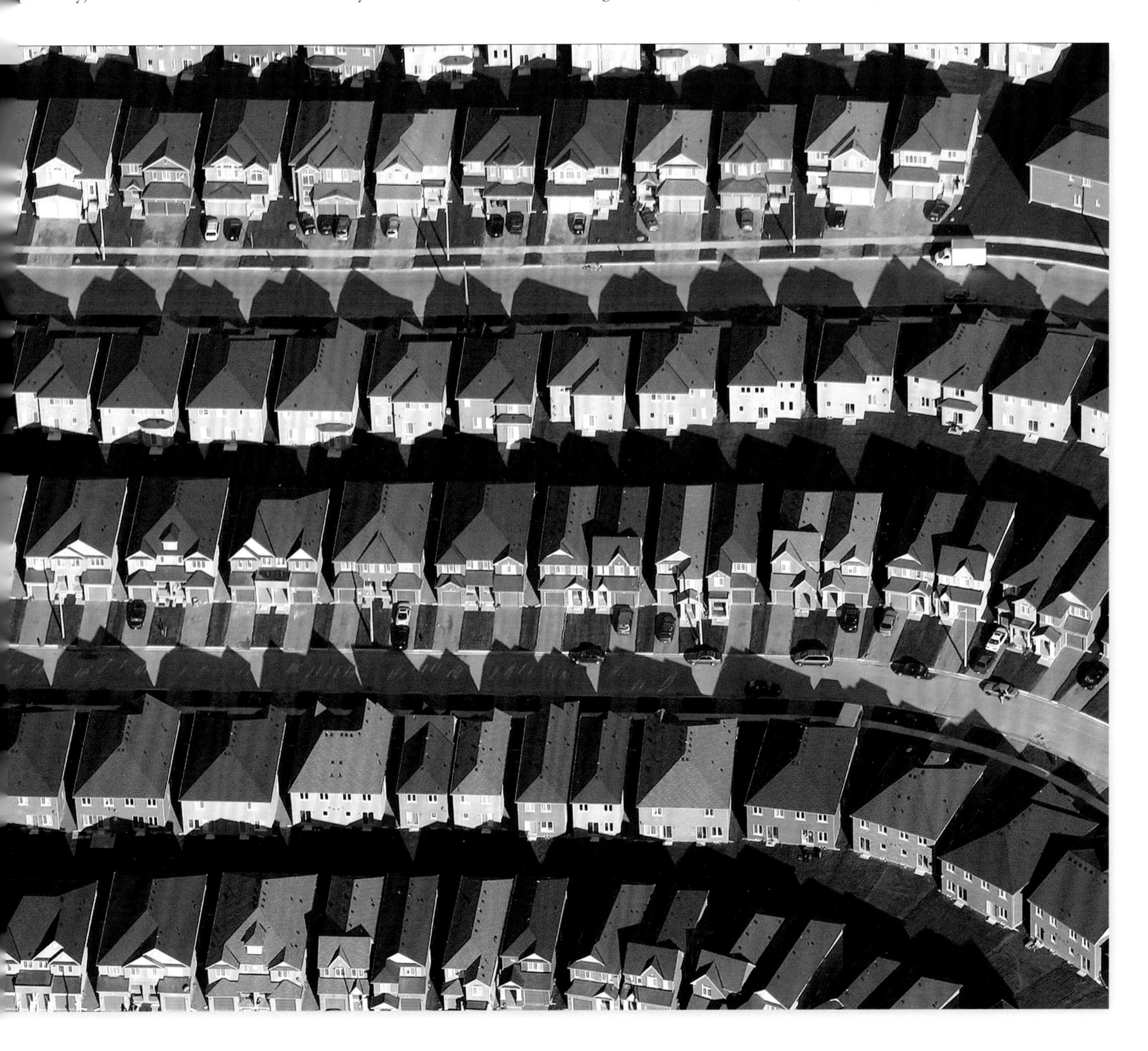

Reebok online store

2014

Today's consumers have the option of designing their own highly customised, yet industrially produced products.

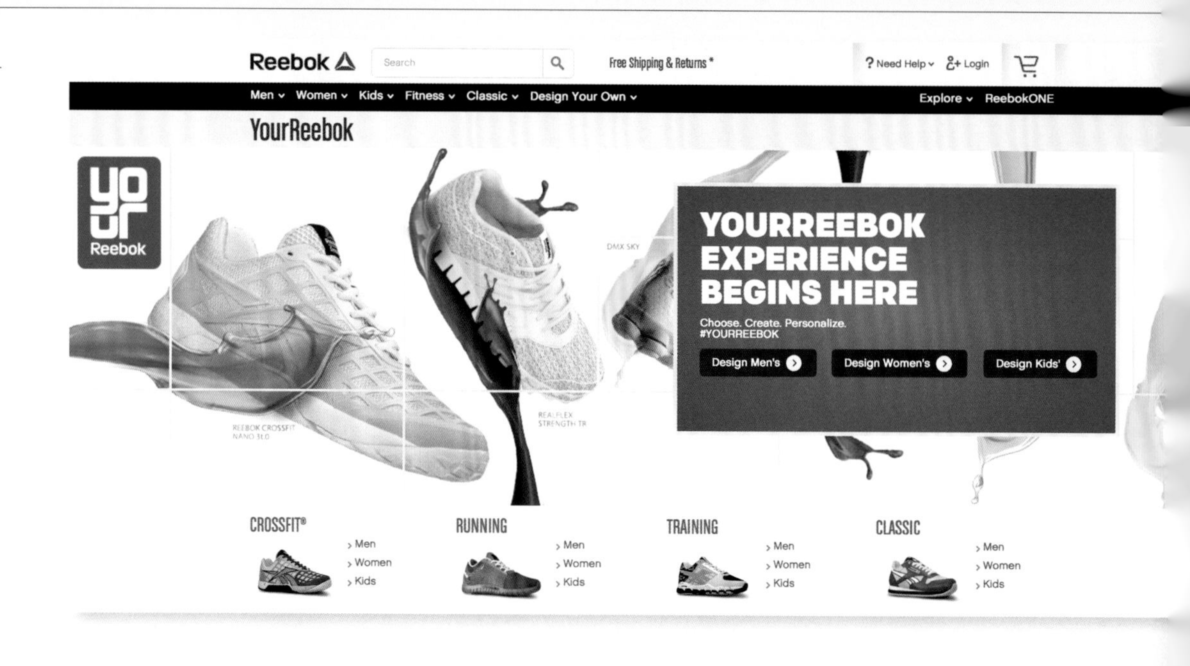

There are websites by architects and/or builders that enable anyone to choose the house design they like, explore available options, and then customise it (within some carefully imposed limits). The 'Design Your Own Home' website by Toll Brothers[3] offers hundreds of stylistically very different house designs; each comes with several options that do not affect the overall geometry of the house, including a choice of various material finishes. The Blu Homes website[4] features several different designs of prefabricated houses with various customisation options; the process starts with 'preliminary delivery assessment', followed by 'conceptual design' (online or in person), with 'code and zoning research' as the final step. The FAB house by Calgary-based Housebrand[5] is a complete design-and-delivery system based on a modular design that provides a considerable degree of freedom in how each house 'shell' can be configured as a one-, two-, three- or four-bedroom house, with considerable cost and time savings. The website by New York firm Resolution: 4 Architecture offers 'modern modular' homes with 'predefined typologies ... formed from a series of standard modules, minimizing cost of production and maximizing possible combinations available for the consumer'.[6] They all offer ways to customise predefined house designs, but none offers dimensional customisation – interactive manipulation of the house's overall geometry – online. Why this is the case is an interesting issue.

Meta-Designing a House

Dimensional mass customisation is a particularly suitable production paradigm for the housing sector of the building industry, since houses (and buildings in general) are mostly one-off, highly customised products. It could also mean that a truly 'custom' house with a unique geometry – shape and form – could eventually become available to a broader segment of society. The technologies to deliver economically mass-produced, yet highly

Blu Homes

'3D Configurator'

2014

left: The site lets any visitor to the website choose and customise a selected house design.

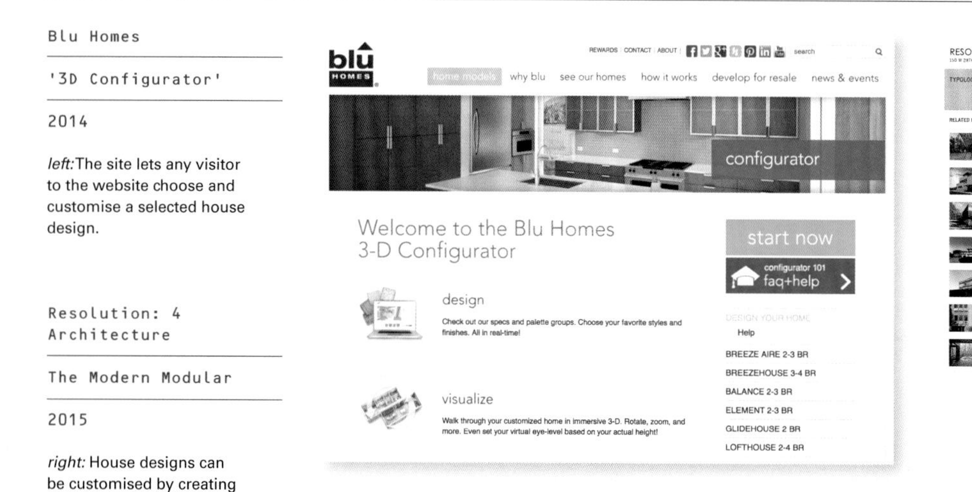

Resolution: 4 Architecture

The Modern Modular

2015

right: House designs can be customised by creating different relationships between predefined modules.

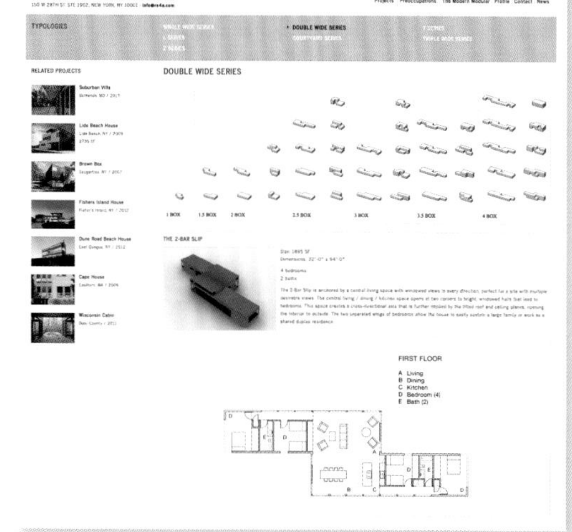

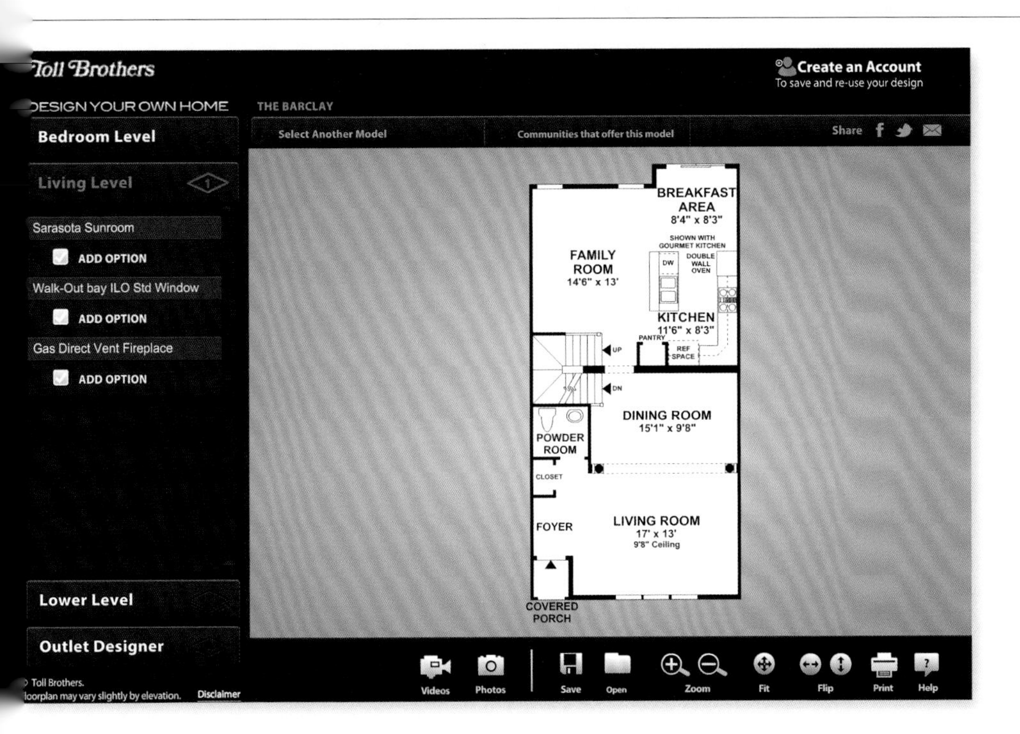

Toll Brothers

'Design Your Own Home'

2014

The Toll Brothers site offers hundreds of customisable house designs, with various options and different material finishes.

customised houses are there: parametric design, digital fabrication, interactive websites for design, visualisation, evaluation and estimating (and automatic generation of production and assembly data). The challenges for wider adoption of house design that can be interactively customised are not technological; as will be argued later on, they are largely social (cultural).

What makes mass customisation of house designs based on parametric variation particularly compelling is that it could deliver homogeneous heterogeneity at the scale of the neighbourhood. Typologically – and topologically – the houses would be very similar, if not identical, yet their layout and geometry could vary considerably. Such typological (and topological) sameness, with differences in the overall layout, shapes, and forms, is what characterises many traditional, historic neighbourhoods. Adding variable geometry – via parametrics – would add elements of difference that would not compromise the overall sense of stylistic or formal unity that might be an overarching design goal at the scale of the neighbourhood.

Such an approach to mass-customised homes requires a definition of a 'metatype' by the designer, as well as a 'metadesign' – a design process that could produce an infinite number of individually tailored variations that differ from each other, yet remain within the metatype defined by the designer. Instead of designing a single house, or creating several slightly different designs, the architect would in this scenario become a meta-designer, creating a parametric definition that can produce thousands of different designs. A parametric definition of a house's geometry could then be made accessible via an interactive website to the masses, who could then design their own unique versions of the house.

Housebrand

FAB house

2015

Housebrand has conceived a complete design-and-delivery system based on a modular house design that is highly customisable.

Thus, a mass-customisable house would be parametrically defined, interactively designed (via a website or an app), and digitally prefabricated, using file-to-factory processes. While this is technologically possible and economically attainable, it is nevertheless socially and culturally questionable. After all, how many of us have designed our own shoes or jackets? How many of us would dare design our own parametrically variable car (if such an option were available)? How many of us would have the confidence that such a car would have good performance characteristics and be aesthetically pleasing? How many of us are prepared to become designers instead of just customers?

'Democratising' Design

The implied 'democratisation' of design – through mass customisation – raises additional questions, such as the authorship of design and the functional and aesthetic quality of products (shoes, tableware, furniture, houses) created by non-designers. It also presents interesting conceptual challenges in the design of software that facilitates customisation. For example, the parametric design 'engine' should ensure that each dimensionally customised product performs well (structurally and environmentally in the case of houses). In addition, the designs should be aesthetically acceptable, requiring that purely qualitative aspects of design be somehow measured and quantitatively assessed within the software.

Bernard Cache was one of the first designers to 'democratise' design by making his parametrically defined furniture and panelling designs publicly accessible over the Internet in 1997. Cache's 'objectiles', as he referred to his designs, were conceived as non-standard objects, procedurally calculated in modelling software and industrially produced using CNC machines. It was the modification of the design parameters that allowed the manufacturing of different shapes in the same series, thus making the mass customisation – the industrial production of unique objects – possible.[7] Anyone could change online the parameter values that controlled the geometry of the objectiles simply by manipulating the sliders, and could immediately see the effects of the changes.[8]

Greg Lynn's pioneering Embryological House project from the late 1990s highlighted the potential of mass customisation based on parametric design and digital fabrication. The 'blobby' geometry of the house was parametrically defined, enabling considerable variety within the metatype. Each house was to be digitally fabricated, with components then assembled onsite. Different house designs were made publicly accessible through a website, where potential clients could see the chosen design in plan and elevations, with additional information if interested, and then choose the materials. The website was at best a sketch, offering rudimentary functionality without any parametric variation, but it was a harbinger of things to come.

Fabio Gramazio and Matthias Kohler went a step further in 2002 with their mTable, a parametrically variable table design (with holes) that customers could 'co-design'.[9] They created an interactive application for mobile phones so that customers could easily specify the size, dimensions, material and colour of the table. Next, by placing 'deformation points' on the underside of the table and 'pressing' them, the customers could create holes with very thin edges. If satisfied with the design, they then transmitted the parameters that defined the table as a simple series of numbers to a website where the designed table was rendered in high resolution. A final step was the placement of the production order, with the table fabricated by a CNC milling machine.

Bernard Cache

Objectiles

1997

below: The online interface for designing 'objectiles' – non-standard objects – featured interactive manipulation of the parametrically defined geometry.

Greg Lynn

Embryological House

1997

right: The website was an early attempt at offering mass-customisable house designs.

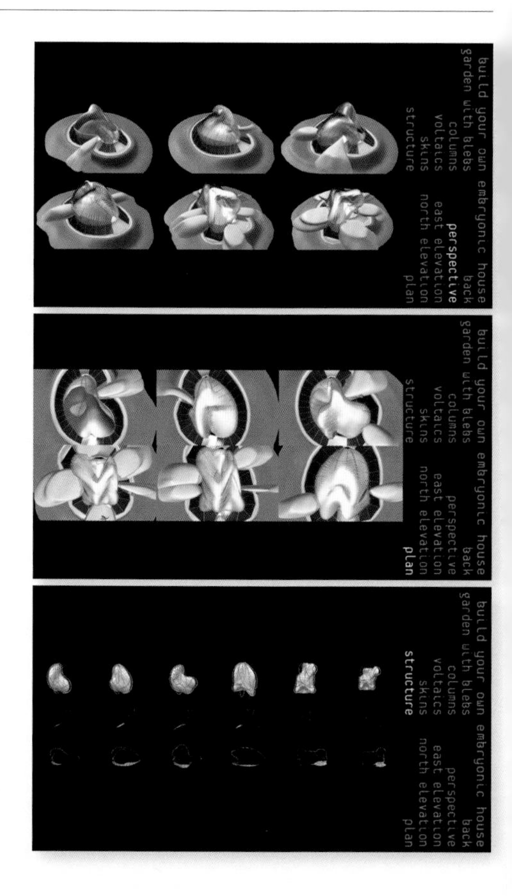

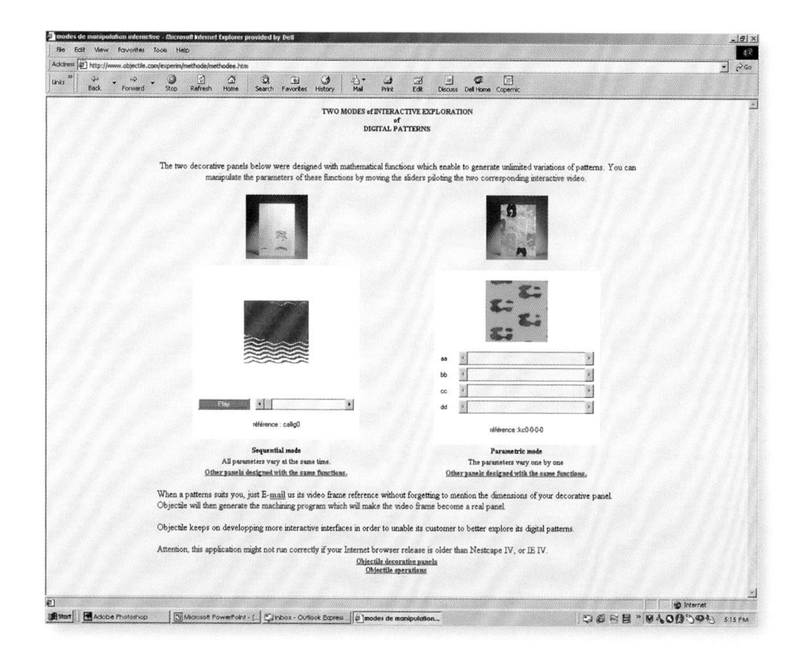

Gramazio and Kohler

mTable

2002

Various mTable designs created by customers using a mobile phone app.

As was the case with Cache's objectiles, a simple interface coupled with parametric minimalism makes customers focus on the most essential design features. While each mTable has a unique geometry, all share an identical 'standard' underlying parametric model – a metadesign. That single parametric definition of the geometry can generate an infinite number of 'non-standard' shapes or forms, all of which belong to the same design family – the same design space.

Gramazio and Kohler were not just interested in parametrics. They wanted to 'examine the consequences of customer interaction when designing non-standard products'.[10] The project raised a number of interesting questions, such as the extent of responsibility that a customer was able and willing to assume in making certain design decisions, and more importantly, who ultimately is the author of the final design – the designer of the parametric system, or the 'customer' who chose the parameter values for the design. It also raised questions about the nature of designing mass-customised products, where the emphasis shifts away from designing a particular form with a discrete set of dimensions, to a parametric system that can produce a range of designs. The designers have to define dimensional ranges (minima and maxima) instead of discrete dimensions, and create design rules that limit the generation of 'bad' designs. While the aesthetic judgement is seemingly transferred to the customer, a designer retains principal control over key elements of the design, deciding which decisions the customer can make.

Such democratisation of the design process has interesting implications for the building industry, especially in its most commoditised sector – the commercial provision of suburban housing, as discussed earlier. It is possible that we will soon see the emergence of websites where customers can dimensionally (and fully) customise the overall spatial layout and appearance of their chosen house design, for example selecting the size of the living room, location of the entry door, right down to the number of mullions in the windows (let alone the materials and finishes, which is already on offer). Such customer-designed homes could be then verified structurally or otherwise, with the geometry of various components generated directly for automated production using digital fabrication and robotic assembly. These technologies already exist, so there are no technological impediments to implementing such design and production systems. The challenges are largely cultural; it is unlikely that most customers would be willing to assume responsibility for the design of their homes.

These scenarios also redefine the central task that architects of mass-customised homes would have to undertake: instead of designing with discrete dimensions, they would be designing with dimensional ranges in mind, with minima and maxima, as already discussed. This also requires a careful definition of parametric hierarchies in the definition of the house's geometry, starting with the 'global' parameters that affect the overall geometry, down to the 'local' parameters that define, for example, the number and the spacing of window mullions. And then there is the most important challenge – ensuring that the designs that emerge out of the operation of the parametric system are not only viable, but also 'good'. The aesthetic challenge will thus remain: as a society and a culture, we do not have a capacity to weed out bad designs in the world of mass-produced suburban housing, let alone in a mass-customised one. ⌂

Notes

1. Karl Ove Knausgård, 'My Saga, Part 1', *New York Times Sunday Magazine*, 1 March 2015, p MM34.
2. Joseph B Pine, *Mass Customization: The New Frontier in Business Competition*, Harvard Business School Press (Boston, MA), 1993.
3. See designyourownhome.com.
4. See bluhomes.com.
5. See housebrand.ca for more information.
6. See re4a.com.
7. For Bernard Cache, 'objects are no longer designed but calculated', allowing the design of complex forms and laying 'the foundation for a nonstandard mode of production'. See Bernard Cache, *Earth Moves: The Furnishing of Territories*, MIT Press (Cambridge, MA), 1995, p 88.
8. The website objectile.com is no longer functional.
9. Fabio Gramazio and Matthias Kohler, 'Towards a Digital Materiality', in Branko Kolarevic and Kevin Klinger (eds), *Manufacturing Material Effects*, Routledge (London), 2008, pp 103–18.
10. *Ibid.*

On Modelling Complexity and Urban Form

M Christine Boyer

As generators of new cities or extensions of existing ones, algorithmic urban models provide a means of designing urban forms of a new complexity. They have the capacity to produce extremely intricate architectural forms, but also to be responsive to scenarios and constraints. **M Christine Boyer**, the William R Kenan Jr Professor of Architecture at Princeton University, reflects on how 'architects acting as an interface between data sets and computer algorithms' might shape distinctive urban environments that lead to the mass customisation of cities.

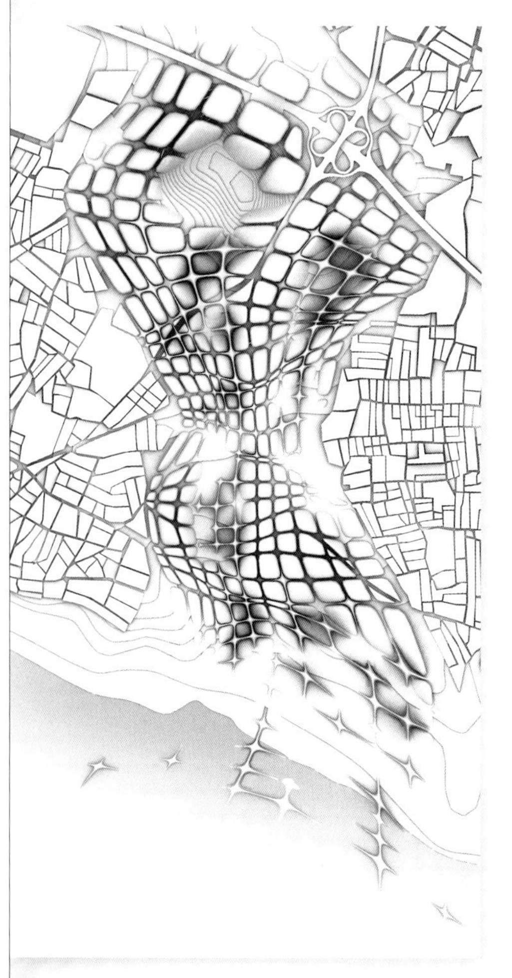

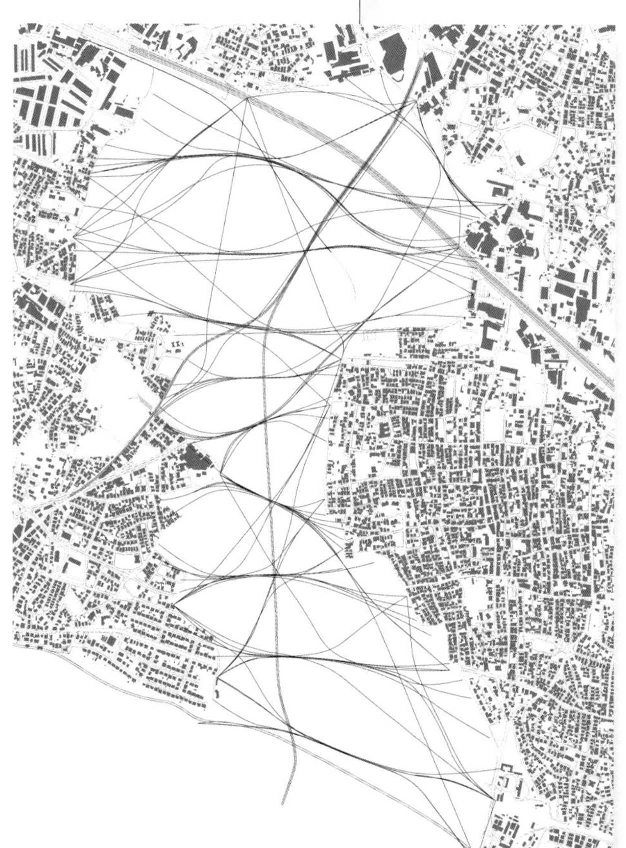

Zaha Hadid Architects
Kartal masterplan
Istanbul
Turkey
2007

left: Commissioned by the Greater Istanbul Municipality and Kartal Urban Regeneration Association, the Kartal masterplan is a 2006 winning competition proposal for a new civic, residential, commercial and transport hub approximately 25 kilometres (15 miles) to the southeast of the city.

Neurons transmitting information

opposite: Neurons transmitting flows of information in a neural network, as a parallel model of an autopoietic system.

... ever since the development of high-powered computers, a method of inquiry has come into use whereby all dynamic systems are equal: the equation of change is not integrated but implemented by the computer. The machine 'simulates' the system and produces, step by step, the trajectory the equations dictate.

— Isabelle Stengers, *Cosmopolitics I*, 2010, pp 165–6[1]

Mathematical models and their related computer simulations are located somewhere between theory and experiment, abstract ideas and pragmatic action.[2] They are objects as well as ideas, judged on the basis of their usefulness in understanding, describing and exploring complex systems. Models thus aim to account for a set of facts, describing and explaining them, how they work together, how they produce their effects. Urban models can be used to design a masterplan for a section of an existing city or a city built on empty fields. They can generate different scenarios based on urban theories as inputs, connect these theories to different data sets, and make predictions about different formal configurations based on alternative sets of constraints. Urban algorithms can take data from sensors embedded in urban fabric either to describe in real time or make future forecasts about infrastructure failures, criminal activities, traffic flows, pollution levels, service breakdowns and so on.

Are their urban models robust enough to simulate complex urban processes and material modifications as these shift and evolve with time?

If architects have been constructors of static architectural types imposed on urban form, now in the era of information and computer algorithms, can they build urban models of sufficient complexity that generate intricate urban forms? Can architects acting as an interface between data sets and computer algorithms generate distinctive urban environments that suggest the 'mass customisation' of cities? Do they have sufficient data sets? Are their urban models robust enough to simulate complex urban processes and material modifications as these shift and evolve with time? As architectural model-makers become manipulators of abstract models of data flows and parametric interactions, it is expected that the shape of urban form will emerge from these unfolding processes. The outputs become 'snapshots' of time representing one slice of continuous variation and correlation of numerous layers of data.

Descriptive Models of Urban Complexity

The city has long been described as a complex set of relationships, asymmetric negotiations and conflicts between human and non-human actors in constant negotiation and change. As a complex dynamic system, the city responds to a multiplicity of forces, transforming over time in an open-ended manner. It is a complicated entity, not decomposable into simpler subsystems; an irritable system perturbed by multiple choices and entangled with material processes. It achieves states that are far from equilibrium. Hence any model of city processes must examine the dynamics of unstable systems full of fluctuations, multiple choices and limited predictability.[3] Is it surprising, then, that urban models of shifting complexity and constant mutation have been likened to self-organising autopoietic systems?

While focused on biological systems, one of the authors of autopoietic systems theory, Francisco Varela, claimed that an autopoietic system is a complex organisation in which information transmittal, reception and interruption proceed recursively through continual feedback and feed forward across multiple levels within the system. In turn, these interactions and the subsequent transformations to the organisational structure of the system they enact, regenerate and realise a network of processes that re-constitute the system by itself. Hence constant communication – or interaction, the relay of information – is essential to every living system; it is what guarantees the emergence of self-organisation and self-maintenance over time.[4]

When applied to the description of how urban form emerges, autopoietic systems theory disavows any intention of a predetermined blueprint, plan of action or rational organisation imposed on urban form, advocating instead that cities are completely determined by their own improvisations and experimental mutations. Without a plan of action laid out in advance, order or greater complexity is expected simply to emerge over time from the myriad flows of information and interactive processes. Form is ever emergent rather than given in advance, evidenced in bottom-up patterns of self-organised urbanisation of informal settlements located in interstitial spaces of third-world cities. It is present in any attempt to describe the conditions of cities in the 21st century.

Nothing exemplifies the concept that autopoietic systems are intrinsically emergent processes more than does climate change: the result of massive entanglements of conscious human actions and inactions, material and immaterial forces. Climate change is today's great threat: the sudden large-scale disruption of self-organising, self-amplifying events such as hurricanes and heat waves wreaking havoc on local communities.[5] The natural environment foments uncertainty, contingency and crisis anywhere, anytime. It can hardly be regulated as scientists once thought. Cities of the 21st century and climate change can no longer be described as an aggregate of their parts; they are complex systems of irreversible states and emergent forms.

Generative Models of Urban Complexity

The ability to generate complex urban forms that model the layers of information a city requires remains an unknown and undetermined endeavour. Models constructed tend to react to a finite set of formal parameters that are far from constituting the completeness required in urban dynamics.[6] In reality, urban processes operate simultaneously, resulting in an assemblage of factors that exhibit nonlinear behaviour, threshold effects, risk and indeterminacy, as do the descriptive models of climate change. Neither simplistic nor tranquil complexities, cities can be described and penetrated only via a multiplicity of conflicting discourses.

In counter-distinction to descriptive models, computer algorithms generating urban form are modes of data modelling: they depend on *a priori* selection of data points, and software that manipulates these points on a relational grid to produce smooth surfaces and spatial patterns. Urban models incorporating multiple layers of data seek to govern future urban form, albeit it in a finite manner. Topological surface manipulations are likened to biomorphic transformations in which evolutionary processes move towards higher levels of complexity, but do so within predetermined forms that grow in scale and form over time.

Parametric urbanism based on generative algorithms is a method of designing city systems where the model is programmed to simulate procedural relations between infrastructural variables.

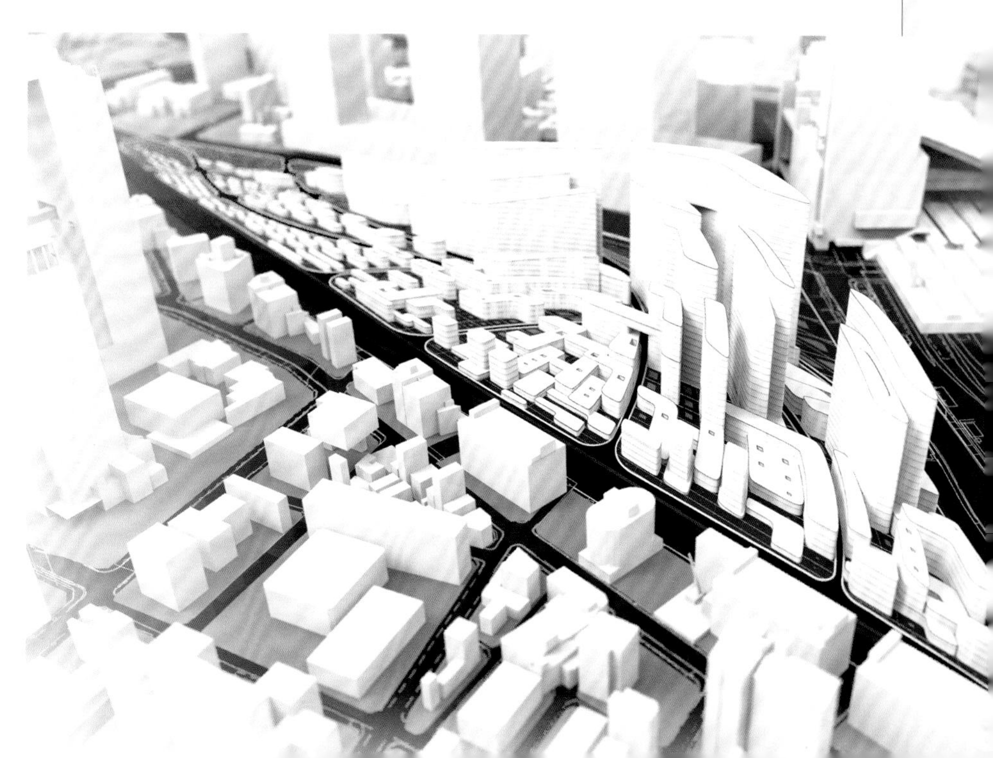

OCEAN CN Consultancy Network and Arup Hong Kong Second Development Zone
Umekita Area
Osaka
Japan
2013-14

Aerial view for a single snapshot in time of a possible formation of the diverse programmatic massing typologies, in which the computational intelligence of the digital model negotiates a complex context comprising small aggregate urbanism and very large-scale deep-plan and deep-section buildings.

What is visualised is the processing of the computer system's iterative meshing and looping, not that of urban dynamics. The designer draws up a finite list of parameters about the visualisation of urban form, the massing and ornamentation of objects, their structure and morphological arrangements, plus a few functional uses of urban space, which by necessity ignores many factors, such as the cultural uses of space, quality of life, public preferences and environmental concerns, not to mention housing needs, poverty issues, population statistics, political mandates – all the myriad factors and conflictual negotiations that comprise a city.

In parametric urbanism, either form follows the design procedures generating hypothetical masterplans on a tabula rasa – morphological patterns of spatial units that can be recalibrated to offer a range of solutions. These generative methods of urban design are based on procedural simulation of space that entails iterative loops and cause–effect relationships. They seek stability, and cannot operate in a less systematic or unpredictable manner. Or parametric urbanism elaborates simple predictive scenarios that instruct decision-makers about the impending state of a city. So-called 'smart' city models are updated by real-time data inputs from sensors distributed on infrastructure across the city monitoring traffic flows and blockages, water systems, energy usage, garbage pickup, parking availability and so on.[7] They offer city managers a proactive role in anticipating problem areas, enabling reaction to the system's behaviour in order to avoid inefficiencies in service delivery and threats of unnecessary costs.

In either case, control is defined as reacting to a set of pre-scripted or predetermined variables. But lacking a master algorithm embodying the theory of urban dynamics to build models of urban self-organisation, parametric urbanism cannot simulate the actual behaviour of a city in real time nor engender new urban designs except in a simplified manner by tweaking its set of variables. But it does allow for exploration of simultaneous processes and sequential actions that determine urban form.

Computational Precedents

It was initially thought by architects in the 1990s that because computation involves complex processes such as recursion, rule-based intelligence and simulation, these could be catalytic in addressing design problems. 'However,' writes Costa Terzidis, 'due to the complex nature of the processes very few designers were in a position to understand and implement them in a meaningful way in design,'[8] Terzidis goes on to explain that computing:

> is about the exploration of indeterminate, vague, unclear and often ill-defined processes ... it aims at emulating or extending the human intellect. It is about rationalization, reasoning, logic, algorithm, deduction, induction, extrapolation, exploration and estimation. In its manifold implications, it involves problem-solving, mental structures, cognition, simulation and rule-based intelligence, to name a few.[9]

It thus requires the elaboration of new modes of thought more in line with scientific experimentation.

What is needed is a more speculative questioning of the theoretical-experimental modelling complex. It is not about finding a set of well-defined data to build a more accurate urban model, nor applying parametric urbanism to any set of data. The danger is explaining away what the model has no need to account for.[10] Nor should the architect simply apply the brute force of computation to generate spectacular visualisations of urban form, or apply the theory of complexity metaphorically or conceptually.[11]

Initiating the concept 'parametric architecture' (1957), Luigi Moretti wrote that:

> [s]cientific research, the enumeration of the parameters, and the quantitative mathematical analysis of these parameters are tasks that the new architecture will have to face, in an a priori manner in every case. In this way what I have long solicited and call 'parametric architecture' will be born. Its ineluctable geometric character, its rigorous concatenation of forms, the absolute freedom of fantasy that will spring up in places where equations cannot fix their own roots, will give it a crystal splendor.[12]

In 1957, Moretti established the Institute for Mathematical and Operational Research in Urbanism (IRMOU) to promote the use of mathematical models for studying traffic flows, the distribution of services, and optimal location of housing in city centres. Some of IRMOU's work became the focus of the 'Parametric Architecture' exhibition at the 12th Milan Triennial in 1960. Moretti's parametric studies of urban stadiums were on display. Sightlines from spectators' seats to points in the field were used to generate 'contour line' graphs reflecting optimum viewing areas, and based on these visibility curves Moretti then constructed butterfly-shaped cavera models.

Frei Otto and his collaborators at the Institute of Lightweight Structures (ILEK) in Stuttgart were another precursor of parametric urbanism. From 1964, Otto conducted systematic form-finding experiments using hanging chains, soap bubbles, plaster and plastic film as explanatory models to predict efficient structural forms. As these projects increased in scale he pioneered the use of computer-based procedures to analyse their shape and behaviour. ILEK also developed theories on the structuring of space and settlement patterns, including the notion of urban networks as emerging and self-organised systems based on laws of attraction/repulsion and occupying/connecting. These were paralleled by experiments that investigated different distancing occupations of magnetic needles, grains of sand, soap bubbles and ink blots as analogue models of settlement patterns.[13]

Another precedent for parametric urbanism stems from efforts at the Architectural Department at Cambridge University from the late 1950s to the 1970s. The research at the Centre for Land Use and Built Form Studies (LUBFS), directed by Leslie Martin and then by Lionel March, tried to establish a rigorous method through which architectural and urban ideas could emerge.[14] Modelling, for these researchers, was based on observing and abstracting relevant characteristics of built form. The purpose of a model was to provide a simplified and intelligible representation of reality in order to understand it better, and to question how the model affected urban form. Translated into architectural terms, it was necessary for rational and speculative thought to make contact. Designers need to understand the structuring framework of cities to be able to open up to a range of choices and opportunities for future development.[15]

Towards a Simplified and Adaptive Urban Model

Although cities generate massive amounts of information, and while our descriptive and generative complexity models are quite sophisticated, what we need today are simplified models of cities and, after experimentation, a greater understanding about which variables engender policies that might affect urban form. Towards such an end, Luís Bettencourt, a complexity theorist, is asking what kind of adaptive system a city is and how this awareness might guide a more scientific approach to urban planning.[16] After collecting data on many cities of different sizes, from megacities to shrinking cities, the evidence suggests they are actually quite simple; their global properties reduce to a few key parameters. Size is the major determinant; history, geography and design play secondary roles. Bettencourt understands cities to be integrated social networks embedded in space and time.

Frei Otto
Munich Olympic Stadium
1972

Roof tensile structures designed by Frei Otto, demonstrating a force-driven approach to the intelligent form-finding of the roof structure of the stadium.

Zaha Hadid Architects
Nordpark Cable Railway
Hungerburg Station
Innsbruck
Austria
2007

One of a series of four cable railway stations, expressing an architectural language of fluidity, along Innsbruck's northern chain of mountains. Lightweight organic roof structures float on concrete plinths.

The key variables are spatial concentration and speed of social interactions:

> In terms of urban design, this conceptualization of cities emphasizes the importance of generative models, where local structures remain to be developed by agents possessing particular goals and information, but must also be constrained by the function of the city as a whole, as an open-ended 'social reactor'.[17]

Understanding the general applicability of these factors, and how the form and function of cities are determined by network principles, is only a descriptive starting point; it does not offer a new model of what cities are. That requires further experimental testing to create designs that are generative of the whole, but leave smaller parts unspecified. Cities, Bettencourt reminds us, are not artefacts to be redesigned or controlled at will; they evolve spontaneously under general circumstances and across scales towards an open-ended expression of human sociality.[18]

Mass Customisation of Urban Form

It is easiest to observe and describe the articulations of information flows, the multiplicity of encounters with matter and actions in the case of cities and climate change. It is more difficult to build simulation models to generate new urban forms of intricate complexity. There remains a distinction to be made between descriptive devices and methodological generators – those that apply a theory to conceptualise urban form and those that try to generate new urban form from a variety of data sets. Yet a new amalgam is being forged by digital computation procedures – from simulation to scripting and agent-based modelling, mixed with biological theoretical descriptions of growth and change from evolutionary theories and genetic coding, to autopoietic systems theory – combined with growing awareness that matter shapes form as much as form imprints matter. This is the beginning of the road towards the mass customisation of intricate individuated urban forms. ᗡ

Designed and Informal Housing
Rio de Janeiro

Housing conceived and implemented as a top-down planning process adjacent to emergent slums.

Notes

1. Isabelle Stengers, *Cosmopolitics I*, trans Robert Bononno, University of Minnesota Press (Minneapolis, MN), 2010, pp 165–6.
2. Sergio Sismondo, 'Models Simulations and their Objects', *Science in Context*, 2, 1999, pp 247–60.
3. Ilya Prigogine, *The End of Certainty: Time, Chaos, and the New Laws of Nature*, The Free Press (New York), 1996.
4. Francisco Varela, *Principles of Biological Autonomy* (1979), quoted in Wolfgang Iser, *The Range of Interpretation*, Columbia University Press (New York), 2000, p 101.
5. Brian Massumi, 'National Enterprise Emergency: Steps Toward an Ecology of Powers', *Theory Culture & Society*, 26 (6), 2009, pp 153–85.
6. Robson Canuto da Silva and Luiz Manuel do Eirado Amorim, 'Parametric Urbanism: Emergence, Limits and Perspectives of a New Trend in Urban Design Based on Parametric Design Systems', *VIRUS*, 3, 2010: www.nomads.usp.br/virus/virus03/submitted/layout.php?item=2&lang=en.
7. Paolo Fusero, Lorenzo Massimiano, Arturo Tedeschi and Sara Lepidi, 'Parametric Urbanism: A New Frontier for Smart Cities', *Planum. The Journal of Urbanism*, 27 (2), 2013, pp 1–13.
8. Costa Terzidis, *Algorithmic Architecture*, Princeton Architectural Press (New York), 2006, p 54.
9. *Ibid*, p 58.
10. Isabelle Stengers, 'The Challenge of Complexity: Unfolding the Ethics of Science: In Memorium Ilya Prigogine', *Emergence: Organisation and Complexity (E:CO)*, 6 (1–2), 2004, pp 92–9.
11. Axel Kilian, 'The Question of the Underlying Model and its Impact on Design', in Emily Abruzzo, Eric Ellingson and Jonathan D Solomon (eds), *Models*, 306090 Inc (New York), 2007, pp 208–13.
12. Luigi Moretti, 'Form as Structure' (1957), quoted in Federico Bucci and Mario Mulazzani (eds), *Luigi Moretti: Works and Writings*, Princeton Architectural Press (New York), 2002, pp 183–4.
13. Frei Otto, *Occupying and Connecting Thoughts on Territories and Spheres of Influence with Particular Reference to Human Settlement*, Editions Axel Menges (Stuttgart), 2009.
14. Altino Joao de Magalhaes Rocha, 'Architecture Theory 1960–1980: Emergence of a Computational Perspective', unpublished PhD, Department of Architecture, Massachusetts Institute of Technology (MIT), January 2004.
15. Leslie Martin, 'The Grid as Generator', in Leslie Martin and Lionel March, *Urban Space and Structures*, Cambridge University Press (Cambridge), 1972, pp 6–27.
16. Luís MA Bettencourt, 'The Kind of Problem a City is: New Perspectives on the Nature of Cities from Complex Systems Theory', in Dietmar Offenhube and Carlo Ratti (eds), *De-Coding the City*, Birkhäuser (Basel), 2014, pp 168– 79; Luís MA Bettencourt, 'The Origins of Scaling in Cities', *Science*, 340, June 2013, pp 1438–41; Luís Bettencourt and Geoffrey West, 'A Unified Theory of Urban Living', *Nature*, 467, October 2010, pp 912–13.
17. Luís MA Bettencourt, 'The Kind of Problem a City is', *op cit*, p 169.
18. *Ibid*, p 177.

Hina Jamelle
and Ali Rahim

Contemporary Architecture Practice

Samsung Raemian Housing Masterplan

Contemporary Architecture Practice
Samsung Raemian Housing Masterplan
Haan River
Seoul
Korea
2011-

A three-dimensional prototype of one of the masterplan buildings showing the inflection of form due to the interior spatial configurations, vertical alignments and maximum variations permitted within Samsung building components.

Haan River
Seoul
Korea

In Seoul, the relentless uniformity of new speculative housing developments is such that it caused the mayor to intervene in 2009 by passing a law requiring differentiation. **Hina Jamelle** and **Ali Rahim** of Contemporary Architecture Practice (CAP) in New York describe the research and design work that they have undertaken for Samsung, Korea's largest construction company, to develop a cost-effective and highly nuanced masterplan that embraces variation.

The Raemian brand was launched within South Korea's apartment industry by Samsung C&T in 2000, to create comfortable, futuristic living environments for city dwellers. Raemian masterplans repeat quantitatively different floor plans in different building typologies ranging from a Flat-Type to an A-Type. At the outset, the buildings all looked the same; so much so that if you drove past them, the only distinguishing feature from one to another was a serial number painted on each building in the masterplan development.

Apartment buildings and blocks in central Seoul

Due to the push for standardisation in housing, the scale and size of unit is the only attribute that is different from one housing development to another. The size is determined on the basis of the tax structure for the scale of apartment unit, ranging from 59.99 square metres to 119.99 square metres.

This cost-effective practice lasted until 2009, when the Mayor of Seoul wrote into law that if there were more than two buildings on the same development site, they must be distinguishable from each other. Initially developers circumvented this decree by altering heights of buildings while keeping the same aesthetics, due to cost-saving measures. Later the ordinance was clarified to include the requirement of a change in look and feel in each building. At this time the largest construction company in Korea, Samsung needed assistance in devising a

below: The generative software for the project was developed on the basis of an understanding of the Samsung Raemian System behind the corporation's dominance in the Seoul housing market. The generative system takes into account all of the building typologies, as well as housing unit sizes, and integrates these with the required regulations to create accurate masterplans that maximise floor area ratios. The coding actually designs the distribution of the masterplan, allowing the architects to adhere to the strict rules and logics provided by Samsung and to combine these with their design intentions.

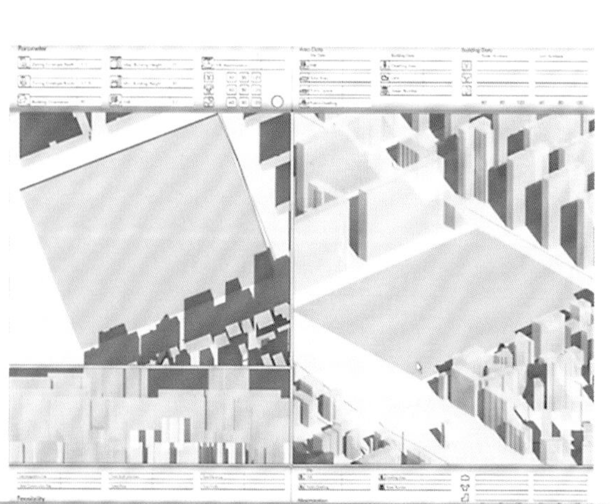

below: The qualities of the masterplan are distinct from typical housing developments in Seoul. Here, the efficiencies of mass-production are circumvented for mass customisation in the production of large-scale building populations within cities.

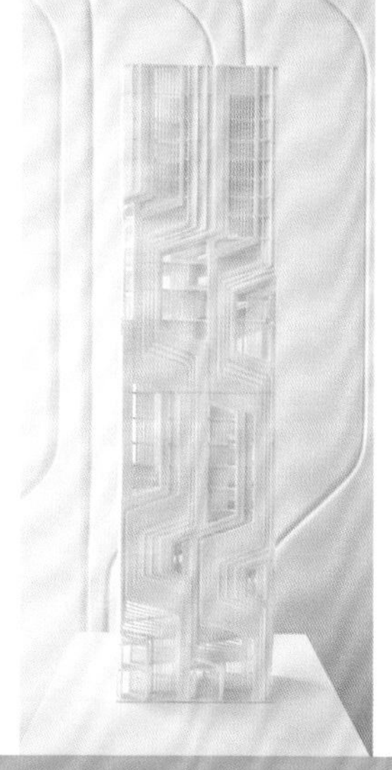

below: The software system is able to generate as many buildings as physically possible on the site to maximise floor area ratio. The configuration shown here was the basis of the later 18-building masterplan.

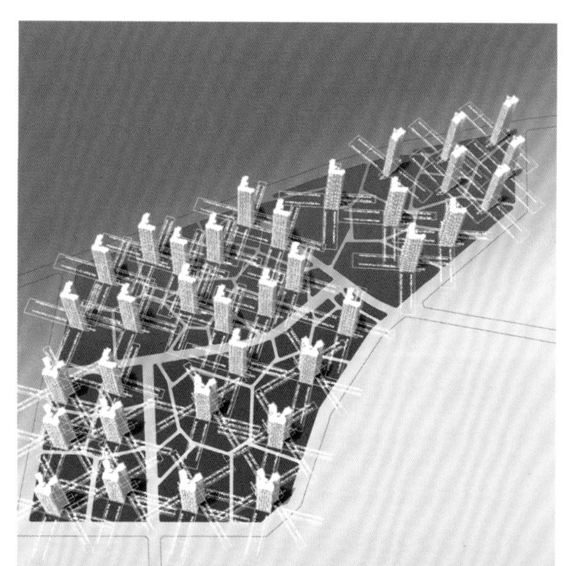

cost-effective alternative that could adhere to their strict rules of plan configurations with variations in the nature and type of buildings. Contemporary Architecture Practice (CAP) provided such an alternative. In addition to utilising all of Samsung's research on housing within Seoul's strict zoning regulations, the practice made use of its own knowledge of writing a design program in C++, as well as of knowledge that it had previously developed with Wharton Business School to calculate costs for different masterplan configurations in real time.

Once the C++ system was developed to include all quantitative regulations, CAP elaborated a design component that worked well within the limitations of the Samsung design strategies, deploying their manufacturing techniques. This interface set the limits of the amount of variation possible within buildings, yet allowed the possibility for there to be enough variation and hence customisation in each. What became apparent is that the integration of the Samsung component logic generated the maximum profit for the housing associations that constituted the clients, yet also yielded qualitative difference between buildings. The interface, its design and the logic of its mechanisms to generate outcomes on the scale of the city are inherently laced with CAP's desire to develop configurations which align with the practice's formal interests.

The design research and the C++ generative system convinced Samsung that CAP's method was accurate enough for them to quantify the results and that these results were reliable. Once this had been achieved, CAP put the system through a tremendous amount of testing under the auspices of the Research and Development Group at Samsung, using it to develop a masterplan comprising 18 high-rise buildings, together with the designs for each individual building. The masterplan incorporates all the programmatic and zoning codes required to maximise views and quality of light within the mid-high-rise development. The proposal reassesses the value of a central recreation area for the entire community, and develops several micro-communities around smaller zones for recreation.

below: The buildings are different yet related. CAP developed the greatest possible variation within the given parameters of regulations determining the overall form of the masterplan as well as each building. The costs had to be kept within an acceptable framework for the client, which required CAP to work within the levels of customisation afforded by Samsung construction.

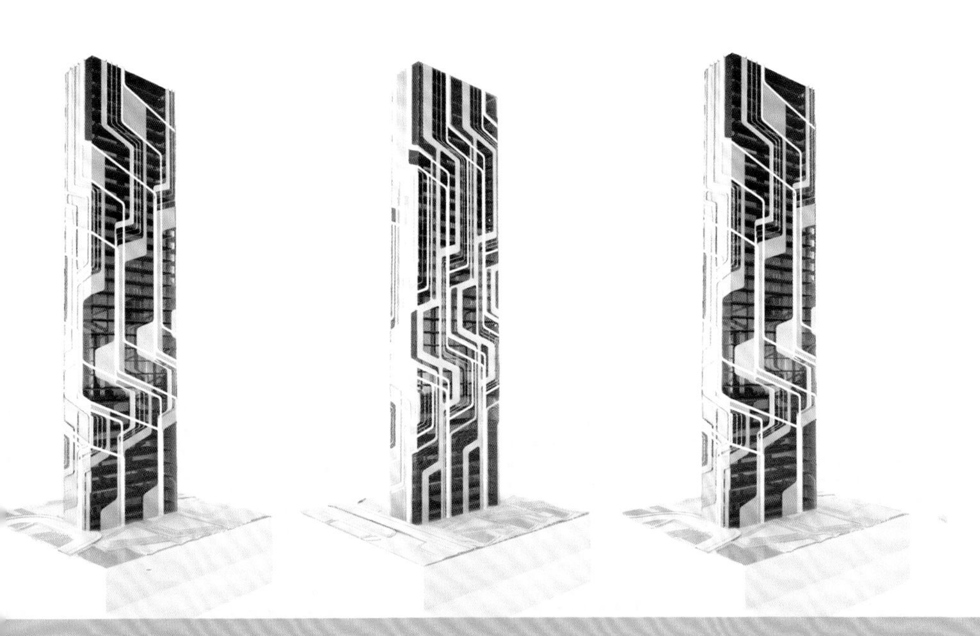

The advantages of this approach include the ability to provide variation within a micro-community, as well as throughout the overall masterplan, through different qualities of buildings and landscapes. The structures adhere to strict building regulations, such as those on unit size, while maximising the amount of variation of views and interior space within the plan configurations. This was determined primarily by the locations of all the buildings' vertical systems, including the circulation as well as dry and wet shafts. The building panels and glass are flat, yet they articulate movement across the facade, enriching the project form. Each unit affects the location of the adjacent units in each of the buildings, thus eventually developing a masterplan with a look and feel based on floor-by-floor regulations and repeatable customised components in its manufacture, instead of typically mass-produced building-to-building relations only.

In summary, the Haan River masterplan was developed using a complex system of rules and programming code that generates masterplan opportunities which adhere to all the required regulations in minutes. Previously these plans would take an architect a year to design, and always led to homogeneous outcomes. CAP's system adds value for the client, as all the pressures of codes and cost are taken into account at the beginning of the design process, enabling the development of a nuanced and elegant masterplan with innovative buildings using cost-effective variation that is mass customised. ⌂

Neil Leach

Is the focus on mass customisation with its emphasis on generating architectural form misguided? Is the future of our cities instead more likely to be directed towards the capacity to accommodate informational systems and the possibilities that new technologies afford to redesign existing buildings? Architectural author, professor and guest-editor of the *Digital Cities* (July/August 2009) and *Space Architecture* (November/December 2014) issues of Δ, **Neil Leach** appeals to architects to turn away from their fixation with the material properties of the built environment and customise their own approaches to analysis and design to fully embrace the computational revolution that has taken place.

What will our future cities look like? Will they be strikingly different to the cities of today, constructed with the latest materials and designed using the most recently developed methods? Or will they look much like our present cities, with occasional new buildings, but with most existing building stock retained and simply retrofitted with the latest information technology? In fact, the most significant driver of change in our future cities is less likely to be new architectural form, and instead informational systems that have already revolutionised other industries.

In his essay 'iPhone City', published in the AD *Digital Cities* issue (2009), American sociologist and design theorist Benjamin H Bratton provocatively challenges half of all architects and urbanists to abandon their traditional role as designers of new buildings and to focus instead on the possibilities afforded by computational systems to redesign existing buildings:

> An experiment: one half of all architects and urbanists in the entire world should, as of now, stop designing new buildings and new developments altogether. Instead they should invest the historical depth and intellectual nuance of their architectural imaginations into the design and programming of new software that provides for the better use of structures and systems we already have. It is a simple matter of good content management. The other half, the control group, may continue as before.[1]

Bratton then goes on to explore how a computational device – the iPhone – has completely changed the way that we operate within the city. Whereas other authors in the issue address the potential architectural forms that could be designed using the latest computational techniques, the future of the 'digital city' for Bratton is based not on new forms, but on new informational systems. In hindsight, his essay stands out as perhaps the most perspicacious in the entire volume, in part because it exposes the shortsightedness of an architectural profession still locked into its traditional role of producing architectural designs for new buildings.

The Problem with Form

It could be claimed that architects have long viewed the world mainly in terms of form at the expense of anything else. They have the tendency to 'aestheticise' the world, seeing it primarily in aesthetic terms and stripping it of any deeper sense of social, political or economic content. Take the question of cost. The generators of any building project – and the foremost concern for any client – are financial resources, and yet one can scarcely find any reference to cost in most of the key books on architectural history, apart from the cost of the book on the back cover.[2] Yet this tendency returns with a vengeance when we think of our future cities. It is not simply that they will probably look much the same as our present ones, albeit with the existing building stock retrofitted with the latest digital communications and control systems. After all, apart from building preservation constraints, it often makes little economic sense to just tear down the buildings of the past to make way for the new. Rather, architects need to rethink their whole approach to design within what Manuel Castells has termed 'the network society' within 'the information age'.[3]

The central issue at stake, surely, is the very primacy of material form. Indeed, when dealing with cities we have to question whether we should be talking solely in terms of their material properties, in that the way that we operate these days is defined less and less by material form per se and more and more by immaterial systems. Paul Virilio, for example, writes about how the materiality of city walls has given way to the immateriality of electronic surveillance systems at airports.[4] Moreover, as Gilles Deleuze has noted,

Uber mobile phone app

Uber has emerged as a market leader in the realm of online transportation services. The capacity to track available vehicles in real time, and to link them with potential customers, has allowed it to undercut the cost of traditional taxis and offer a highly efficient alternative way of booking transportation.

we are increasingly being controlled not by the physical forms of buildings, but by immaterial constraints such as credit.[5] As such we might detect a certain erosion of the hegemony of the physical in our contemporary age. To this we could perhaps add the challenging claim made by Reyner Banham back in the 1970s in the context of Los Angeles, that form is largely irrelevant, provided that cities function adequately.[6] Indeed, we should also question whether we can still refer to cities today in such straightforward material terms. For a city understood solely in terms of its 'material' manifestation becomes an increasingly problematic concept when many of our operations have shifted into the 'immaterial' realm of computational interfaces. Can we even refer, for example, to the notion of a 'community' as though it were constituted by a given number of people living in a given physical location when our friends and associates today are far more likely to be found in the immaterial proximity of our Facebook pages than in the material proximity of our neighbouring apartments?

Against the primacy of material form, we might posit an alternative logic, and make a distinction between form – as in 'form for the sake of form' – and information. Whereas 'form' implies a concern for a static condition governed largely by aesthetic issues, 'information' implies a dynamic condition that is informed by a range of factors, many of them also including the word 'form', such as 'per*form*ance'. The shift towards performative (such as structural or environmental) concerns implies a radical shift away from purely aesthetic issues. As such it opens up important questions of optimisation and efficiency. It is here perhaps that we might begin to glimpse the most likely driver of change for our future cities.

Intensive Cities

One way to question the limitations of the obsession that architects have with form is through the distinction that Gilles Deleuze makes between 'intensive' and 'extensive' qualities. Put simply – in terms of space – it is the distinction between the material properties of a space (extensive space) and the immaterial properties associated with that space (intensive space). Manuel DeLanda describes these as the difference between the material characteristics of a space – a country, city, neighbourhood or ecosystem – and its immaterial characteristics, such as pressure, density and speed.[7] He illustrates this with the difference between an extensive property such as volume, and an intensive property such as temperature. If we take a litre of water at 50°C and double it, what we get is two litres of water at 50°C and not 100°C. An everyday example of this would be the standard meteorological chart that we see in a weather forecast. The extensive properties of this chart would be the material or geological properties – the mountains, rivers and oceans. The intensive properties would be the immaterial or meteorological ones, such as zones of high or low pressure, warm fronts, cold fronts etc. Of course, the extensive and the intensive properties often relate to one another, in that the physical properties of the landscape can influence patterns of weather, but intrinsically they are quite different.

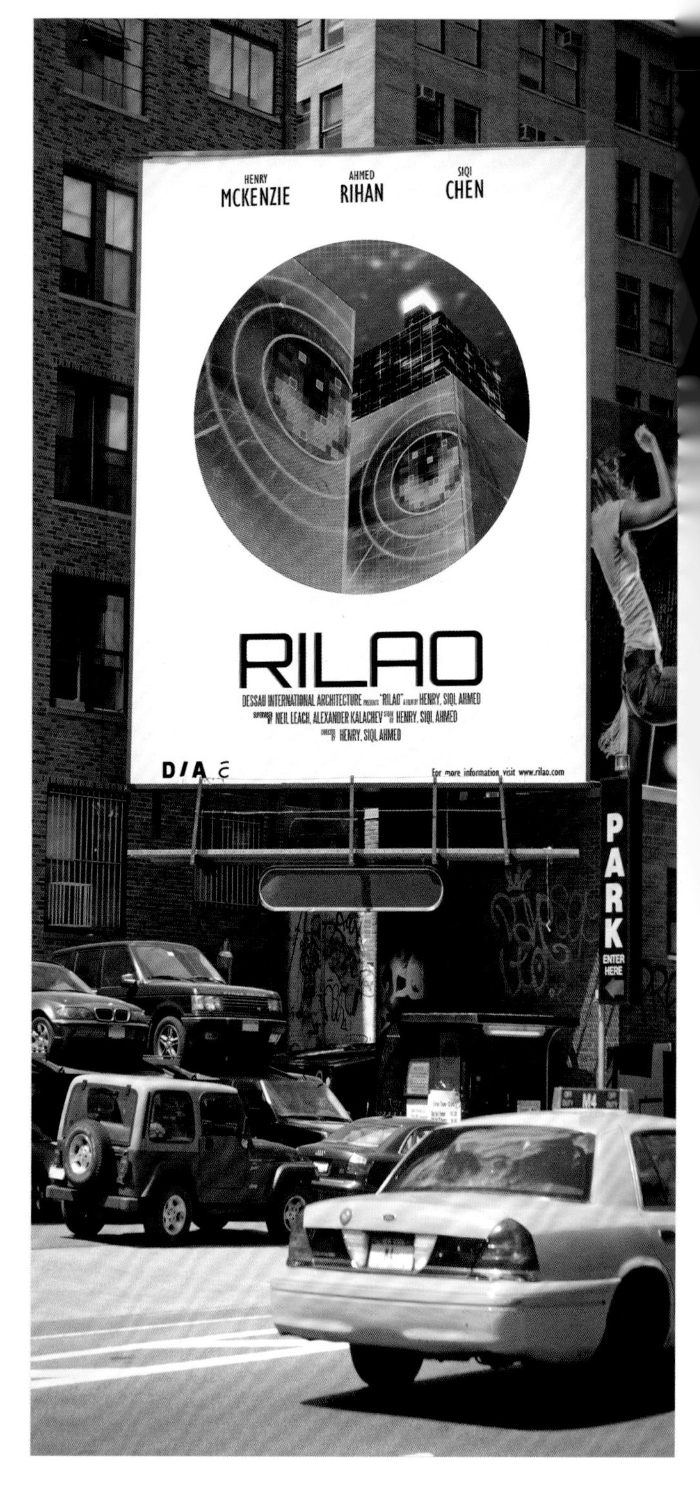

Siqi Chen, Henry McKenzie and Ahmed Rihan, RILAO, Master's in Architecture, Dessau Institute of Architecture, 2014

above: This project captures the potentially sinister side of data ownership. Figures such as Julian Assange, Chelsea Manning and Edward Snowden, who have attempted to leak information, are already either imprisoned or effectively trapped in temporary safe havens. But what happens when all transactions are conducted online and a nefarious government could seize online data for its advantage? Will there be any escape? This project addresses such problems.

Sheehan and Partners, Facebook Data Center, Prineville, Oregon, 2012

opposite top: The interior of the Facebook Data Center offers an architectural manifestation of the physical space required to house servers for the storage of big data. While the move towards big data will shift the emphasis in design methodologies increasingly from (pure) physical form to informational search processes, there will nonetheless still be a requirement for the design of physical spaces in order to house big data facilities.

In terms of cities, we might think of this distinction as being between the material form of our cities – the buildings, roads and so on – and the immaterial information associated with that material fabric: factors such as 'desirability'. In other words, we might imagine that just as a meteorological map might reveal zones of intensity that dictate the weather patterns, so an intensive map of a city might track the ever-shifting patterns of desirability as one area becomes highly sought after while another loses its appeal, prompting a shift in real-estate prices. Such concerns are often excluded from architectural discourse that tends to 'aestheticise' forms and rinse out any economic associations, but they nonetheless have an important impact on form itself. For without the 'intensive' factors that make one area more 'desirable' than another, there would be little incentive for developers and others to commission new buildings. As such, we might extend this difference between 'extensive' and 'intensive' space to a broader set of concerns: the difference between simple 'form' and other factors that 'inform' that form.

Informational Cities

What this begins to hint at is another way of understanding cities. With the advent of so-called 'big data', there is now an almost endless supply of raw data available. Given that all online transactions are recorded, we potentially have a source of important information that was previously unavailable pre-Internet. As such, it is as though the days of 'marketing surveys' – where typically agents would be dispersed on

Laura Ferrarello, iBus, Master's in Architecture, University of Brighton, 2008

right: The project explores new ways of making cities more sustainable. Instead of simply planting more trees, it encourages citizens to use public transportation by linking various online information sites and tracking buses in real time, so as to provide a more comprehensive and user-friendly guide to bus use. This situation is now not far from becoming a reality in some cities.

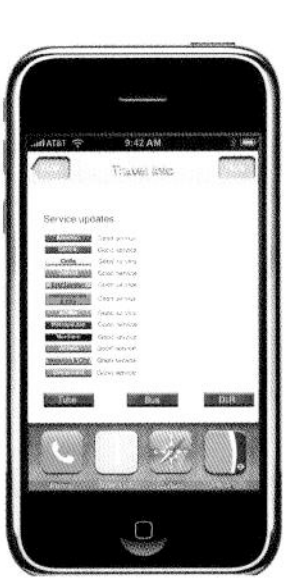

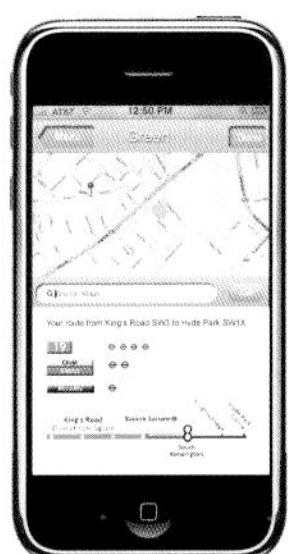

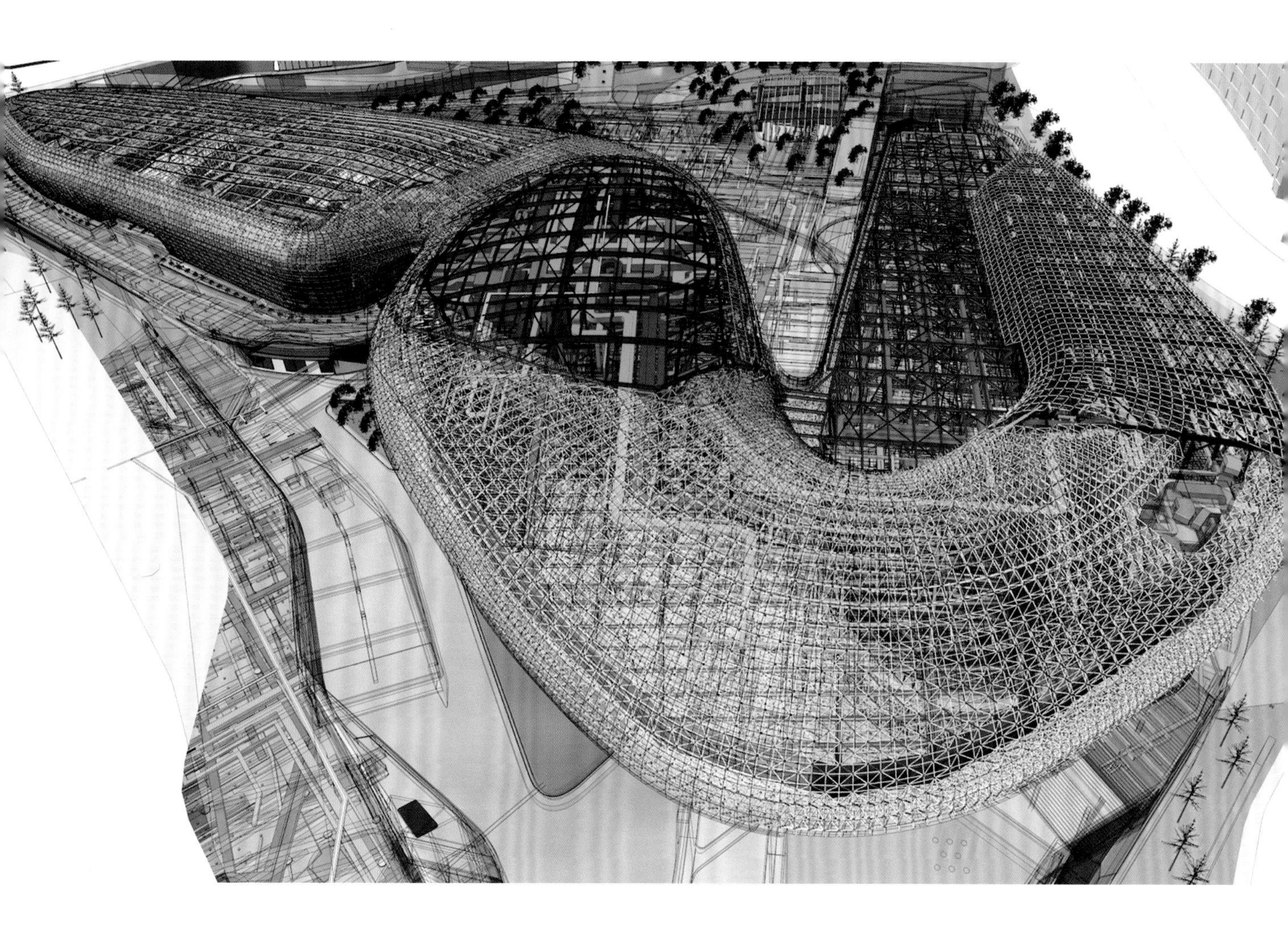

to the streets, clipboard in hand, in an attempt to glean information – are all but over. There is less need to search for new information when almost all trends are discernable online. However, access to information depends on ownership, and data is not necessarily always available to be shared.[8]

In itself, however, raw data means relatively little. What becomes crucial, then, is the way in which that data is processed in order to extract useful information. Moreover, access to that information depends on interface systems. If, therefore, we are to locate the most important domain in terms of influence, we might look towards computational interfaces that allow the data to be shared potentially within different informational systems.[9] Moreover, it is clear that information systems have already played a significant role in redefining the operations of the designer, from building information modelling (BIM) used for the logistics of construction of individual buildings, to geographic information systems (GIS) used at an urban level. Furthermore, we might point towards the introduction of new hi-tech industries, such as Lyft and Uber, as evidence of the fact that computational interfaces can allow for transportation systems that are more efficient than the previous model offered by taxis, through their ability to track in real time and link potential drivers to potential customers. Likewise we can see how information-based smart devices, such as the NEST self-learning thermostat, can introduce energy-saving efficiencies within the domestic home. This is the decade surely of the informational interface.

What impact, then, might this have on design? We might even go so far as to suggest that our whole notion of design needs to be reconfigured based on the availability of such information. If, for example, we look at the logic of the search that has come to dominate many online operations, we might observe that the true potential of computation lies in introducing tools that could allow us to search for design information. As noted previously:

> Of the many potentialities afforded by the computer, one of the most significant is its capacity to operate as a search engine. If, then, we think through the logic of the search in the context of 'design', what such an approach suggests is that if all possible solutions already exist, it is simply a question of defining a set of constraints and conducting a search, and then selecting one of the many outcomes. The potential implications of this are far reaching. Not only does it challenge the traditional notion of the 'genius' of the architect/designer and the originality of the work of art, but it also suggests that if there is still any creativity in the 'design' process, it should lie, firstly, in defining the constraints that generate the range of possible solutions to a problem, and, secondly, in developing an effective method of filtering or evaluating them.[10]

As design itself shifts inexorably towards the harnessing of informational systems dominated by the logic of the search, how far away might be the day when we will 'search' for

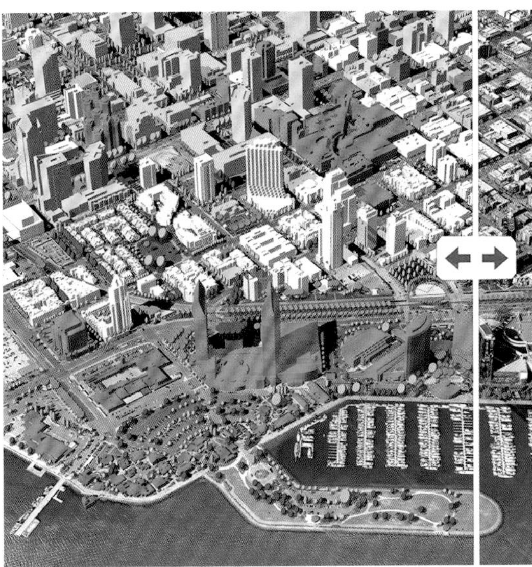

Environmental Systems Research Institute (ESRI), Geographic information services study, San Diego, 2014

left: Geographic information services (GIS) have revolutionised the way in which we can visualise information about the city. Here a study by the Environmental Systems Research Institute (ESRI) shows how we can visualise the programmatic activities that lie behind the physical form of the city.

Zaha Hadid Architects, Dongdaemun Design Plaza, Seoul, South Korea, 2011

opposite: The image shows how Digital Project (DP) – a form of building information modelling (BIM) developed by Gehry Technologies – allows the various professionals in the construction industry to coordinate and share information.

designs computationally, in the same way that now we use Google to search for information, or Uber to search for transportation? Some indication of the potential of such a project can be found in Flux, a recent start-up that actually emerged out of Google X, the radical think tank within Google dedicated to finding innovative solutions to everyday problems.[11]

This brings us back to Bratton's original proposition. Should half of all architects today abandon the traditional notion of designing new forms, and focus instead on computational operations to redesign existing forms? Perhaps Bratton does not go far enough. It is not just a question of designing form in a traditional manner versus redesigning existing forms in a new, computational way. Rather it is a question of how computational information will revolutionise all kinds of design. It is not just the design process that needs to be reappraised. So too design theory needs to be rethought. As such, the figure of Deleuze, for so long the 'philosopher of choice' of the new 'digital' architects, comes back to haunt the space of design, not as the apologist for progressive form, but as the champion of informational processes over mere formal inventiveness, and of 'intensive' qualities over 'extensive' quantities.

Architects like to think of themselves as progressive designers, but one domain they have largely failed to redesign is their own approach to design. The architectural profession needs to open up to the full implications of the computational revolution that has engulfed so may other industries. Instead of simply designing new forms in the traditional manner, architects should be designing new approaches based less on form per se than on informational systems, in order to harness the full potential of big data in our 'information age'. ⌂

Notes

1. Benjamin H Bratton, 'iPhone City', in Neil Leach, AD *Digital Cities*, July/August (no 4), 2009, pp 90–7.
2. Neil Leach, *The Anaesthetics of Architecture*, MIT Press (Cambridge, MA), 1999.
3. See Manuel Castells, *The Rise of the Network Society: The Information Age – Economy, Society and Culture*, Vol I, Blackwell (Malden, MA and Oxford), 1996; Castells, *The Power of Identity: The Information Age – Economy, Society and Culture*, Vol II, Blackwell (Malden, MA and Oxford), 1997; and Castells, *End of Millennium: The Information Age – Economy, Society and Culture*, Vol III, Blackwell (Malden, MA and Oxford), 1998.
4. Paul Virilio, 'The Overexposed City', in Neil Leach (ed), *Rethinking Architecture: A Reader in Cultural Theory*, Routledge (London), 1997, pp 380–90.
5. Gilles Deleuze, 'Postscript on the Societies of Control', in *ibid*, pp 293–6.
6. See *Reyner Banham Loves Los Angeles*: https://vimeo.com/22488225.
7. Manuel DeLanda, 'Space: Extensive and Intensive, Actual and Virtual', in Ian Buchanan and Gregg Lambert (eds), *Deleuze and Space*, Edinburgh University Press (Edinburgh), 2005, p 80.
8. See Anthony Townsend, *Smart Cities: Big Data, Civic Hackers, and the Quest for a New Utopia*, WW Norton (New York), 2013.
9. See Branden Hookway, *Interface*, MIT Press (Cambridge, MA), 2014.
10. Neil Leach, 'There is No Such Thing as Digital Design', in David Gerber and Mariana Ibanez (eds), *Paradigms in Computing: Making, Machines, and Models for Design Agency in Architecture*, eVolo Press (Los Angeles, CA), 2014, pp 148–58.
11. On this see Randy Deutsch, 'Google's BIM-busting App for Design and Construction', BIM + Integrated Design, 24 October 2014: http://bimandintegrateddesign.com/2014/10/24/googles-bim-busting-app-for-design-and-construction/.

David Gerber, Shih Hsin Lin and Bei Pan, Design Optioneering: Variation, Exploration, Correlation, University of Southern California, Los Angeles, 2011

This project for a high-rise tower reveals how an informational search-based approach to architectural design using HDS Beagle can generate a range of possible solutions from which one can be selected based on a further process of filtering or evaluating outcomes.

EPFL Media x Design Lab and Convergeo

Seventy-two Growth Typologies – Houses

Shanghai

2010

Various instances of a zoologically inspired house from the 'Home 2.0' exhibition, a collaboration between the Media x Design Lab and Convergeo (Jeffrey Huang, Muriel Waldvogel andTrevor Patt), generated for the Swiss Pavilion at the World Expo in Shanghai.

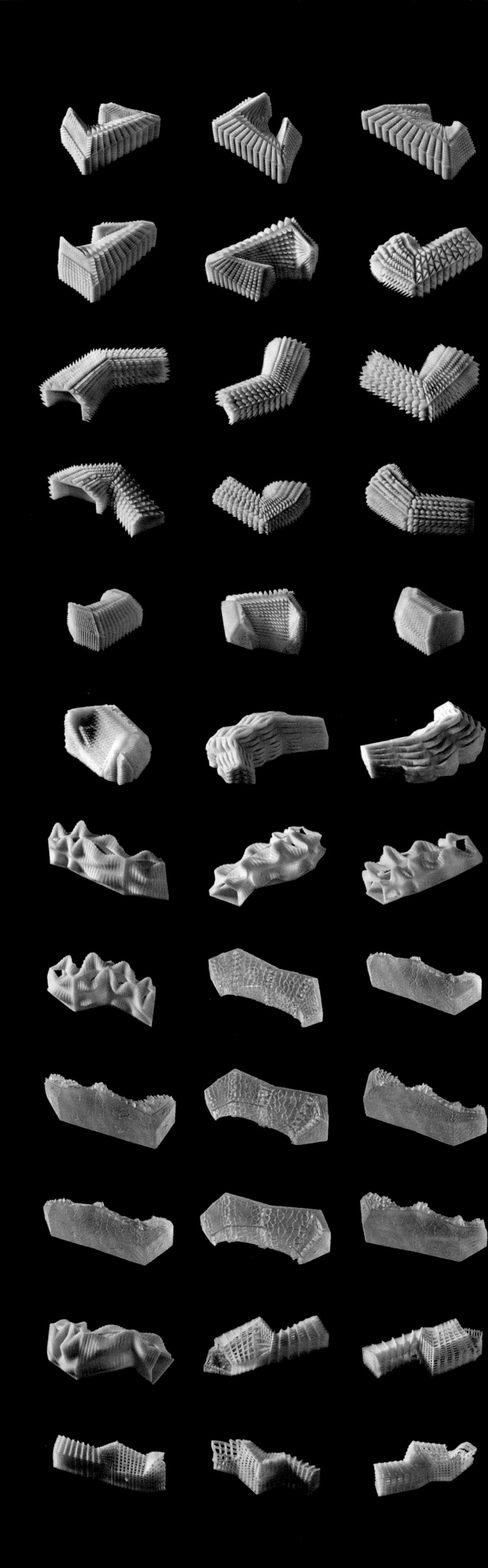

Jeffrey Huang

Growth Typologies, Localities and Defamiliarisation

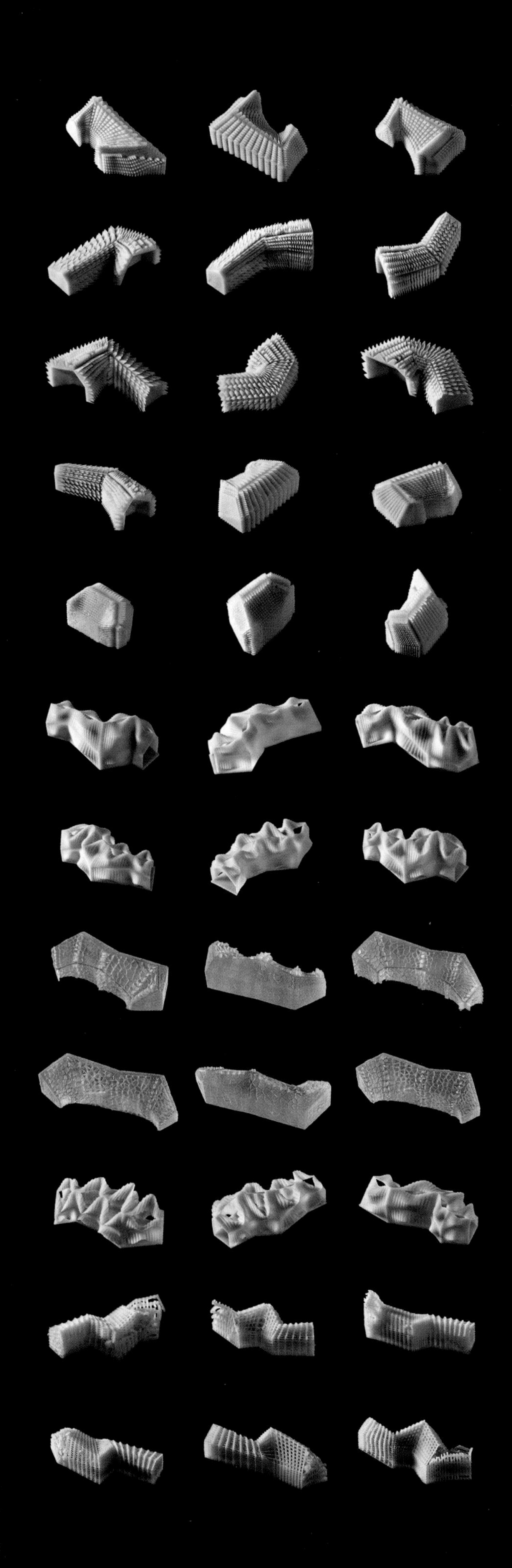

For the last 8 years, the Media x Design Lab at École Polytechnique Fédérale de Lausanne (EPFL) has been engaged on research into 'Artificial Urbanism'. **Jeffrey Huang**, Director of the lab, describes how generative computer codes and algorithms are employed in pursuit of an accelerated design process; with the aim of not only meeting the demands of rapid urbanisation, but also being responsive to the ecological and contextual conditions of a particular locality.

Experiments with Artificial Urbanism in Sichuan, Guangzhou and Beijing

The unprecedented speed and scope of rapid urbanisation in Asia calls for a fundamental rethinking of urbanism. Conventional urbanism in Asia is slow and static, often based on imported, top-down visions, incapable of responding to site-specific microclimatic, topographical and social conditions.

'Artificial Urbanism' is a key concept being explored within the Media x Design Lab at the École Polytechnique Fédérale de Lausanne (EPFL) in Switzerland. The goal is to fundamentally rethink and accelerate the design process to cope with the pressures of rapid urbanism. The approach is motivated by a desire to empower artificial machines to generate responsive, almost real-time urban solutions that are sensitive to the unique features of individual localities.

Since 2007, the Media x Design Lab has been investigating generative computer codes and algorithms for architectural design and ecological urbanism. The work has undergone several stages of progress, evolving from experiments with artificial morphogenesis and computational landscape urbanism to the current work on growth typologies.

Initial projects focused on the use of bio-inspired algorithms to drive geometric form-finding processes in architecture and urbanism, starting with the creation of an open-sourced, object-oriented geometry library called anar.ch (written by the late Guillaume LaBelle with Julien Nembrini in Java/Processing and Scala),[1] which provided geometrical codes that could be used, adapted and combined to design and grow novel architectural shapes. The resulting forms included variations of a zoologically inspired house for the World Expo in Shanghai, organic skyscrapers for an exhibition in Florence,[2] middle-rise buildings and urban housing fabric that resemble and pay tribute to the philosophy, spirit and formal vocabulary of the Metabolist movement of 1960s Japan[3] and the experiments with evolutionary architecture by John Frazer at the Architectural Association (AA) in London between 1989 and 1995.[4]

While such results at different scales were formally intriguing and interesting as volumetric and sculptural propositions, the experiments also exposed the limitations of using an approach driven by bio-inspired code for creating effective architecture and urbanism. Two limitations in particular became evident. The first was related to the passiveness of landscape and context. Neglecting to integrate external landscape and ecological parameters into the initial definition of the design codes resulted in several shortcomings: rather than exploiting the potential of landscape and contextual vectors as proactive drivers of the design, they remained reactive constraints for correcting an already formulated design. The second involved neglect of traditional architectural typologies. Because of the bio-inspired code's indifference to local typologies,

EPFL Media x Design Lab (Organicités Studio), Four Growth Typologies (High-Rise Towers), Florence, 2009

Organic skyscrapers from the Organicités Studio generated by geometric code from the anar.ch library. Organicités Studio: Professor Jeffrey Huang; assistants Nathaniel Zuelzke, Julien Nembrini and Guillaume LaBelle; and students Olivier Wyssmueller, Olivier Ilegems, Osamu Moser and Alberto Fiore.

EPFL Media x Design Lab, Computational Reading of a Site, Leshan, Sichuan, China, 2013

Identification of potential building sites with minimal impact on paddy farms – low runoff impact and steep slopes, from Trevor Patt's PhD dissertation at the EPFL Media x Design Lab.

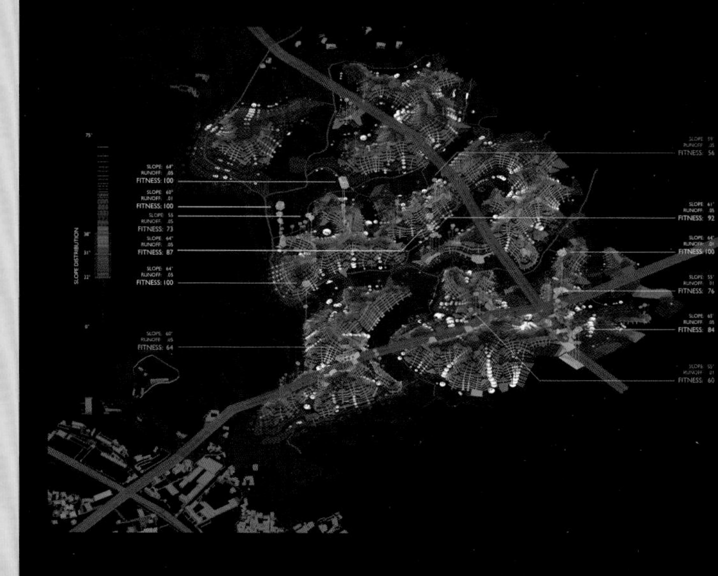

the organic shapes, derived from biology and other scientific (non-architectural) fields needed to be artificially and forcefully adapted into livable, desirable, meaningful spaces. The opportunity to activate the architectural knowledge embedded in existing architectural typologies was therefore missed.

Growth Typologies

To address these two constraints, in 2012 a new series of design research studios entitled 'growth typologies' was initiated to more actively integrate landscape parameters and typological concerns. 'Growth typologies' have an intrinsic ability to encompass planning for a whole city as well as for individual buildings – that is, to scale – directly translating the diversity of local constraints into the designs, and adapting to changes in context. They take into account future extensions of the design, the actual realisation representing only a transitory state promised to further developments. The resulting form thus loses its arbitrariness to become a spatial representation of the set of constraints enforced on it.[5]

The case studies for testing growth typologies are the emerging cities in Asia, and particularly the problems associated with rapid urbanisation in China, and the expanding role of the design professions in developments of increased scale, scope and speed. Rather than passively following the criteria of top-down planning, the design research studios are interested in developing bottom-up typologies that structure and inform the urban organisation around them. Accordingly, typologies are not seen as static, identical copies, but adapt to their local situation, such as site conditions and landscape, and their collective milieu. This design strategy can be considered a response to the growing dissatisfaction with the imposition of unconsidered, top-down, 'cookie-cutter' Western planning in Asia.

The initial research studios investigated three specific sites with idiosyncratic contextual and typological conditions: 'foothill typologies' in Beijing, 'hilltop typologies' in Sichuan and 'floodplain typologies' in Guangzhou. In collaboration with architects Trevor Patt, Peter Ortner, Soohyun Chang and Nathaniel Zuelzke, the studios also benefited from external cooperation, data inputs and joint site visits with parallel design studios offered at the Harvard Graduate School of Design (GSD) and Peking University (PKU) led by Professor Kongjian Yu. In 2013, the Artificial Design Lab at the Singapore University of Technology and Design (SUTD) joined as an Asian partner, and the work received a larger research grant from the MIT-SUTD International Design Centre (IDC) in Singapore.

Localities

Each project began with a computational analysis of the ecological and contextual data of the existing site, including topography, sun, wind, water, humidity,

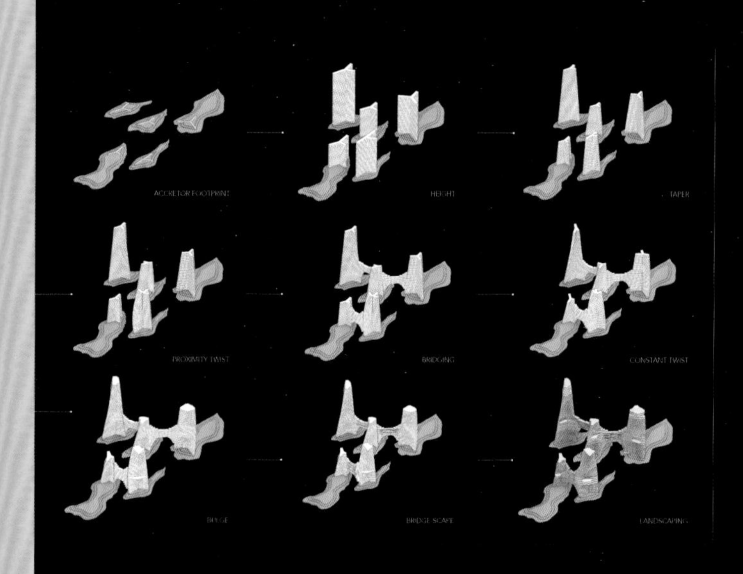

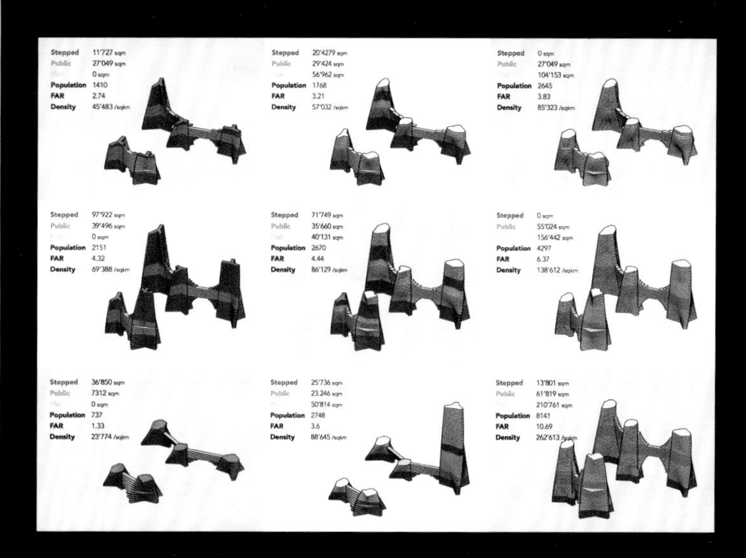

EPFL Media x Design Lab (Guangzhou Studio), Emerging Typologies, Haizhu, Guangzhou, China, 2013

The landscape parameters drive the development of potential typologies in a morphogenetic process according to shape, programme, population, floor area ratio and density. Guangzhou Studio: Professor Jeffrey Huang; assistants Trevor Patt and Peter Ortner; and student Alex Sadeghi.

'Growth typologies' have an intrinsic ability to encompass planning for a whole city as well as for individual buildings – that is, to scale – directly translating the diversity of local constraints into the designs, and adapting to changes in context.

available infrastructure and circulation flow. The data was then indexed and transformed into maps in the form of generative diagrams. An example was the computational reading of the Leshan site in Sichuan for the hilltop typologies studio. Landscape data pertaining to slope steepness and runoff impact was here mobilised as an ecological site force, and the data mapped in order to identify future built densities that minimise impact on the existing paddy farms. In a further step, massing scenarios were derived from the data, and growth typologies emerged.

Data constitutes the fuel of an artificial design paradigm and anchors a design to a specific locality. Taking landscape data as a starting point and driver for the generation of urban form – similar to that already proposed by advocates of landscape urbanism – constitutes a grounded process that can be easily rationalised. The linearity of the landscape-driven morphogenetic narrative – the almost step-by-step form-generation process that takes environmental data as an input to output urban form according to pre-specified rules – makes the process easily decodable.

Yet this landscape-based, data-driven design process inspired by a 'negative' planning approach[6] – where the non-built space is designed rather than the built – needs to be confronted with a positive typology when applied in an architectural or urban design context. Here, typologies must act as a kind of necessary 'inertia' to provide resistance and challenge the linear, data-driven morphogenetic process, turning it into an iterative loop. But what should be the origin of the typologies? Is the local typology, for example that of the urban villages found on the sites, generative enough to be copied and intensified? Or should a 'working' typology be imported from the larger region or other, climatically related parts of the world? Is there an opportunity to artificially compose completely new typologies based on new parameters?

In the Qinlonghu Beijing Studio in the southwestern suburbs of Beijing, the adaptability of the basic courthouse typology was tested. The hutong-like typology found in traditional villages in the region was analysed and decoded, and varied along dimensions of height, density, interstitial space, connectivity and diversity. The liquefied growth typology was then mapped onto the Qinlonghu site. The connectivity of the courtyards (the inner workings of the social fabric) was computed and made explicit, as scenarios of the proposed population of the site were explored.

Iterative Defamiliarisation

The experiments also combined growth typologies with a process of iterative defamiliarisation, which can be seen as a local, tactical design operation that aims; on the one hand, to subvert the linear data-driven morphogenetic process, and on the other hand, to estrange the generic growth typological code and give it

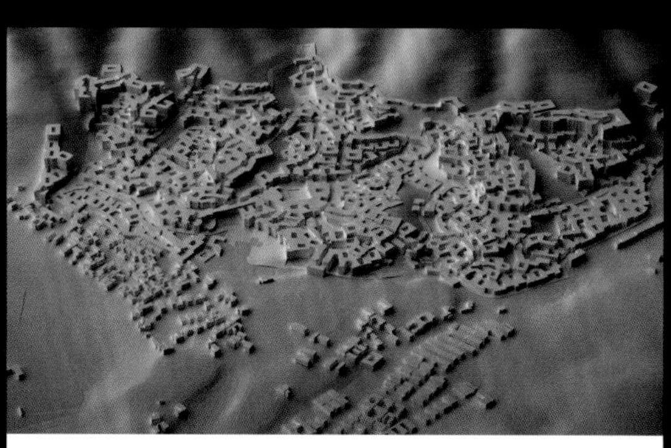

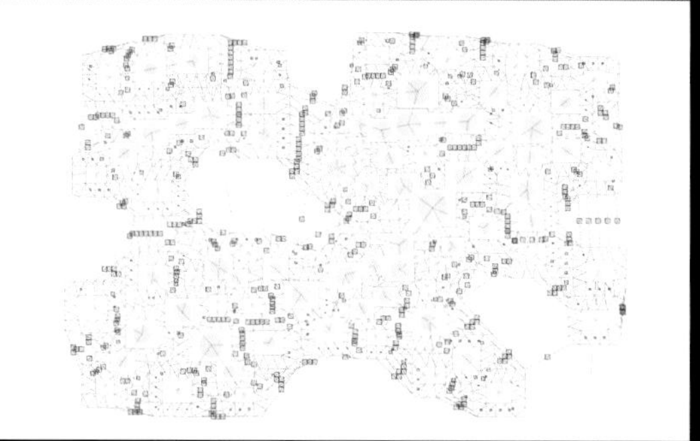

EPFL Media x Design Lab (Qinlonghu Beijing Studio), Growth Typologies Based on the Traditional Courtyard Type, Qinlonghu, Beijing, 2013

top: Variations of a basic courthouse typology along the dimensions of height, density, interstitial space, connectivity and diversity. *centre:* Growth typologies mapped onto the Qinlonghu site. *bottom:* Network analysis of interconnections.

Qinlonghu Beijing Studio: Professor Jeffrey Huang; assistants Trevor Patt and Nathaniel Zuelzke; and students Christophe Hotz and Johann Watzk.

a certain local specificity. Estranging familiar typologies – prolonging the process of recognition – allows not only a heightened perception and appreciation of the familiar, but also buys a certain freedom (from the typological and landscape-driven code) for local algorithmic adaptation.

The plan, section and axonometry of a typology derived from the existing urban village examined different instances and varying initial conditions. Volumetric and aesthetic relationships were investigated in the process of defamiliarisation, and the performance of the different iterations was evaluated and measured against intentional criteria in an iterative feedback loop, resulting in defamiliarised instances of the growth typology. In a final process, local sculpting and trimming operations were introduced to finesse the architectural and urban form in order to further respond to micro-contextual conditions.

Towards Artificial Urbanism

With a view towards a future Chinese urbanism in which the pressure to cope with the speed and scope of rapid urbanism will continue to increase, radically new approaches to urbanism that do not rely solely on the bounded rationality and capacity of humans seem inevitable. Humans may still design a few selected iconic buildings and boutique cities, but most architectural and urban design tasks will need to be handled artificially in order to respond to the challenges of rapid urbanism, and to generate urban solutions that are sensitive to the unique features of individual localities.

In order to artificialise the process of creating such a 'mass-customised' urbanism, then, some groundwork is necessary to define the kinds of design algorithms that can constitute the building blocks of a future, semi- or fully automated urbanism. With this goal in mind, the work of the Media x Design Lab and SUTD is focused on three distinctive types of code – growth typological code, localities-driven morphogenetic code and defamiliarisation code – which, taken together, could prove to be productive categories for a nascent, shared planetary library for artificial urbanism. ⌂

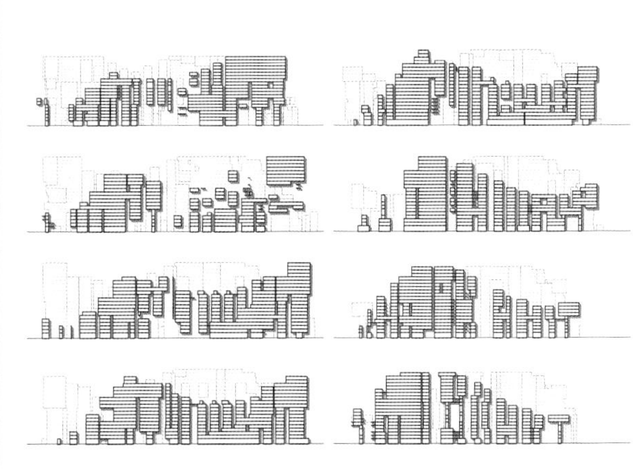

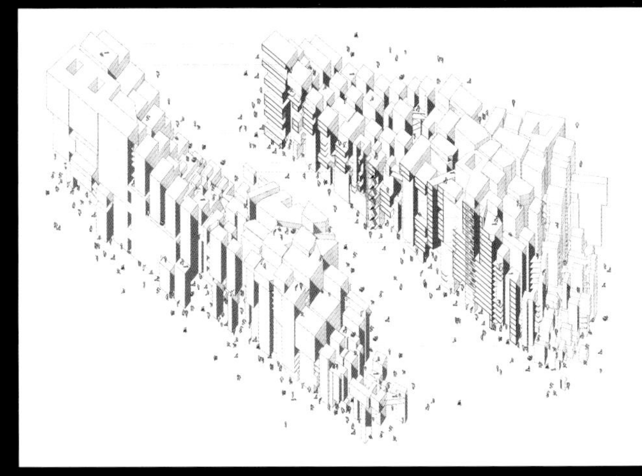

EPFL Media x Design Lab (Guangzhou Studio), Iterative Defamiliarisation of an Urban Village, Haizhu, Guangzhou, 2013

Plan, section and axonometry of a gradual densification and defamiliarisation of an existing urban village. Guangzhou Studio: Professor Jeffrey Huang; assistants Trevor Patt and Peter Ortner; and students Christina Haas and Jana Scharli.

Notes

1. Guillaume LaBelle, Julien Nembrini and Jeffrey Huang, 'Programming Framework for Architectural Design ANAR+: Object Oriented Geometry', in Temy Tidafi and Tomás Dorta (eds), *Joining Languages, Cultures and Visions – CAADFutures 2009: Proceedings of the 13th International CAAD Futures Conference*, Les Presses de l'Université de Montréal (Montreal), 2009.
2. Jeffrey Huang, Nathaniel Zuelzke, Guillaume LaBelle and Julien Nembrini, 'Organicités', in *Visions: Catalog of the 9th Edition of Beyond Media*, Image Publishing (Florence), 2009.
3. Noboru Kawazoe (ed), *Metabolism 1960: Proposals for a New Urbanism*, Bitjsutu Shuppan Sha (Tokyo), 1960.
4. John Frazer, *An Evolutionary Architecture*, Architectural Association Publications (London), 1995.
5. Nathaniel Zuelzke, Trevor Patt and Jeffrey Huang, 'Computation as an Ideological Practice', in *Proceedings of the ACSA*, Boston, Massachusetts, 2012.
6. Kongjian Yu, Dihua Li and Hailong Liu, *The 'Negative Planning' Approach*, Chinese Building Industry Press (Beijing), 2005.

Rocker-Lange Architects
Shanghai Lilong Tower Urbanism
Shanghai, China

Rocker-Lange Architects
Shanghai Lilong Tower Urbanism
Shanghai
China
2014

Aerial view of a prototypical tower. Flexible in form, the towers evolve out of a ground figure that adapts to the site and the specific input settings (access, height, courtyard size and so on).

In Shanghai, rapid urbanisation has made the high-rise the predominant building type – supplanting traditional low-rise row houses. Here **Christian J Lange,** founding partner of Rocker-Lange Architects, based in Boston and Hong Kong, describes an alternative model for the generic housing tower. By employing a computational adaptable system, dense housing is created that recreates the courtyards and access lanes of the original city through an ingenious use of a podium.

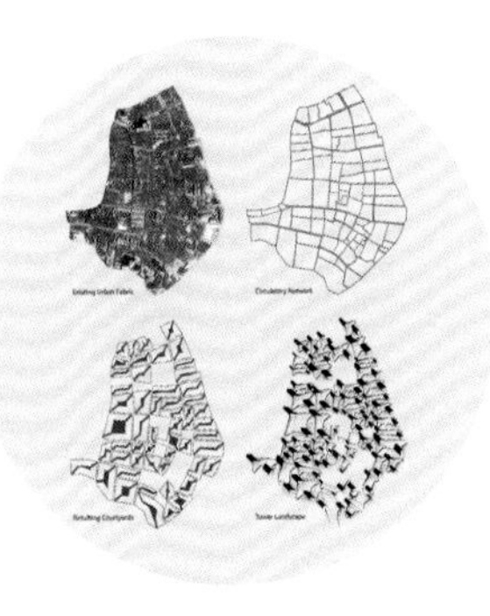

top left: The building type follows the specific morphology of the plot and respects the existing street network. The dimensions of towers and urban courtyards are based on the specific site parameters.

top right: Different density scenarios show the relationships between the new typology and areas that should be, or could be, preserved.

bottom: Site, historic change and concept diagrams. The site for this theoretical project is located adjacent to the old town of Shanghai, close to the Huangpu River. The past 15 years have seen the transformation of the area's previously low-rise urban fabric into a predominantly high-rise environment. Rocker-Lange's project seeks to maintain the existing circulatory network while introducing a new adaptive high-density courtyard tower typology.

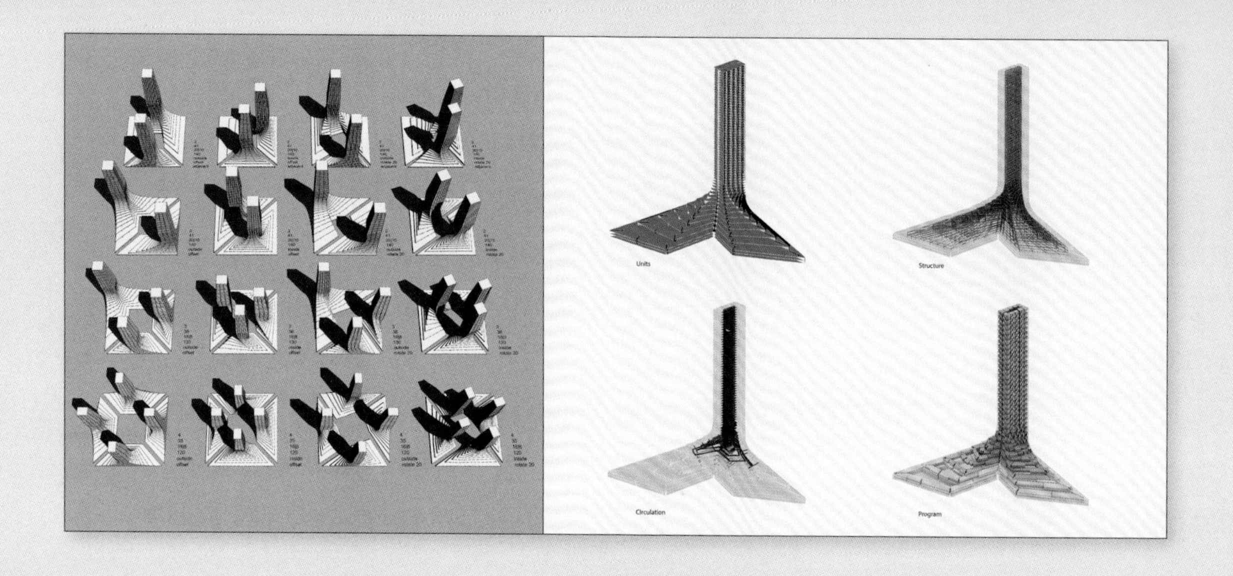

Shanghai is the largest city in China with a population of over 20 million in its greater metropolitan area. In the last two decades it has undergone rapid economic and urban expansion. It now boasts thousands of buildings labelled as 'tall', with many more to come within the next few decades. Such development has irreversible effects on the quality of urban space and the way people live. In large parts of the city the traditional urban fabric of low-rise, low-density row houses has already been replaced by generic high-rise typologies. These are significantly transforming urban life and neighbourhood relationships, and if the trend continues, the original character of the city will be in danger.

Rocker-Lange Architects' Shanghai Lilong Tower Urbanism research project attempts to offer a counterproposal to current models of urban development in Shanghai, which are largely based on either the generic point-block tower in an open green landscape or the podium tower typology dominating and internalising an urban block. As China's economy

top left: Unit, structural, circulation and programme diagrams. Based on a column-and-beam structure, the typology provides two separate circulatory systems: one for the residents in the tower, and one for the commercial and office zone in the lower landscape.

top right: The project is based on a catalogue of adaptive tower typologies that emphasise the urban space. The matrices show tower configurations with varying parameters, resulting in different access strategies, orientations and densities.

bottom: The inner courtyard is surrounded by a commercial perimeter, activating the more intimate public space. The cascading levels animated with trees and urban greenery are an extension of urban public life.

began to burgeon in the late 1990s, both became the predominant building models of efficiency and economy for high-density housing in the city.

The premise of the project is to establish an alternative building type with the capacity to maintain parts of the original character of the city while also offering new types of urban spaces. Based on a computational adaptable system, it suggests solutions that have the ability to preserve the identity and urban quality of Shanghai without neglecting the call for densification. Indeed it aims to find a compromise between the need for compaction, the desire to protect as much of the historical city as possible, and the idea of an architectural organism that combines vertical built volumes with ground-level public open spaces.

Until the early 1950s, more than 60 per cent of the total housing area in Shanghai consisted of lilongs. These communities are characterised by an outer perimeter along the main streets dominated by commercial programmes (workshops and shops), and an inner circulatory system that gives access to two- to three-storey residential units and provides a high degree of security and privacy. Rocker-Lange's project takes these ideas as a point of departure to generate a two- to three-storey podium that adapts to the eaves height of the traditional context, while implementing access lanes to a variably sized inner courtyard that provides a more private urban environment. The landscape of the podium that terraces from the roof of the second level before merging into the tower provides an open public space that is half park, half promenade. The algorithmic architectural-urban system underlying the project is thus able to adapt to any of the city's plot topologies, while offering flexible tower morphologies that can be oriented independently. All of the urban and architectural features important for the overall outcome can be altered through integrated feedback processes.

The testing ground for the project was a larger urban context around Shanghai's Xiaonanmen Subway Station. Between the old city centre and the Huangpu River, over the last 15 years the area has been heavily affected by the tabula rasa mentality that continues today, and in a few years will have lost all of its historical references. To understand the influence of the new typology on this context, different density scenarios were developed that took as their basis the area's urban situation in 2001. While each version reveals different relationships between the new typology and the areas that should be or could be protected, where to draw the line between healthy preservation of the city's architectural heritage and the need for densification rather than urban sprawl is still very much left open for discussion. ⌂

top left: Oblique aerial view of a prototypical tower. The typology is the synergy of a podium and tower that in between the two conditions generates publicly accessible urban terraces vertically, and urban courtyards horizontally.

top right: Street view. The height of the outer perimeter eaves aligns with the existing urban fabric. The access lanes to the inner courtyard provide a more private environment.

An Interview with
Mark Burry

Donald Bates

Permanence and Change

Mark Burry is Professor of Urban Futures at the University of Melbourne. He is renowned internationally for his work employing digital techniques to advance the completion of Antoni Gaudí's Sagrada Família in Barcelona. What happens, though, when architects shift the focus from designing buildings to cities? **Donald Bates**, Chair of Architectural Design at the University of Melbourne and Director of LAB Architecture Studio, asks Burry this question about scalability and discusses with him further the viability of mass customisation in an urban context.

Antoni Gaudí
Basilica Sagrada Família
Barcelona
1882–

Aerial view from the southeast.

Embedded within the proposition for a 'mass-customised city' sits a progression or sequence. Beginning in the early 1990s with the introduction of digital and computational techniques into the design process, the sequence was later extended to include fabrication and manufacturing. This lineage has been relatively easy to manage with singular objects or multiples of objects, elements and components. However, more recently, production through digital fabrication has shifted from objects/components of a certain product scale to the possibility of being able to digitally print/fabricate a complete house or high-rise tower.

The move to a mass-customised city might be seen as a logical extrapolation of this process. If mass customisation has been achieved at the level of objects, then it might well be achieved at the scale of architecture (in terms of buildings or precincts). Can this logic also then be extrapolated to the scale of the city? A recurring trope in architecture posits that the design of a house is similar to that of a piece of furniture, and that the design of a city is similar to the design of a house, though at larger scales.

Mark Burry, Professor of Urban Futures at the Faculty of Architecture, Building and Planning, University of Melbourne, is internationally recognised for his groundbreaking work on the translation of digital techniques into the design resolution and material construction for the completion of the Sagrada Família in Barcelona. As an expert on Antoni Gaudí, he has been deeply involved, as Senior Architect and Researcher, in the design and work programme that now sees the potential for the completion of the basilica by 2026 (the centenary of Gaudí's death).

Burry's work and research is practice based, exploring the incorporation of new processes and technologies (digital or otherwise) within contemporary architectural practice. His research is increasingly focused on the broader aspects of design beyond architecture, and especially on the future urban condition. Reacting to the proposition of scalability from object to building to city, he notes: 'I might actually start with the opening gambit about scalability. I have to say, I have always had difficulty in understanding why an architect would ever claim ownership of urbanism, as in urban design. The proof of that difference is that you don't ever get a chair with a screwdriver still sticking out of it or a house with a tarpaulin permanently over part of it (unless you are talking about the Australian film *The Castle*). Cities always have cranes sticking out of them. There is no such thing as a completed city. I have always looked at cities as being arrangements of buildings, streets, parks and squares etc, constantly changing in ways that architecture cannot. We may well aspire for that constant change, but it is not really the case that architecture is in a state of constant change. Materially, on the whole, it is started and it is finished.'

Aerial view from the northwest.

View from the southeast looking up towards the Nativity Facade, completed just after Gaudí's death in 1926.

This cliché of direct scalability of object–building–city would appear to fail from its very inception. At the level of a singular object, there is little, if anything, that requires the organisational spatiality that defines a work of architecture. For a house, building or precinct, what is at stake is not simply the materiality, the details or the formal massing and composition, but also the organisational structuring and the consequences of this for, among other things, social relationships. Likewise, the essential nature of a city is profoundly more than simply taking sets of relationships and underlying spatial orders, and projecting these into larger, more complex formations.

Burry counters: 'What this means is that at a design level, cities are systems, rather than objects. This understanding is fundamental to my personal sensibility, which also means that I have difficulty in thinking that architects can claim the urban territory entirely on their own. The city therefore is a system that requires inputs from all sorts of skill bases. If we are talking about design, then the designer may have the predominant role (but has to have all those other inputs as well) in terms not of "scalability", but of "changeability".'

In the context of mass customisation, two divergent lines would appear to be implicated. As discussed already, there is the linear increase of scale and the extrapolation of that scale and its consequences – object to building to city. The second line is the transition from mass repetition to mass customisation, and the speculation on how that plays out in terms of the production of cities. Beyond contemplation of the technological feasibility of such a proposition, Burry raises what might be seen as an existential question regarding the nature of customisation, adaptation and 'fitness-for-purpose': 'We're talking about cities being "mass-customisable", and the implication is that you get the city you want to fit the way you are; the way you want to live. Much more so than we've had in the past – because of the technologies at our disposal. What we are arguing about is to what extent do people want things to be perfectly customised to their needs? Is it not the case that having to adapt to circumstances is an important part of the human condition?'

This reframes the issue of adaptation and customisation (mass or otherwise) and re-focuses examination not on the technology and opportunity, but on the emotional status of change and permanence. The thesis of 'mass-customised cities' is partially predicated on a notion that we are actually getting good at changing things around us. Not only can we make them non-repetitive, but we can change them ever faster and more often. If our advances in software, in programming, allow for ever more rapid cycles of change and alteration, is there a social and psychological shift that is inducing in us a sense that the last thing we need (or desire) to pay attention to is longevity or long-term planning?

This may not be what Burry implies by 'changeability': 'I am already in my 50s so it could be that the generation of our children has no sense of durability or longevity or constancy. I think it's been a human condition for generations though, that there is "place", this thing called "home". You can change. You change by physically moving from the building, but not by the building changing.

As an expert on Antoni Gaudí, Mark Burry has been deeply involved, as Senior Architect and Researcher, in the design and work programme that now sees the potential for the completion of the basilica by 2026 (the centenary of Gaudí's death).

'There is no such thing as a completed city. I have always looked at cities as being arrangements of buildings, streets, parks and squares etc, constantly changing in ways that architecture cannot.'

AMP
Far East
UPPER WEST
P

'I admit I was assuming that the non-negotiable, the sine qua non of existence, is a sense of place, and that we as humans, as nomadic humans, enjoyed shifts in place by moving literally from one place to another. I have always assumed that because there is a place that is permanent (in German, *heimat*) that you can do what you like in terms of seeking change as long as there is something; a root, an anchor.

'That is why I would say that granny, rather than moving from the family home that she has been in for 50 years to somewhere more suitable for her age and occupation, might have an option where the place stays the same, but not the environment. If we're going to be looking at technology, I would be looking at the system as the driver, not the pure mechanics.'

Advocating for the mass-customised city is also to advocate for greater differentiation in the fabric of the city. Repetition, standardised materials and techniques, prefabricated elements and facade systems – in the name of industrial production – have allowed for increased speeds of erection and cost savings. Nonetheless, it could also be argued that such advantages have been outweighed by an impoverishment of the built environment, where repetitive details and features have become overly simplified and far too monotonous and devoid of specificity.

The hope of mass customisation is that the texture of the city will regain its variegation and formal diversity, providing a richer, more engaging material palette for the city. But is it the advances in digital technologies that will achieve this architectural and urban effect? According to Burry: 'In (Melbourne) Victoria recently, we've had a set of policies that have allowed a rather extraordinary rash of tall skyscrapers for apartments. I am not convinced that all the ramifications are being considered in terms of what that means, such as at the pavement level. I am sure the rules (such as they are) have been observed. But that's policy, that's not design. They're making short-term decisions.' The problem is a political condition, not a formal or technological impasse. 'The politicians put the policies that set the economics. The builders, the developers are responding to the opportunities those policies offer.'

'I am much more interested in how we get greater agglomeration in the cities without the loss of individual expression,' Burry continues. 'I think it will be politics before technology. The technology might help drive decision-making by politicians, but at the moment the problems are evident, yet the signs of the solutions aren't clear as being something that technology will lead or aid and abet. The question is: "what is it that we're not doing as designers that can help the politicians feel comfortable about making longer-term decisions?"' ⌂

This article is based on an interview by Donald Bates with Mark Burry in February 2015 in Melbourne.

Central business district (CBD) Melbourne

above, opposite and below: Melbourne's CBD and adjacent precincts have witnessed unprecedented high-rise apartment development in the last 15 years. The trend continues unabated, with the population doubling in the last nine years to over 54,000.

David Erdman and Clover Lee

davidclovers
The Repulse Bay
Repulse Bay
Hong Kong

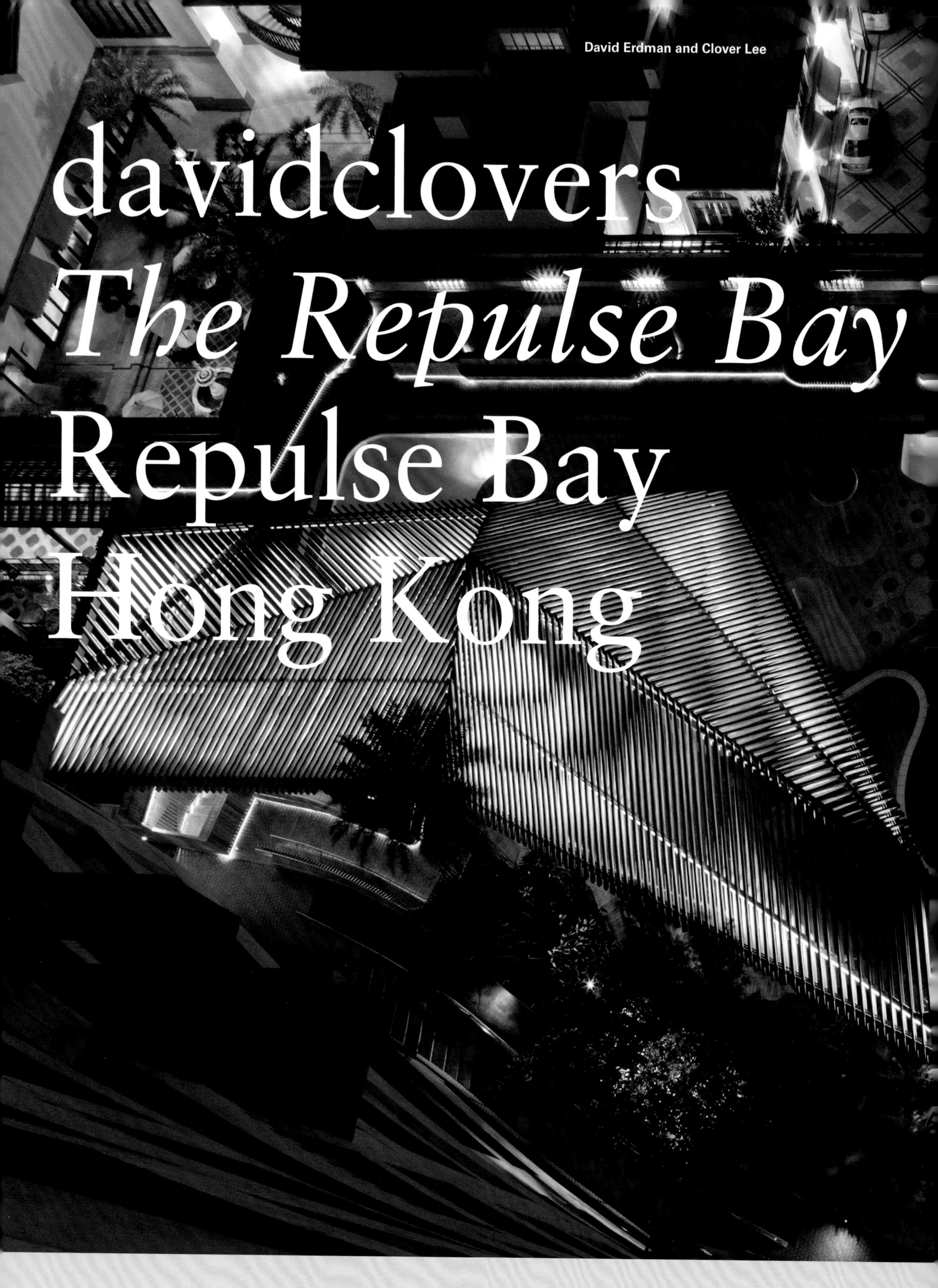

davidclovers
The Repulse Bay complex
Repulse Bay
Hong Kong
2013

Aerial view of the waterscape from Tower 01. The gradient spacing, tapering and widening of the canopy play off the curvature of the tower and the pool. Working in concert with the existing pedestrian walkway, this forms a dense, newly established zone of activity connecting the lobbies of all four towers (each redesigned by davidclovers) to the Waterscape.

Complex

View along the main pedestrian pathway linking all four towers, depicting the Waterscape pool and Tower 01 behind. Executed concurrently, but designed with very different constraints, geometry and materials affiliate the interiors of Tower 01 with the waterscape experience.

Adaptation and alteration of existing building are a fertile area for mass customisation, as well as new builds. With growing land values and an increasing maturity of building stock in Southeast Asian cities, this has become a more viable option than carte blanche development. **David Erdman and Clover Lee,** founding directors of davidclovers based in Hong Kong, describe how they employed a composite of technological approaches when undertaking the 'gut renovation' and alteration of The Repulse Bay Complex in the city.

The glass facade of the Tower 03 lobby intervention along the main pedestrian walkway gently pushes inwards while the stone from the interior spills outwards, wrapping columns and the retaining wall. The design plays off the large-scale curvature of all four towers, while intensifying and interiorising it into a dense, textural, interior/exterior object along the pathway.

The project illustrates the potential of the disjunctive producing a new spatial fabric that is cohesive yet agile, and formed out of a series of disconnected interventions. It is therefore distinct from an adaptation, which requires and perhaps strives for the production of a singular, autonomous whole.

Mid- to late 20th-century obsessions with digital technology often relied upon biological models to understand how architecture could adapt to its changing context. While there have been some notable advances in this field in a host of formal, parametric and geometrical architectural experiments, it is difficult to ignore adaptation's infestation of the profession à la 'adaptive re-use'. Used more often as a marketing ploy than a conceptual opportunity, adaptation is ripe for theoretical expansion and interrogation, particularly in the context of customisation and the production of cities.

Alteration opens up fresh discursive territory that builds upon the ideas of adaptation by similarly affronting standardisation – with a few distinctions. For the most part, architectural adaptation projects are conceived from the ground up, introducing a comprehensive and whole architectural system into a specific context. The contemporary field of design software similarly favours this continuous, smooth, singular, fully integrated approach. Alteration, on the other hand, is somewhat more restrained, fine grained and interiorised, a more centripetal than centrifugal approach to design that involutes, pulls and tucks the architecture into shape rather than deforming it to adjust it to its adjacencies.

The potential of alteration within digital architecture has not yet been realised. However, its episodic characteristics mean it is open to a reconsideration of the theories of disjunctive or fragmented architectures prevalent in the 1980s. To a large extent, these theories are absent from digital architecture today, the result of an obsession with continuity and an intellectually stubborn insistence on designing the whole.

The distinction between adaptation and alteration is central to davidclovers' renovation of an existing residential complex in Hong Kong for The Repulse Bay, a wholly owned subsidiary of Hong Kong and Shanghai Hotels Limited, which owns and operates the city's famed Peninsula Hotel. The original, mid-1980s complex, including four towers of mid- to up-scale, unfurnished rental units, is an Arquitectonica 'knock-off' infamous for the gaping hole between the third and fourth towers. Each tower was standardised and homogeneous, surrounded by landscaping, outdoor recreational areas and a clubhouse that were designed without an overall identity and experience of the complex at large.

Tower 01 was unique in Hong Kong, being one of the first comprehensive 'gut renovations' of a tower coupled with extensive revamping of the podium, clubhouse, lobbies of the adjacent three towers and the overall complex. This type of project reflects a number of broader themes such as the city's maturing building fabric and its sobering economy, and is emblematic of the challenges that need to be faced in response to the rapidly decreasing availability of undeveloped land. The collection of interventions that includes the residential Tower 01 (or Ricou Tower), the Waterscape (a pool atop the podium), the lobbies of towers 02 to 04, portions of the clubhouse including Breakers cafe, other recreational areas and collective spaces was designed and completed incrementally by davidclovers between 2011 and 2013. The project brief aimed at simultaneously augmenting the heterogeneity of the tower units of Tower 01 while imbuing the overall complex and three adjacent towers with a greater sense of cohesion.

In the simplest terms, each intervention is a physical alteration of an existing structure, focusing on changes to the common areas of a residential complex that alter inhabitants' perception of and interaction with these spaces. The project illustrates the potential of the disjunctive producing a new spatial fabric that is cohesive yet agile, and formed out of a series of disconnected interventions. It is therefore distinct from an adaptation, which requires and perhaps strives for the production of a singular, autonomous whole.

right: The clubhouse ground-floor lobby as seen from the shuttle stop. Drawing upon similar techniques to those used for the Tower 03 lobby, the clubhouse entry acts as another semi-autonomous, intensified intervention on the site. The extension of the interior stone limits the boundaries of the design while reinforcing the texture and rhythm of the tower lobbies across the street.

above: The shuttle stop and bench with the waterscape canopy beyond, viewed from the clubhouse entrance. Notions about the negative space between elements acted as a device to bind without connecting them. The shuttle stop and waterscape, constructed with similar materials but very different techniques, can be seen here to figure and form foreground and background voids cultivating an affiliation between each intervention.

right: The communal seating area of Breakers cafe. The six-sided design principles used in Tower 01 were experimented with further in this intervention, which is the focal point and gathering nexus of the clubhouse. Algorithmically manipulating a photograph, washes of deep blue and white augment the geometry and interrelationships of the cafe's columns. While each column is autonomous, the colouration and pattern work in concert to define the space of the cafe as well as open it up to the traffic flowing through it.

pposite middle right: The living ·rea of a typical three-bedroom ·partment. The six-sided design ·chnique allows for relationships ·etween built-in elements and ·ithin rooms to slide across ·alls, floors and ceilings, ·mphasising the volumetric and ·ertical characteristics of the unit. ·laster, glass-fibre-reinforced ·eiling elements are prefabricated ·hroughout the tower.

below: The wood and plaster texture of the interventions permeates each floor of Tower 01, as well as the common areas and the units. The lobby is just one example that demonstrates how a series of prefabricated plaster elements peel away to reveal a luminous wood surface beyond. The design of the lobby is a six-sided intervention that affiliates with nearly 100 different six-sided interventions distributed vertically throughout the tower.

While each of davidclovers' interventions in the Repulse Bay complex significantly alters existing structural, mechanical and visual arrangements, each also has its own discrete limits and can never be a continuous whole. Often regarded as a deficiency or a diluted architectural opportunity, alteration is seen in this project as a robust opportunity that also reflects forthcoming trends for development in Asia, where buildings are over-structured and being redeveloped with increasing frequency.

The convergence of technological approaches and the parallel streaming of design techniques in each of the Repulse Bay projects proliferates a high degree of specificity, dexterity and heterogeneity, while avoiding episodic fragmentation. A composite of technological approaches are deployed, ranging from digitally prefabricated construction to algorithmically generated graphic design and colouring techniques. The designs alter a series of autonomous landscapes, interiors and architectural elements into a rhythmic texture that appears and disappears throughout the site. Working in this manner has developed a finely grained yet open system. Each intervention opens up to, and simultaneously alters, existing structures and relationships, and is a result of a disciplinary plurality – integrating techniques from product, graphic and landscape design, and further altering the stable 'reading' or perception of any single technique. The ensemble of designs never fully integrates or makes the site whole, yet incrementally they produce enough pressure and tension to tether together remote and unconnected experiences.

Perhaps it is fruitful to consider whether or not a focus on alteration can allow for more diverse ways for architectural design and its associated digital praxis to mature and develop. Regardless of the outcome of such a debate, it may be useful to consider how the use of digital technologies in architecture and its interior condition might transform concepts of the singular whole. Experimenting with the limits of continuity and fragmentation through alteration could enable a greater degree of compatibility with existing architectural systems and an even greater plurality of experience and effect. The Repulse Bay complex serves as an interesting testing ground in this light, where diverse material assemblies and moods augment the heterogeneity of experiences while at the same time producing enough cohesion to give the property a new identity. Alteration can subsequently be seen as a way to re-situate digital architecture, highlighting its disjunctive capacities and ushering in post-digital themes that are more relevant to broad cultural trends in the industry. If we can abandon the obsession with the whole, shifting from adaptation to alteration may allow for fertile theoretical and practical projections. ⌂

right: Diagram showing the locations and scope of interventions throughout the Repulse Bay complex.

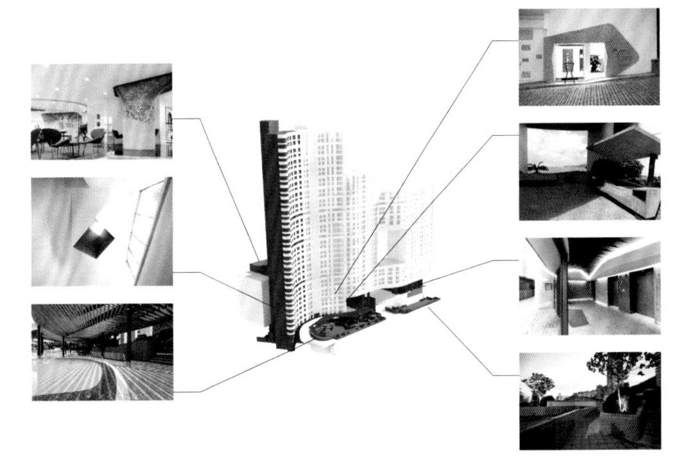

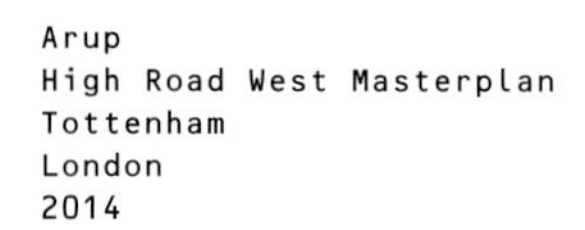
Arup
High Road West Masterplan
Tottenham
London
2014

Axonometric view showing the sensitive integration of existing heritage, workplaces and social infrastructure into the masterplan and the creation of a well-connected, attractive, mixed-use neighbourhood alongside the Tottenham Hotspur football stadium.

Catal Urba

The Role of Customised Design Solutions in Delivering Transformational Urban Change

Elad Eisenstein

Arup
Physical Development Framework
Tottenham
London
2014

Strategic diagram highlighting the five key regeneration focus areas in Tottenham and strategic connections to the wider context.

Elad Eisenstein is a Director at Arup, leading the firm's urban design and masterplanning practice from London. Here he describes how through a highly customised approach, 'catalytic urbanism', Arup is working internationally in cities undergoing rapid change in a manner that is tailored to both global and local forces – accounting for climate change, macroeconomics and mobility. This bespoke method is illustrated in three diverse contexts: in North London, Pretoria in South Africa and Wanzhuang in China.

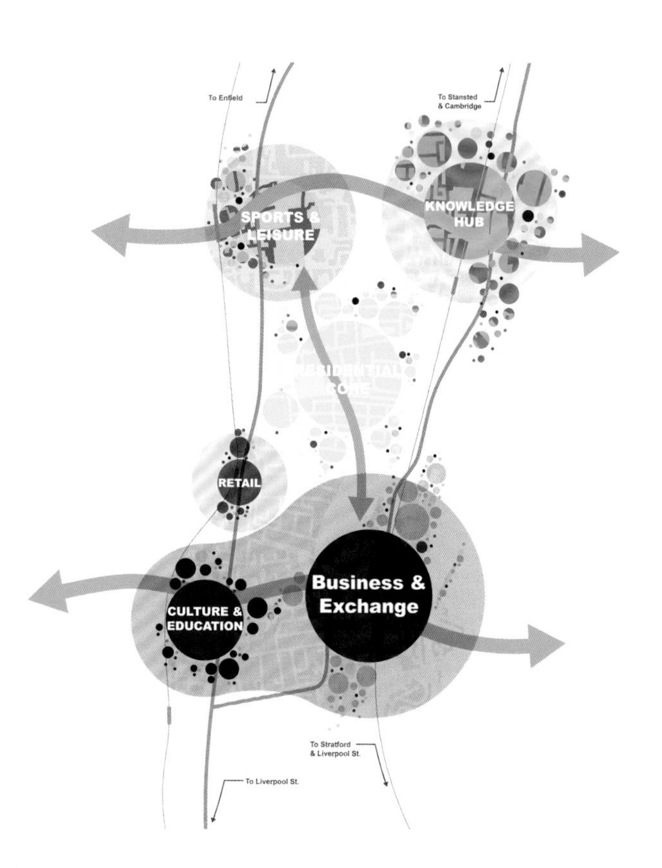

The scale and speed of urban change continue to grow. While the need to address the challenges of urbanisation is urgent, the way in which these should be addressed remains unclear both in terms of productive design solutions, and of effective models for delivering quality large-scale urban change.

The challenges of delivering successful, sustainable and long-lasting new urban environments at a large scale require a unique approach – one that can effectively balance physical and social conditions particular to a place with the impacts of global forces and practices such as climate change, macroeconomics and mobility.

Arup has been working closely with global cities undergoing rapid change. Operating both at global and local scales, Arup applies global knowledge and practices to sensitively address radically different urban contexts. Catalytic urbanism – the methodology applied to city design – prioritises custom, rather than standardised urbanism, to focus strategies around critical local issues and stimulate wider impacts.

Projects presented here from Arup's work on cities in Europe, Africa and Asia showcase the catalytic impact of custom design solutions in radically different contexts and the tools, innovation and strategic thinking applied to deliver meaningful transformational change.

The Case of Tottenham

Image showing improvements to White Hart Lane including new public realm, reuse of existing heritage buildings, new cycling lanes and active frontage.

The 2011 riots brought Tottenham in North London into the national headlines, resulting in investment from the Mayor of London and the local Council for rebuilding damaged properties and in the development of long-term regeneration plans for the area. London is expected to grow significantly to a population of 10 million by 2030, and Tottenham is one of the city's main opportunity areas for accommodating this growth.

In recent years, low skills and levels of education created barriers for communities to accessing economic opportunities and jobs in London. These have contributed to social unrest and crime. Nonetheless, Tottenham has all the right ingredients to be a successful place, with excellent transport connectivity to wider London, attractive parks and open spaces, legible Victorian street hierarchy and urban structure, and a strong history of manufacturing that continues to grow.

The regeneration strategy for the area capitalises on these assets to create an overarching framework for change that includes a range of spatial and policy interventions. By improving the performance of the existing urban condition, the strategy joins together a range of projects customised for specific local conditions to deliver growth and attract investment into the area.

A focus on transport infrastructure was used as a tool to unlock new investment potential, primarily through the redistribution of economic activities into key nodes and around major transport interchanges. A road improvement scheme to release development sites near Tottenham Hale station by dismantling the one-way gyratory system created opportunities to attract new investment into the area. A comprehensive redevelopment of Tottenham Hale tube, rail and bus station delivers operational efficiency, significantly improves accessibility, and turns the station and surroundings into a major mixed-use centre, capitalising on its position along the Cambridge–Stansted–London corridor.

Localised interventions to improve connectivity, permeability and public realm strengthen the growth and productivity of the high road and support the delivery of sustainable residential neighbourhoods. Three centres of different character are reinforced along the high road, with a leisure-led mixed-use centre around the new Tottenham Hotspur football stadium attracting new residents and investment into the area.

Over the next 10 years, Tottenham is expected to deliver a transformation on a scale that is larger than the area around the Olympic Park, or a new town, but at a fraction of the cost – building on the infrastructure, connectivity and communities in the area. Regeneration initiatives, as in the Tottenham example, demonstrate the way in which customised commitment towards improving opportunities for local communities can make a significant contribution in supporting the challenges of urbanisation.

The Case of Tshwane

Arup
City of Tshwane Masterplan
Pretoria
South Africa
2013

While many highly urbanised areas across Europe are undergoing large-scale inner-city regeneration, in Africa, many cities are suffering from the reverse process, as political instability and personal safety concerns redirect investment away from the centres of cities.

The capital of South Africa – Pretoria – reflects the enormous change within the country, historically and today. In recent years, the central area of the city –Tshwane – has seen an exodus of residents and businesses to the outer city suburbs. As a result, the performance of the urban environment has suffered, with crime levels increasing. As Johannesburg and other centres in the region continue to grow, Tshwane is struggling to compete, with fragile growth opportunities and a continuing undermining of investor confidence in the city.

Despite this trend, a number of areas of the city show stronger social and economic activity than others. The plan for Tshwane is centred on these zones. The regeneration of the city centre will take place through strengthening existing activities and pointing public and private investors towards these priority geographical areas, where their combined activity will most effectively deliver change and create market conditions for wider transformation.

Infrastructure is at the heart of the plan. A new rapid transit system has been put in place, and many of the major streets have been invested with new public realm to create a walkable city. Green spaces and recreation areas have been improved, with a green infrastructure network running throughout the city, helping to deal with the effects of climate change and improving livability of neighbourhoods.

At the local scale, many of the long urban blocks have been opened up, improving connectivity and safety. Small-scale urban spaces stimulate cultural activities and create opportunities for a range of businesses to cluster in different locations. More efficient servicing and parking arrangements unlock new development opportunities and encourage the use of more sustainable transport modes.

The plan for Tshwane maintains the culture and creativity of the city and generates new opportunities for affordable urban redevelopment. Through focused interventions customised to different locations and conditions, the plan creates opportunities for innovation and entrepreneurship, inviting the market to come forward and work closely with the city to deliver sustainable places.

Photograph showing the current condition of Belle Ombre station – one of the city centre's main transport interchanges.

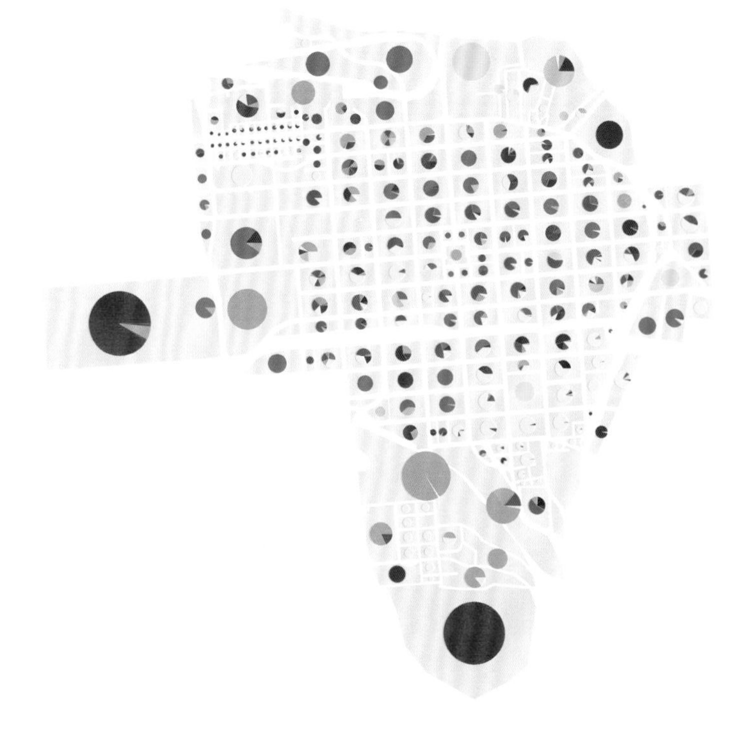

Economic analysis map showing Tshwane city blocks and their existing range of use mix, pointing to geographic areas of regenerative potential.

below: Aerial view showing the regeneration focus areas in Tshwane and their connection to the existing urban grid and new green infrastructure network.

bottom: Tshwane framework plan illustrating the regeneration of focus areas as well as specific interventions in key locations and wider city networks, including connectivity, open space, heritage, social infrastructure and education.

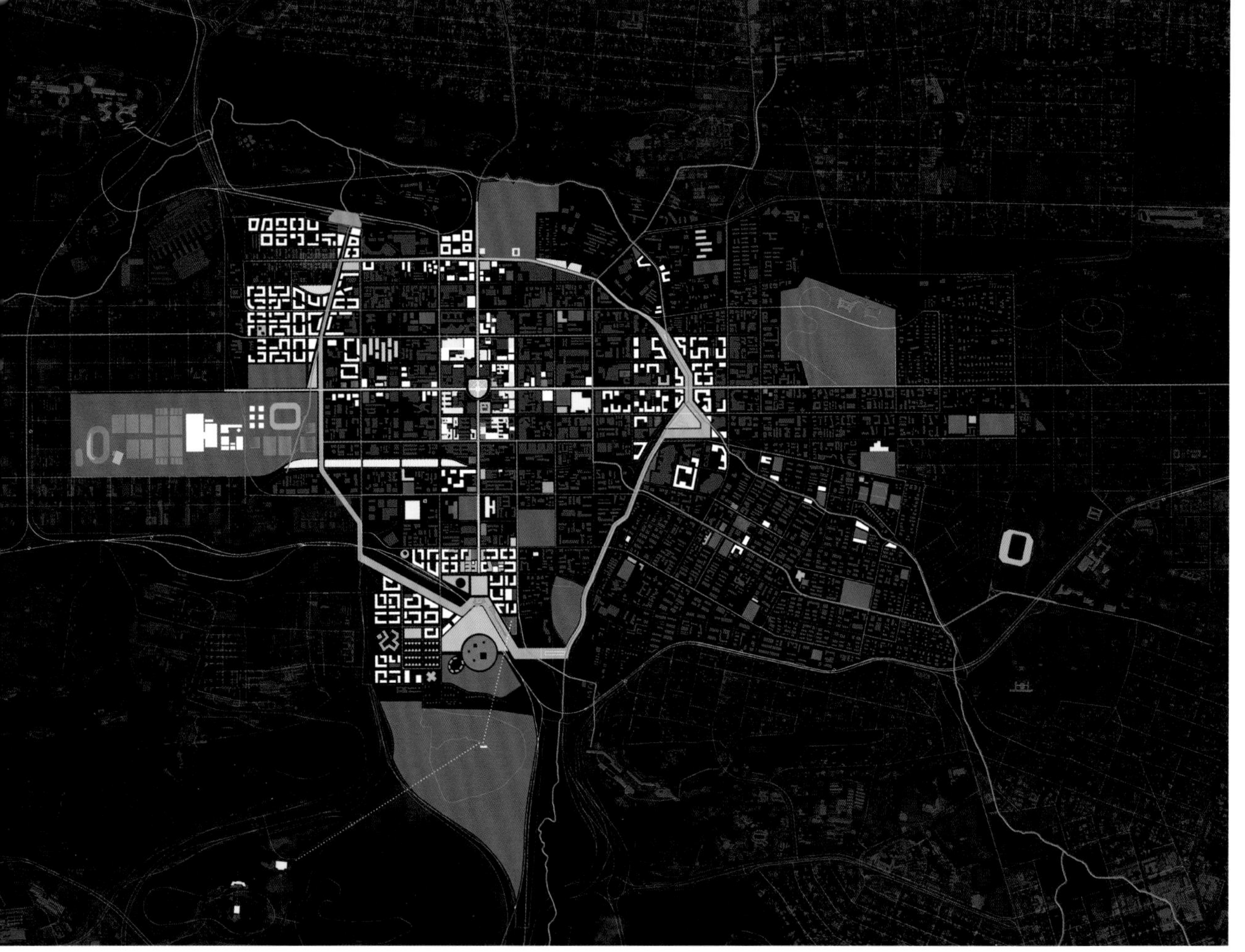

The Case of Wanzhuang

Arup
Wanzhuang Eco-City
China
2010

Aerial view looking into one of the local centres of Wanzhuang, illustrating the strong relationship between agricultural intensification, the existing villages and opportunities for new development.

The urbanisation of China is one of the biggest shifts in economic outputs and trends being witnessed in modern times. In the next five years alone, China will see an additional 100 million people living in cities. As recently published in its urbanisation plan, China's main focus in the coming years is to mitigate some of the social and environmental impact caused by the pursuit of rapid and large-scale urban expansion.

Wanzhuang eco-city is located halfway between Beijing and the port of Tianjin. The 80-square-kilometre (30-square-mile) area, which currently contains 42 villages in an agricultural setting, has been selected by the Chinese government for development into a city that will accommodate up to half a million people by 2025. This offers a unique opportunity to explore new directions in eco-city development, with a focus on agriculture.

Preserving, utilising and enhancing the knowledge and farming skills of local residents is central to the strategy. This creates new economic opportunities by building on the existing agricultural skills base while helping to manage the balance between the need for new development and the desire to retain a functional rural context.

Compact development combined with the intensification of areas around the existing villages allows for the conservation of important productive land and agricultural heritage as well as the incorporation of characteristics of the existing urban fabric into the new development areas. Sustainable farming systems incorporating new technologies are integrated into the more urbanised areas, attracting other uses such as research and business and thus creating a mixed-use environment. A new Town Centre located along the Beijing–Tianjin corridor connects Wanzhuang to the region's other major economic centres.

The rural landscape plays an important part in the character of Wanzhuang. Parks, large recreation areas and mature urban landscape create a unique environment where health and wellbeing are central to urban living. Human-scale streets and a city-wide cycling network, supported by efficient public transport, help redefine urban–rural relationships, creating a dynamic, thriving environment that achieves harmonious urbanisation.

The plan for Wanzhuang exemplifies how large-scale urban development can be catalysed through a series of solutions customised to address local needs and purpose. Focused around preserving and strengthening the agricultural heritage in the area, the variety of strategies and interventions, delivered at multiple scales and locations, create an urban environment that is unique, productive and sustainable.

Global Practices and Local Transformation

Arup's global practices are deployed within the specific constraints and contingencies of the different cities in which it operates. With urban environments becoming increasingly complex, there is a need to help cities prioritise their efforts in balancing the global challenges and potential of urbanisation with local issues and the aspirations of communities.

The cases illustrated here demonstrate how customised urban strategies catalyse the delivery of large-scale meaningful change: in Tottenham, how the focus on resolving transport issues unlocks opportunities for wider growth; in Tshwane, how the strengthening of the informal economy delivers city-wide change; and in Wanzhuang, the way in which strengthening agricultural heritage creates a prosperous regional economy. All strategies are applied locally but are strongly underpinned by global practices, tools and innovations.

City making is a process, not an imagination of an end-state condition. Arup's approach helps bring stakeholders together, develop community support, focus external investment and minimise long-term risk. This is done through Arup's use of modelling and consultation to monitor impacts and identify synergies between parameters, and through applying foresight and innovation to help identify future trends and to deliver strategies with wider long-term benefits in mind.

In addressing rapid urbanisation, long-term success will be measured primarily through the prosperity of local communities. Creating places where people will choose to live, can afford to live and stay, and will be productive remains one of the critical challenges of our generation. ⌂

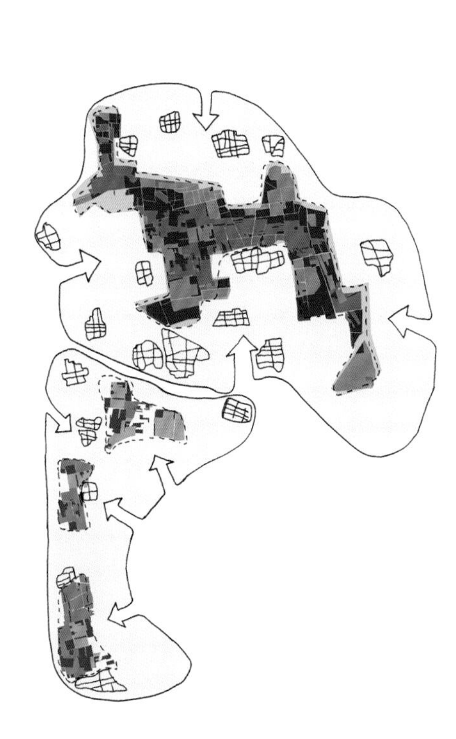

Hand-drawn sketch diagram showing the intensified agricultural areas within the Wanzhuang area.

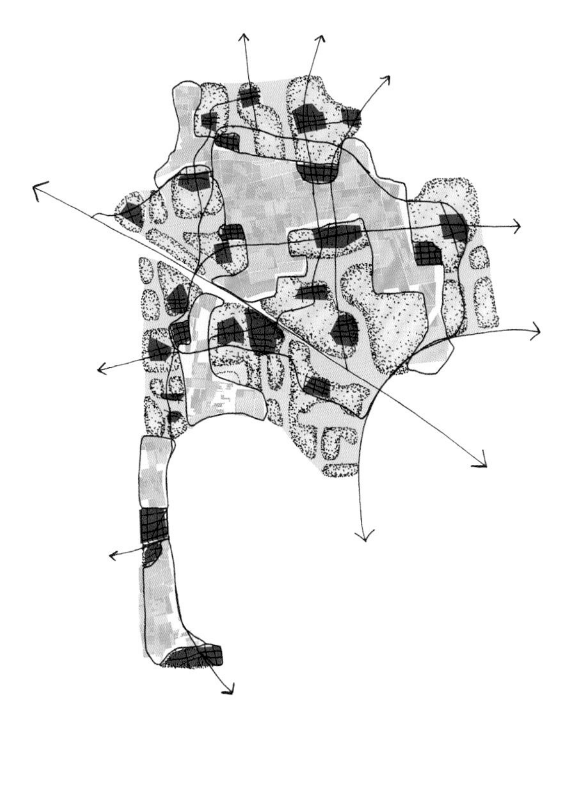

Hand-drawn sketch diagram showing the relationships between the expanded existing villages, local agricultural activities and the wider connectivity networks.

OCEAN CN Consultancy Network

Second Development Zone

Umekita Area, Osaka, Japan

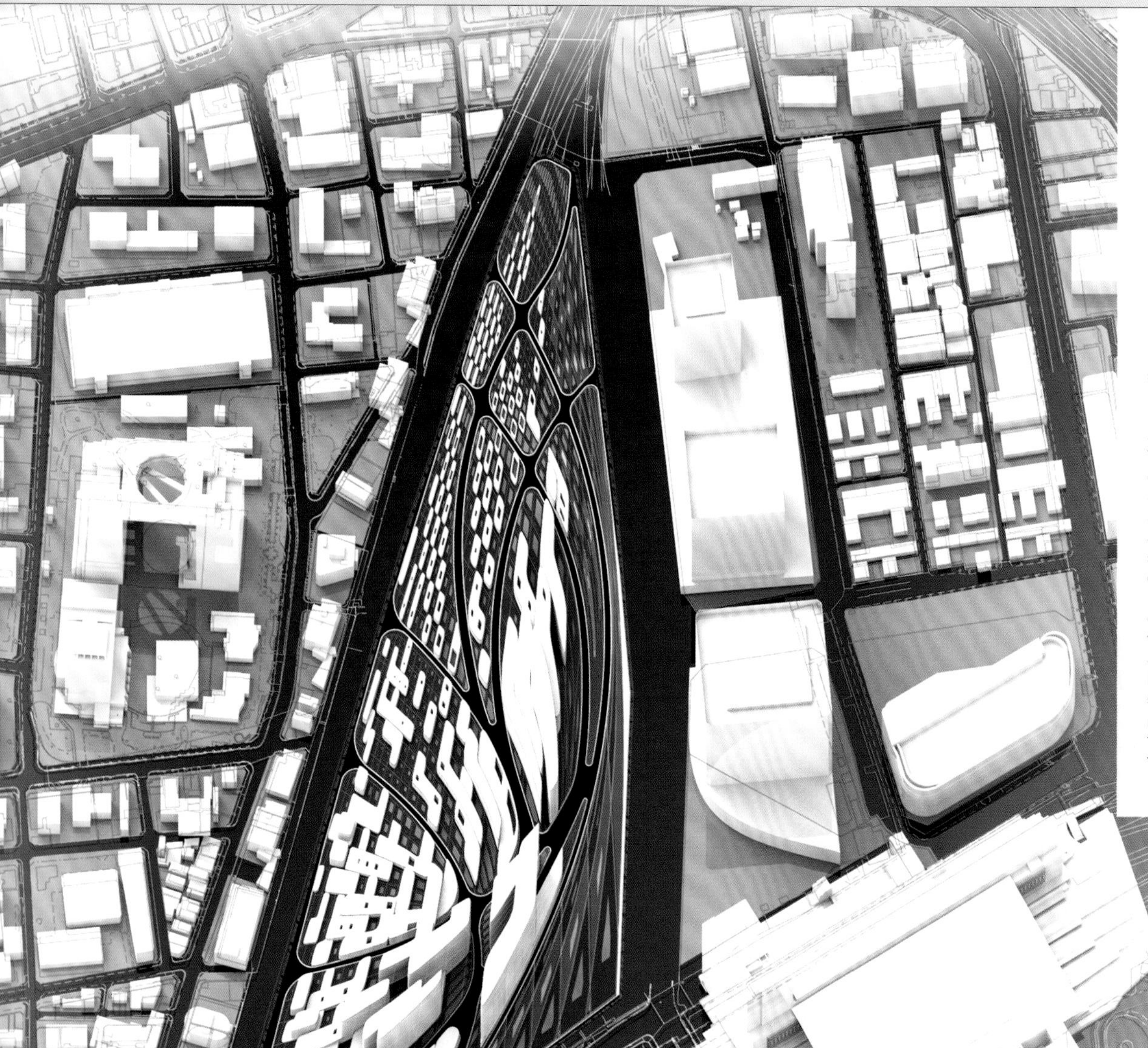

OCEAN CN
Consultancy Network

Second Development Zone

Umekita Area

Osaka

Japan

2013-14

left and opposite: Aerial views and a masterplan proposal for a single snapshot in time, as an instant in a process of formation and information to be developed and adapted to future contingencies. This urban model emphasises a concrete description of massing and open space, configured by a variety of programmatic uses and massing typologies. Varied scales, densities and types of extruded, granular pixilated massing are contrasted with diverse public open spaces with varied planting, material textures and orientation. The traffic and infrastructural management of the site is embedded within a porous, pedestrian-focused urbanism flowing around, under and through fields of building mass.

OCEAN CN Consultancy Network is a Hong Kong-based specialist design consultancy with links to Beijing, Shanghai and London. Its work spans architecture and urbanism. In Asia, an adaptive and interactive approach has been developed for urban masterplanning, as well as for infrastructural and cultural projects. Here Guest-Editor and Creative Director of OCEAN CN **Tom Verebes** describes the network's invited competition entry for the Second Development Zone of the Umekita Area in Osaka, which in its adaptive approach embraces local specificity and variable futures scenarios in its adoption of customisation and new technologies.

OCEAN CN's future vision for the Second Development Zone of the Umekita Area in Osaka is based on two related aims: to achieve a distinctive urbanism predicated on the design of unique and memorable spatial experiences, as well as to develop an adaptive and responsive urban interface. Although the invited competition entry for this 7-hectare (17-acre) urban scheme proposes a single design outcome, its significance is found rather in the intelligence of the back-end modelling environment, which encapsulates the potential to design multiple outcomes based on complex parameters and contingencies.

The proposal first aims to create an identifiable character for Umekita's urban precinct while confidently augmenting the existing conditions of the specific urban locale. Customisation of the 21st-century city will not therefore erase its preceding order, but rather embrace its diverse site forces and contingencies as the basis of urban complexity. The second aim of the project is more elusive and indefinite. Under the false pretence of permanence, a discrete architectural project can be deemed to be enduring and finite, thereby disregarding any temporal forces of change. A large urban site, on the other hand, requires a design approach and methodology with which to mediate indeterminate future circumstances. Thus, the design methods and models of OCEAN CN's proposal for Umekita target ways in which the area's attributes can be adapted to both foreseeable as well as unforeseen conditions. Understanding the emergent properties of city formation makes it possible to effect its evolution over time.

The principal strategic objective is to develop diverse future scenarios and configurations for the site that can be adapted to diverging patterns of future investment and planning. Although one single design scheme is presented, the proposal is rather for an adaptive process of mediating many possible futures, each contingent on how economic, political, social and environmental considerations play out in time.

Given this paradox of planning for growth and change, typically the two-dimensional plan, when

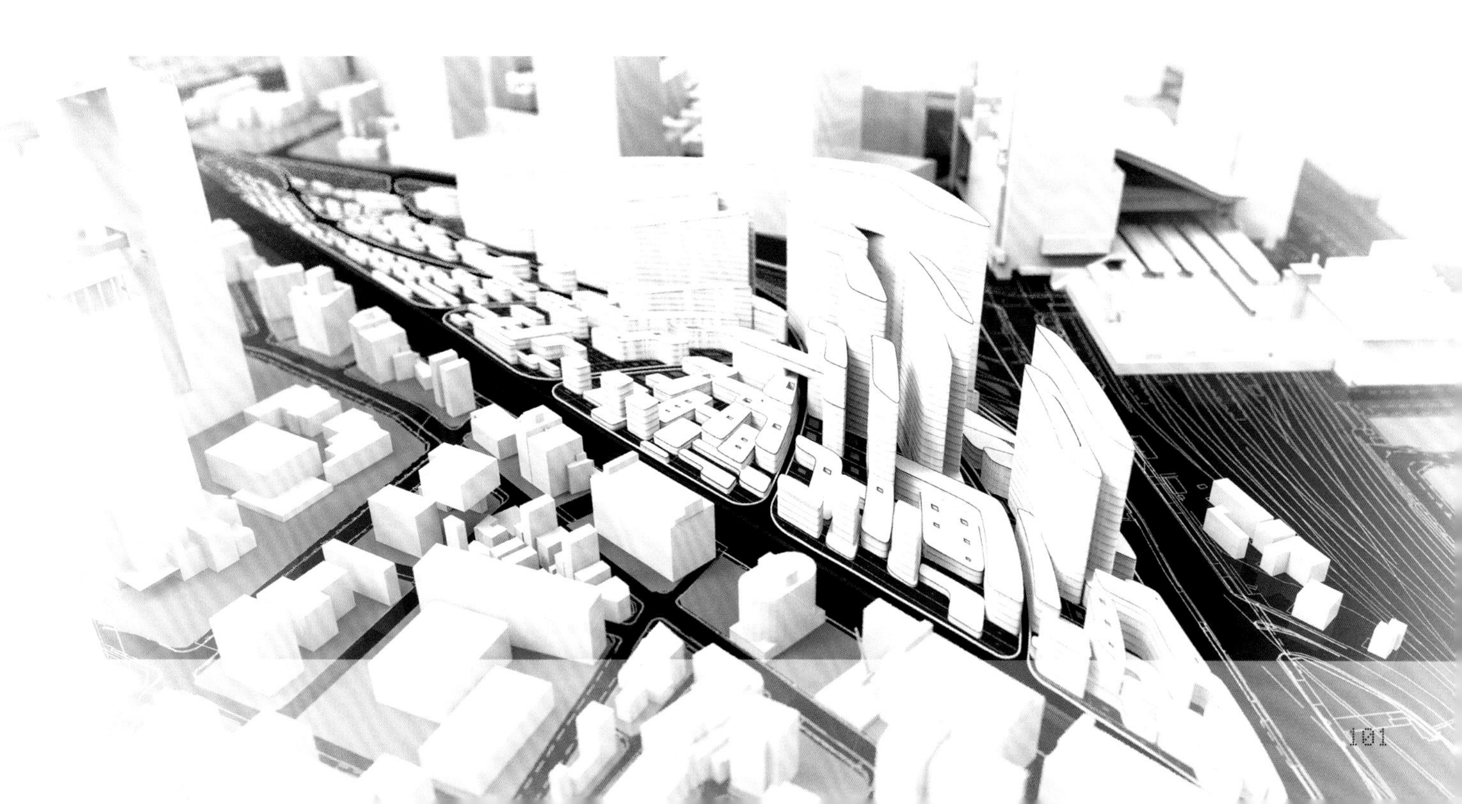

top: Six zoning scenarios, each outlining a varied mix of programmatic ratios, are deployed as instruments to yield six different diagrams of massing and open green spaces. These six models and corresponding urban plans describe the land utilisation, programme areas and composition of six schemes, demonstrating the metrics of built and open space. The resultant diverse urban morphologies demonstrate the urban model as an interactive tool within a methodology that is responsive to the contingencies that will shape the development of the Umekita area.

bottom: One of several plan diagrams indicating driving parameters such as point and field attractors, relations to roads and rail infrastructure and the immediate urban contextual morphology, programming and density. Through this data-driven approach to contextual specificity, the associated massing densities, heights, footprints and setbacks of each of the urban models generated is determined. With the 'back-end' computation of algorithms, linked to 'front-end' computational interfaces, these methods help to order variegation of models, the initial status of which is that of un-designed, raw output from a 3D modelling environment.

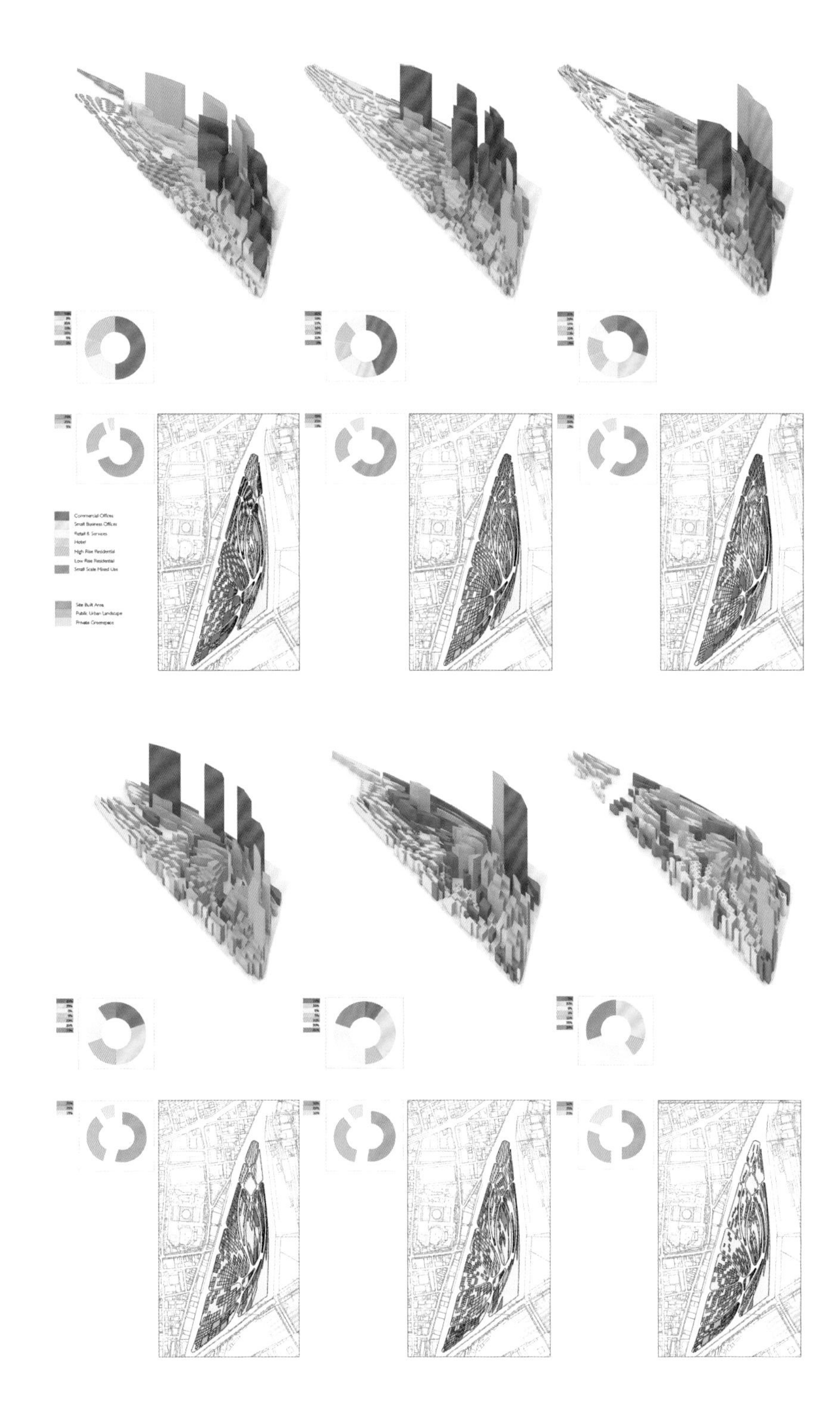

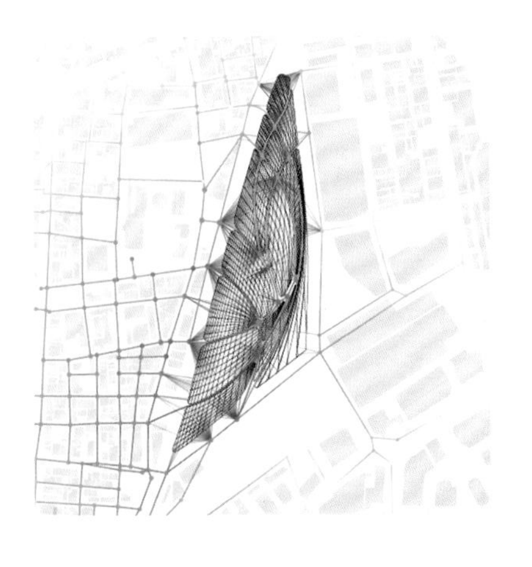

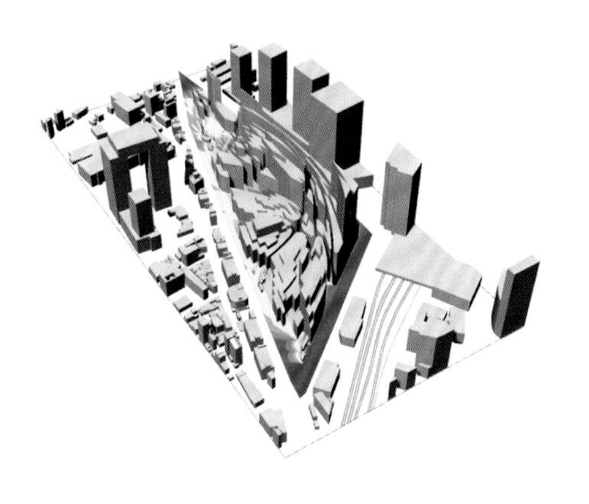

understood as a static and final representation of the singular – and even ideal – outcome of a design process is often obsolete before it is built. In contrast, the urban model is posited as an interactive machine for issuing variance of a multitude of front-end design outcomes, with intelligence embedded in its back-end computational drivers. As an alternative to a static masterplan, the shepherding interactive model as proposed by OCEAN CN for Umekita is generated by multifarious influences and associations over time, and projects a future that is unknown and indeterminable. Computational coding and modelling are deployed as vehicles for generating multiple possible future conditions through the machining and prototyping of masterplans that rather than being merely images or representations, are provisional configurations of interactive models shaped by many different contingencies and information-based inputs. Umekita is thus conceived through customising prototyping processes instead of the Fordist legacy of uniform and repetitive production.

In OCEAN CN's proposal, high-density massing is mitigated by public green corridors and plazas to create a sense of openness within the intense metropolitan urbanism of the site. Hovering above existing railway tracks, this topside development is connected to a complex three-dimensional network of rail, road and pedestrian infrastructure. The proposed mix of programmes, typologies and densities has the capacity to adapt to divergent patterns of investment, the needs of the public and infrastructural planning considerations. The machining of various possible futures aims at a more customised, perhaps even optimised urbanism that in turn may also further articulate the specific contextual identities of the cities of tomorrow. ◇

bottom left: A series of model morphologies demonstrating the principles of a data-driven contextual method of driving the proposal with direct inputs from the immediate urban context. The design potential of the associative modelling of urban information to configure specific spatial differences enables each model to have a distinct identity and character. Possible applications of this modelling approach include ways for designers, commissioners and authorities to interact with the development of a large urban site so that it can be more flexible and responsive over time.

bottom right: Plan of the overlap of open spaces, canopied spaces and interior landscapes illustrating the patterns and textures of materials and planting that can be applied to any of the generated schemes to accommodate a variety of building footprints and densities. These green spaces can be at ground level, under cover, interior or elevated on the roof of the building mass.

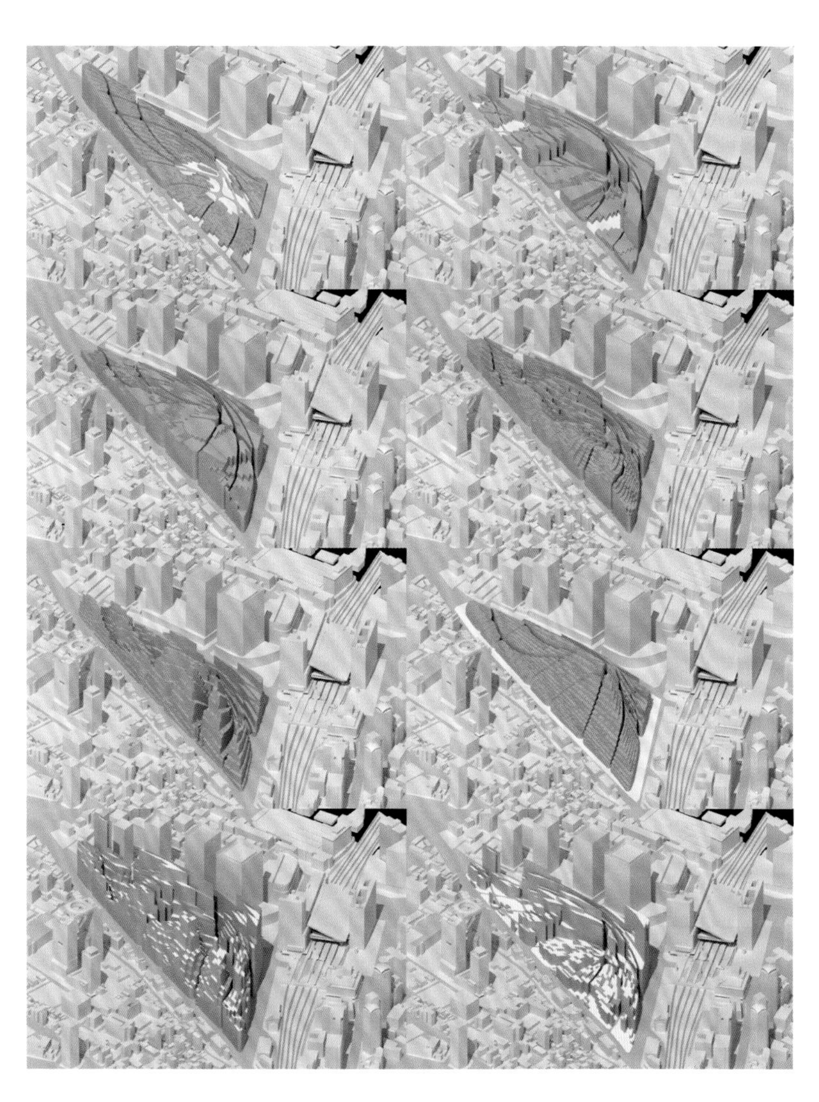

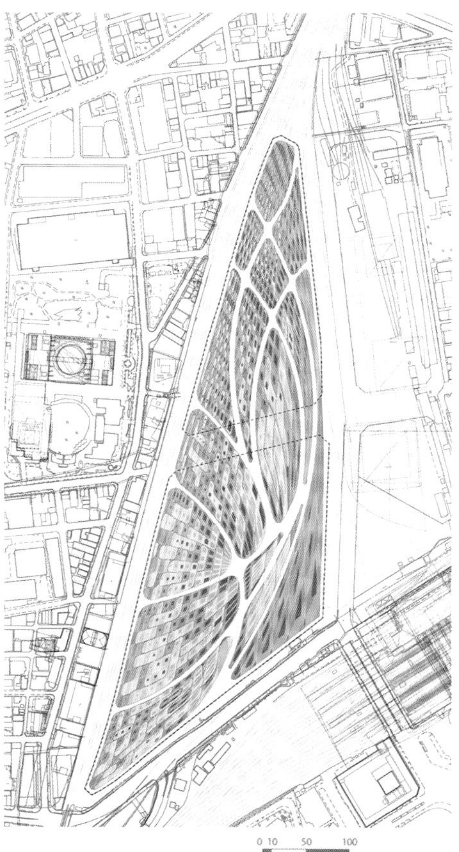

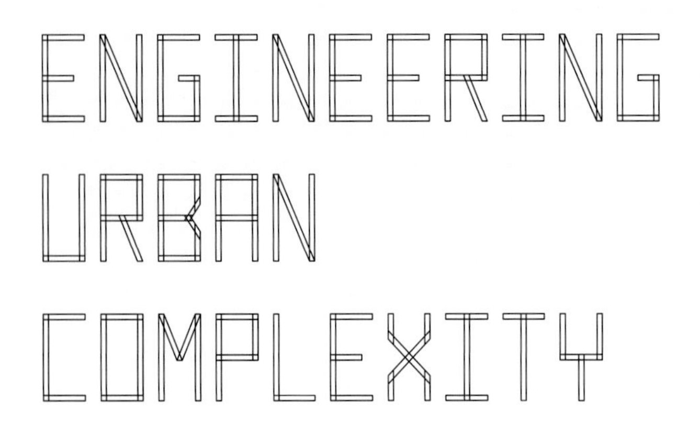

BESPOKE INTEGRATED DESIGN

Rapid urbanisation across the globe and far-reaching technological changes are transforming urban design. Building Information modelling (BIM) is combining 3D modelling techniques and the employment of rich datasets, which is eliding the gap between the disciplines of architecture and engineering. This is enabling the introduction of a new level of complexity in the modelling of cities and the simulation and testing of urban and environmental conditions. **Rob May**, an Associate Director at BuroHappold Engineering and the leader of the structures team in Beijing, reflects on the potential of complex bespoke processes for creative problem-solving in the urban context.

BuroHappold Engineering, Structural BIM models for the HENN Architekten, OCT Tower competition, Shenzhen, China, 2013; spatial practice, Twin Towers competition, Harbin, China, 2008; and Aedas, Northstar Changsha Centre competition, Changsha, China, 2014

opposite: Structural BIM models rapidly and parametrically generated for simulation and illustration.

The application of computational design and production tools for the built environment has never been more powerful or progressive. At the same time, the fields of architecture and engineering have not been closer since the days of the master builder, as an increasing flow of information between design disciplines is enabled through data exchange and information-rich communication. Alongside parametric design and building information modelling (BIM) software, increased knowledge and use of open-source programming – both visual and text based – is providing engineers with unprecedented capability to simulate and test unique solutions and concepts. As technology has advanced, so have the urban scale, ubiquity and prevalence of digital design, simulation and analytical tools for the engineering of complex architectural spaces and systems. As a result there are huge opportunities to maximise the potential of the interdisciplinary and holistic digital design approaches that are shaping our cities while avoiding mass-produced design.

BUILDING INFORMATION MODELLING

For millennia we have been communicating our designs and ideas by making two-dimensional patterns and diagrams, attempting to create reproductions of our imagination. Vector-based drawing software applications have not offered much more to the design process than this, other than the ability to communicate designs neatly and more efficiently than can be done using pen and paper or charcoal and rock. While digitised two-dimensional design processes initially gave the impression of progress or process innovation, they have had the opposite effect as designers have become slaves to machines — drawing coloured lines on a black background to meet the requirements of governing bodies and conventions entirely abstracted and disconnected from the physical world around us. However, as the global building industry is beginning to adopt three-dimensional design processes on a larger scale, and in particular technologies such as BIM, information is becoming less abstracted, and communicated in languages that much more closely represent their physical counterparts. As more information is modelled explicitly in the computer from early on in the process, it is easier to test and therefore optimise the design and engineering, or intuit alternative solutions informed by project-specific requirements, not to mention downstream uses for construction and facilities management.

By generating data for our designs beyond two-dimensional drawings and handwritten calculations, we are now also embedding rich information in models such as design rules and engineering data that can be used for rapid simulation. At the building element scale, for example, a feature spiral staircase can be represented by a basic parametric design model and customised for different projects and settings. The fundamental principles of setting out the stair geometry do not vary significantly between designs and can therefore easily be programmed, while the detailing, structural materials, support points, finishes and balustrades can all be customised for each unique design. At the urban scale, entire cityscapes can be modelled to assess the impact of new buildings on wind flow, and information can be embedded in models to help simulate traffic and crowd flows to assist designers working with complex urban spaces.

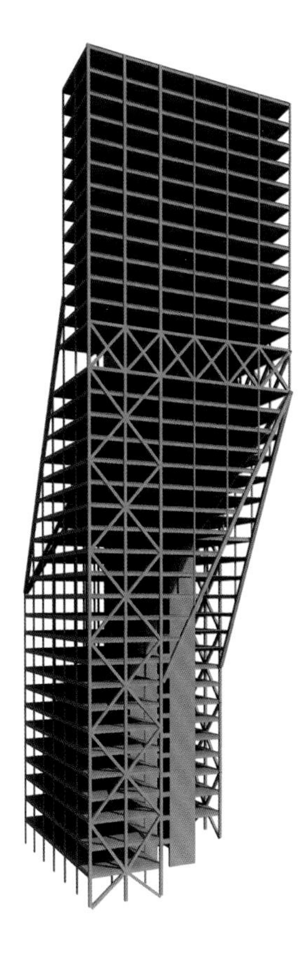

RETHINKING URBAN DESIGN PROCESSES

As has been widely reported recently, more of the world's population is moving from rural to urban areas. According to the World Health Organization (WHO), the urban population in 2014 accounted for 54 per cent of the total global population: so more than half of the world's population now lives in towns or cities.[1] The trend is perhaps exemplified by China, where the urban population is predicted to have grown to almost a billion people by 2025.[2] China's cities are growing at a rate equivalent to one new Beijing every year. To support the pace and scale of this urbanisation as sustainably and organically as possible it is important to analyse and, in some cases, rethink our design processes, to make best use of the tools available to us. As engineers, architects and clients working in the urban environment, the challenge ahead is clear: we must approach urban design in a holistic way, reducing dependence on carbon and the motor car, creating walkable cities and safe, sociable public spaces that people will enjoy living in for years to come, and placing cultural buildings back at the heart of the community. With a backdrop of increasing scale yet reduced time for design and careful thought, we must leverage technology to assist these efforts, while simultaneously avoiding simply mass-producing similar solutions that are out of context.

If 'mass production' is defined as the production of large amounts of standardised product, and 'product' describes an object that satisfies a market demand, it could be argued that a large portion of the building stock developed during phases of excessive growth is the result of mass production. In this analogy, the assembly line is not the project site or the fabricators' yard, but design offices themselves who organise teams to mass-produce drawings and calculations for similar buildings. Software developers in the building industry respond to this by developing applications not only with standardised building components, but with standardised engineering calculations for building typologies. Without strong architectural or engineering design intent, it follows then that building designs become repetitive, in using standardised software to produce standardised drawings and calculations economically.

The idea of mass-produced building designs is again exemplified by China. Apart from the incredible feats of architecture such as OMA's CCTV headquarters (2002) or Herzog & de Meuron's National Stadium (2008), both in Beijing, standardisation and repetition is prevalent — from national-standard structural analysis software down to national-standard construction detailing manuals. But while these standards have provided a safe and easy-to-use system, they can be restrictive for more adventurous clients and designers who have sought international assistance to challenge the norm. In Hong Kong, customised design has another obstacle: commerce. With some of the highest urban densities in the world, repetition is almost a requirement in itself as floor area is at such a premium.

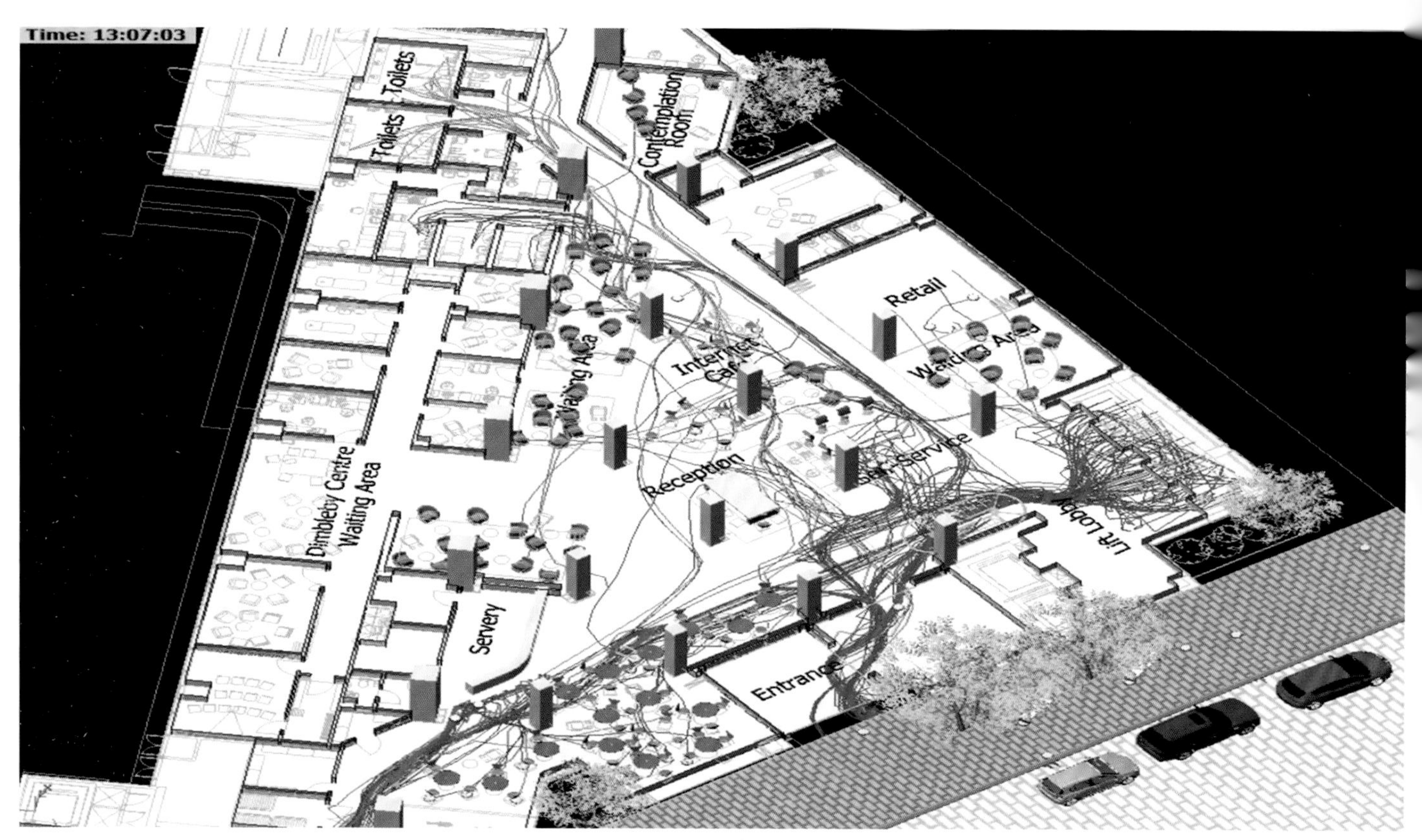

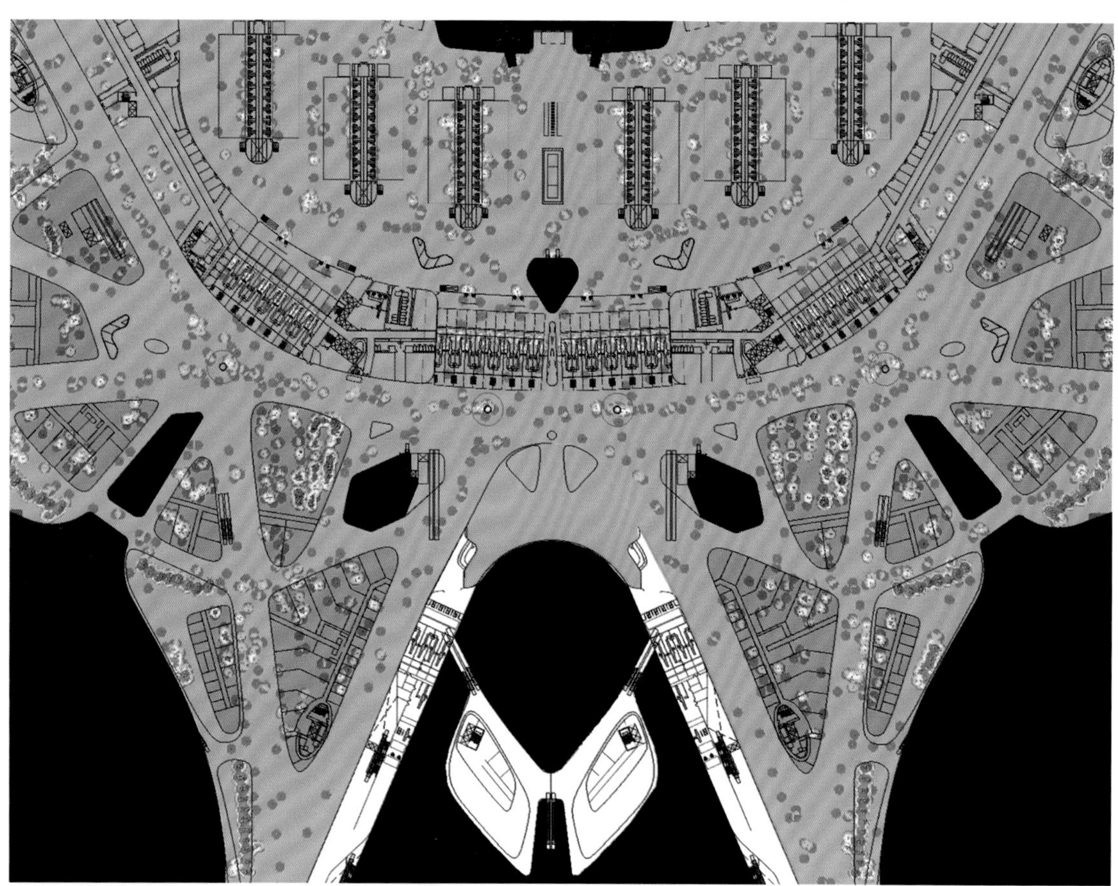

BuroHappold Engineering, SMART space technology, people flow modelling for a proposed new airport (below) and a cancer hospital in London (above), 2014

Simulation tools are increasing in both power and scale – simulation of crowd flow is becoming more popular as urban spaces become more crowded and complex.

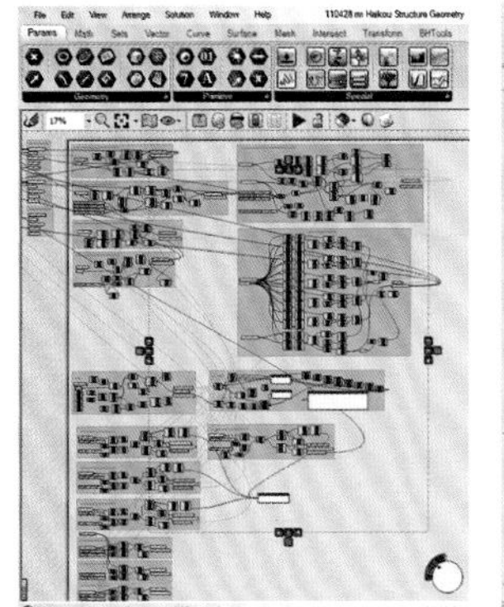

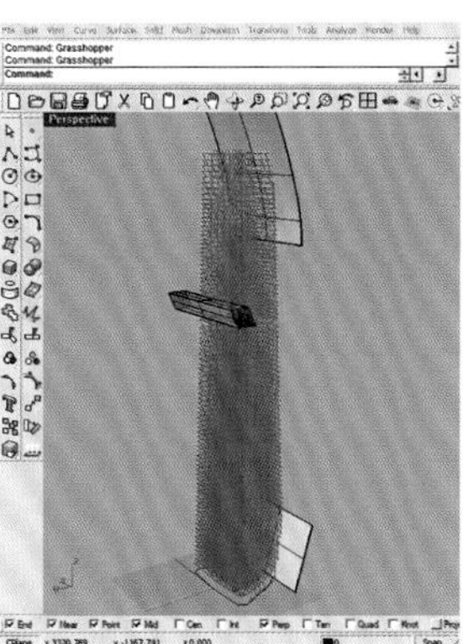

The now widespread use of visual programming tools such as Grasshopper for Rhino or Dynamo for Revit is enabling architects and engineers to visualise and test designs so readily that many design options can be generated and studied in a short amount of time. Importantly, these tools are also forcing us to consider our design and thought processes. As engineers we like to take things apart, understand how they work and put them back together. By using visual programming in a three-dimensional environment, this physical process can be replicated computationally with some engineering logic. This can be anything from rationalised geometry to simply embedding structural objects that we use to simulate performance and illustrate spatial requirements for different design options. The process has proven particularly useful in providing quick simulations of tall building concepts in China, which are often required to demonstrate to a review panel that the building structure meets some minimum requirements using complex structural analysis models, even at the very earliest stage of a project. It is important to note that the ability to do this quickly is not driven by a standardised tool that analyses or produces standardised solutions, but by experienced engineers leveraging powerful tools to create bespoke engineering strategies.

The same analytical techniques can also be used further along the design process. For a 238-metre (780-feet) tall building in Changyuan city, near Zhengzhou, London-based architects Urban Systems were keen that the exterior was informed by factors including natural light and both gravity and lateral forces acting on the building. The spatial arrangement of atria is therefore influenced by daylight studies, and the perimeter frame is the result of several structural additive and reductive optimisation studies. The additive processes allowed for an increase in column sizes to predefined maximums, then the addition of columns on preset grids adjacent to overstressed columns, while the reductive process reduced sizes and removed under-utilised columns. Such is our capability now, we are able to run each iteration of a full building model on a standard computer in around 10 minutes, including sifting through and analysing large data sets of seismic analysis results, to create a structure that is visibly influenced by the forces acting on it, and optimised to reduce the amount of steel and concrete.

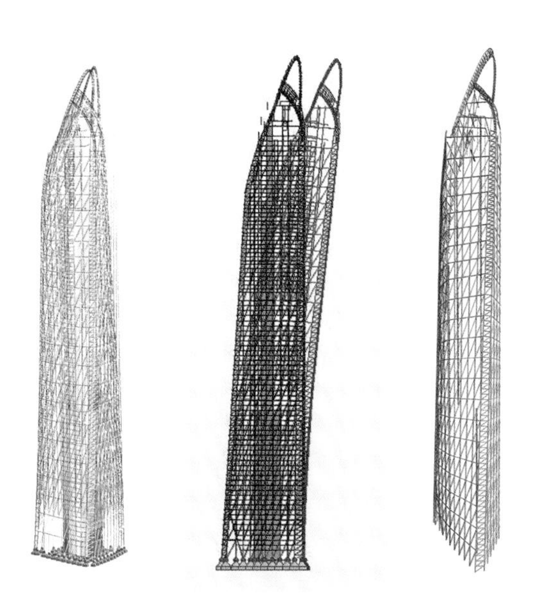

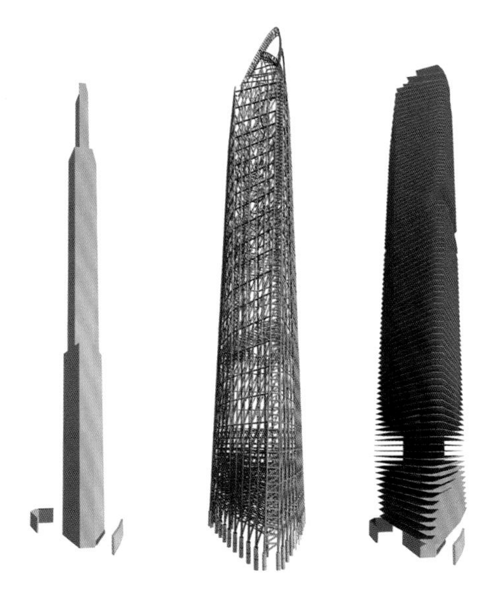

Broadway Malyan Architects with BuroHappold Engineering, Haikou Tower competition, Hainan, China, 2011

Using McNeel Rhino and Grasshopper (top left and top centre) linked to Autodesk Revit and Robot Structural Analysis software (top right and above), it is possible to quickly deconstruct architectural models and reconstruct the structural skeletons based on setting out principles to rapidly test the designs.

As technology develops and evolves, it should be utilised ... to free up designers' precious time to think, sketch and create.

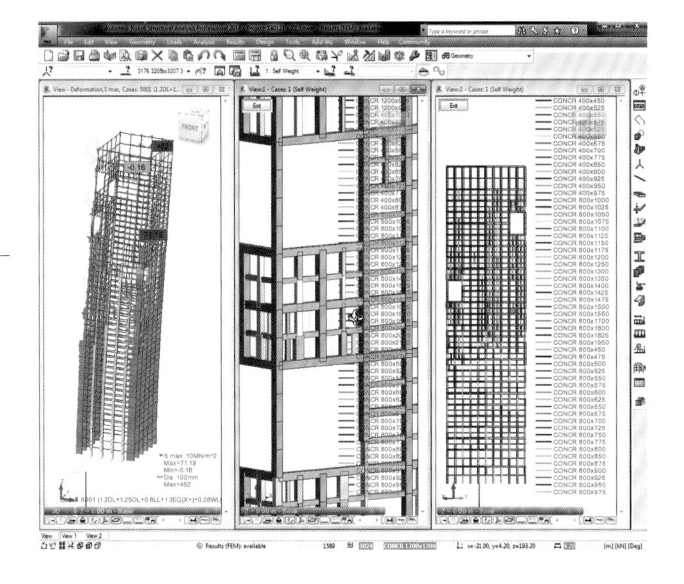

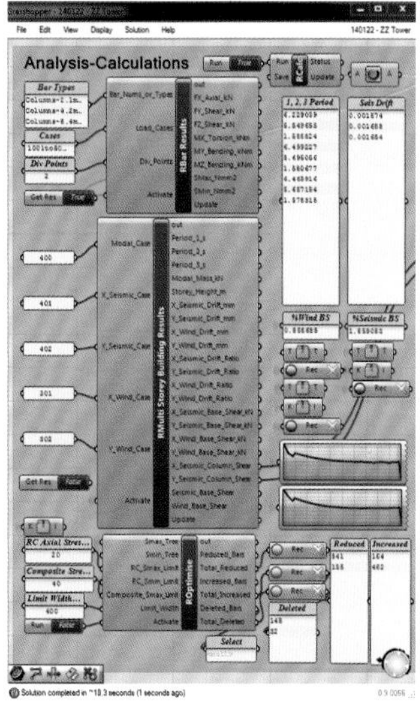

Urban Systems Architects with BuroHappold Engineering, CBD Tower, Zhengzhou, China, 2014

top: Twin towers linked together with a high-level bridge, a design influenced by engineering optimisation.

right: Optimisation of the perimeter frame structure of the CBD Tower based on geometric rules, gravity, wind and seismic loading.

While complex bespoke processes can be used to optimise regular or orthogonal buildings, they are a necessity to realise complicated or freeform buildings without significant simplification or programme delay. For freeform buildings such as Zaha Hadid's City of Dreams Hotel Tower in Macau (due for completion in 2017), which has very few internal columns, a primary structure consisting predominantly of two reinforced-concrete columns and a perimeter steel exoskeleton, these tools are imperative. To ensure connections are capable of transferring the complex load paths and maximise repetition in the steel detailing for ease of fabrication, the computer was programmed to recognise similar connections based on spatial arrangement, curvature, steel size and shape, and load intensity by accessing, interrogating and then manipulating large data sets.

The skills used in developing these strategies for solving complex problems are both transferable and scalable, and must be drawn upon to provide smart solutions to the engineering challenges of urbanisation globally across all design disciplines. The ubiquity of these technologies for the buildings must be leveraged and scaled. Existing platforms need to be developed and enhanced to allow larger and more associative and interactive data-driven simulations of design iterations in order to realise a sustainable and holistic interdisciplinary design approach at the city – or city information modelling – scale. With great power also comes great responsibility: as technology develops and evolves, it should be utilised not to increase standardisation for the sake of simplicity or mass production, but to free up designers' precious time to think, sketch and create. ⌂

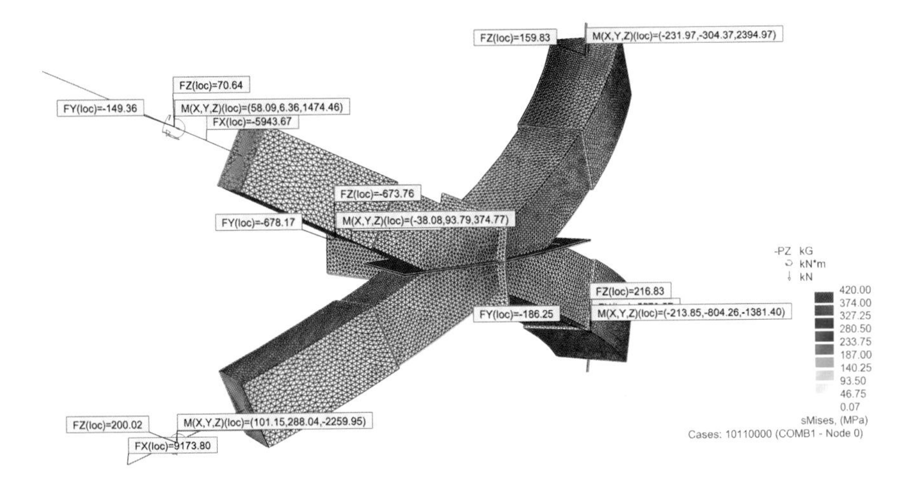

Zaha Hadid Architects with BuroHappold Engineering, City of Dreams Hotel Tower, Macau, China, due for completion 2017

top: As well as optimising the structure by linking architectural form to structural analysis in the early stages of design, the complexity of over 2,500 primary steel connections in the exoskeleton required analysing and modelling individually.

above: Complex modelling and analysis of the steel exoskeleton structural connections of the City of Dreams Hotel, using bespoke tools that recognise similar geometry, structural element sizes and loading conditions.

Notes

1. World Health Organization, Global Health Observatory (GHO) data: www.who.int/gho/urban_health/en/.
2. McKinsey Global Institute, 'Preparing for China's Urban Billion', February 2009: www.mckinsey.com/insights/urbanization/preparing_for_urban_billion_in_china.

Philip F Yuan

Archi-Union Architects

City of Breeze

Shenzhen Bay, Shenzhen, China

Archi-Union Architects
City of Breeze
Shenzhen Bay
Shenzhen
China
2014

The project site is located in the central zone of the Shenzhen Bay Ring, which will become the main economic area in the Shenzhen-Hong Kong metropolitan region. Archi-Union's proposal includes three high-rise office towers to improve the locality both economically and culturally. As such, balancing the economic requirements and local environmental performance became the main task of the design.

What happens when ancient cultural practices are combined with the most current design technologies? Archi-Union Architects used the opportunity of their entry to the 2014 Shenzhen Bay 'Super City' International Competition to develop a bespoke generational method that integrated feng shui with advanced environmental simulation techniques. **Philip F Yuan**, the founder and director of Archi-Union Architects, who is Associate Professor in Architecture at Tongji University, Shanghai, here describes the City of Breeze project and the design methodology behind it.

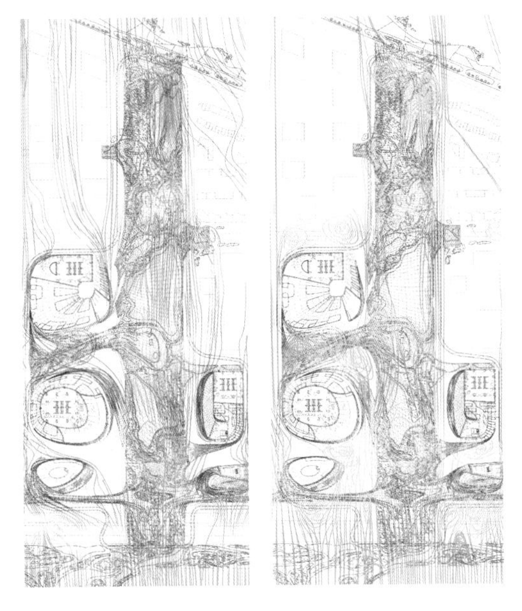

The topography of the landscape is generated by wind analysis combined with the stack effect of the towers, which in turn improves site ventilation.

The outdoor space formed by the twist of the towers' podiums creates a continuous urban landscape. The 'green carpet' can be pulled out at particular spots of the park to reach the public spaces on the podiums.

In contemporary urban design, ancient Chinese geomantic omen theory, or feng shui, can be potently combined with state-of-the-art techniques. Derived from Taoist philosophy and developed in China more than 3,000 years ago, feng shui draws on laws of existence based on natural phenomena (such as the energy of the land) to provide an overarching system for determining site selection and spatial arrangement. The most current design processes, in juxtaposition, with their emphasis on environmental performance and computational techniques, can provide important evaluation criteria and act as the primary drivers of urban form.

Given these complementary cultural and technological research interests, in their City of Breeze entry for the 2014 Shenzhen Bay 'Super City' International Competition Archi-Union Architects decided to redefine the meaning of environmental performance in urban morphology. The design draws on the unique subtropical marine climate and wind conditions of Shenzhen, on the south coast of southern China, to optimise the natural ecology of the super city. Wind performance was the main factor driving the processes of urban formation for the project. The simulation of urban environmental performance was employed as a design-generating tool rather than as a mere evaluating system.

The project site is the heart of the Shenzhen Bay Ring in the Shenzhen-Hong Kong western passage. Based on the collection and analysis of local environmental data, the main strategy of generating a comfortable urban space was established at the beginning of the design process – adapting the wind speed and temperature to different seasons by manipulating the formation and distribution of the urban space in a synchronised system.

top: The stack effect of the double-skin system enhances the ventilation of both the building interiors and the urban public space.

bottom: Each of the buildings of the high-rise massing design strategy contributes to improving the wind performance of the site by applying different formal and technical functionalities.

Working as a synchronised system, the City of Breeze uses wind as a form-generator while simultaneously modifying the forces of the airstream.

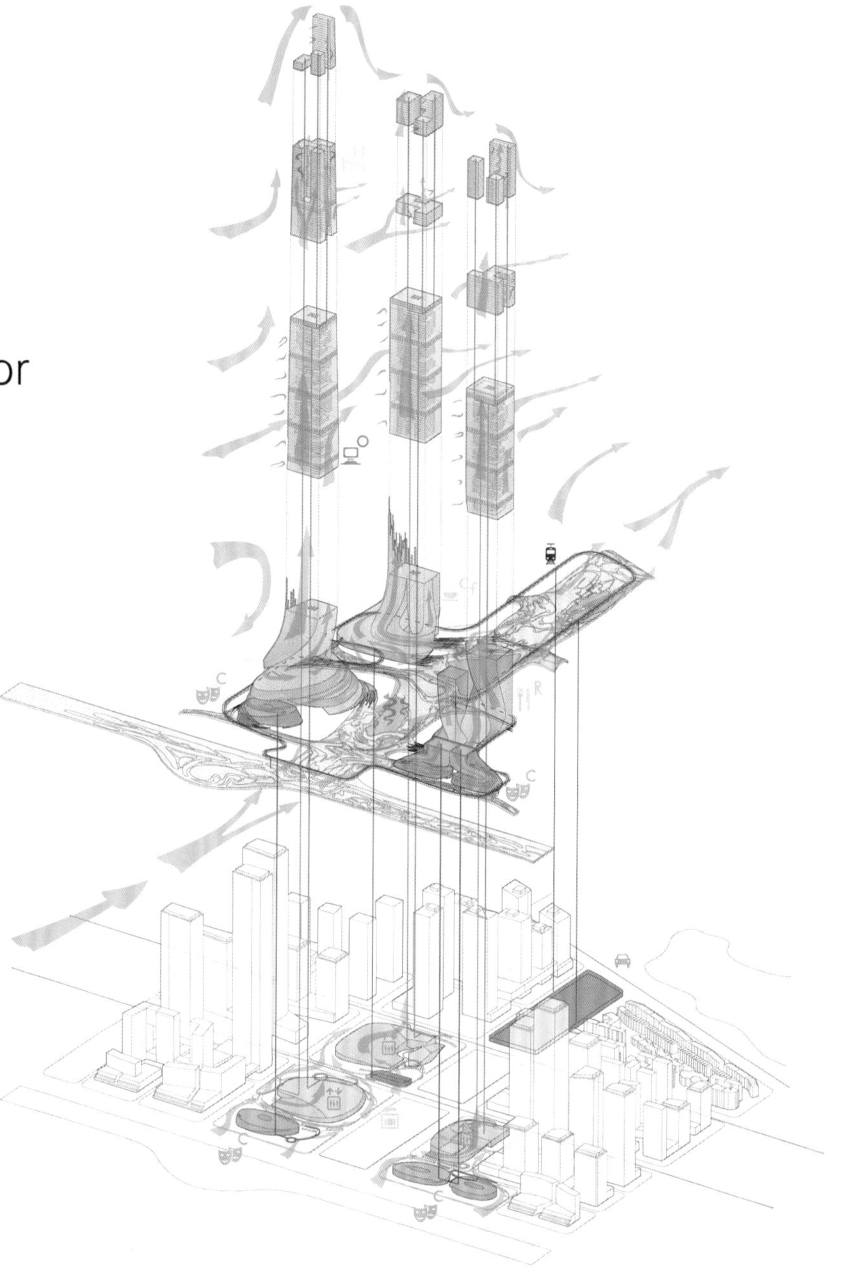

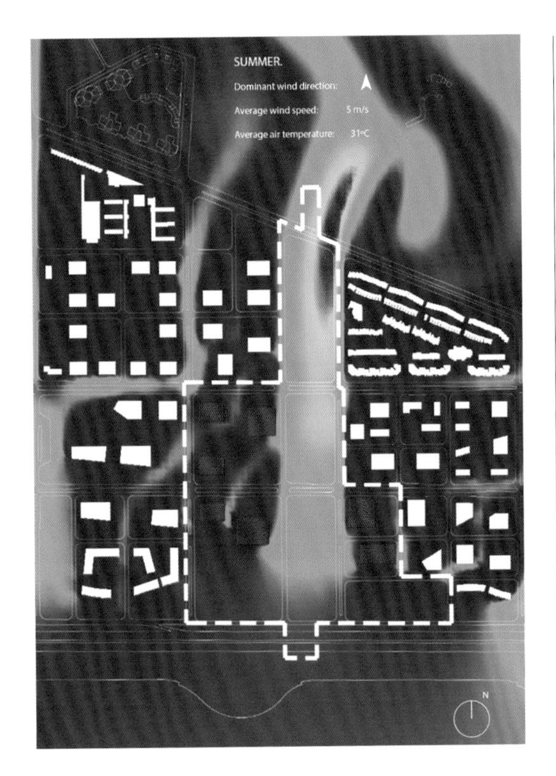

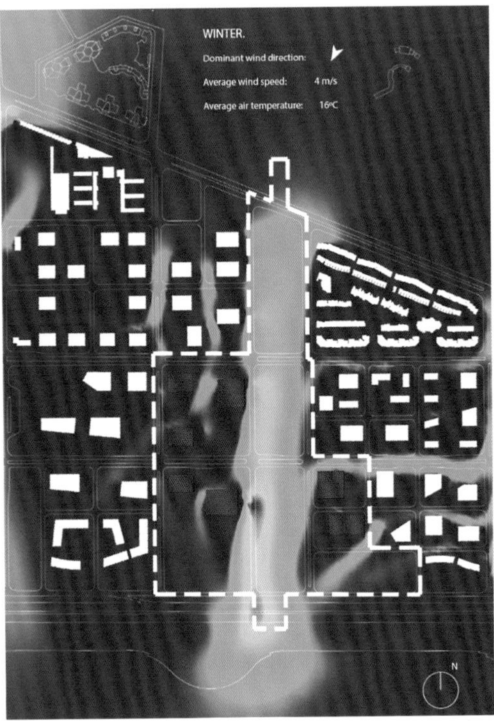

The wind speed and temperature parameters shown at different points of the gradient map were used to generate the topography of the central landscape.

A wind-controlled park zone for public activities was created through the positioning of three high-rise office towers distributed to the east and west of the site. The central park area was left empty as a wind tunnel in order to connect the south waterfront to the northern mountains both geographically and environmentally. Within this environment-controlled public area, the synchronised system was unfolded at three different scales – topography, building form and skin detail. These were determined by the environmental strategy, while simultaneously being employed to improve environmental performance.

Based on wind analysis of the project site, the environmental parameters were extracted from the gradient map and translated into geometrical data to generate the landscape topography of the central park. The podiums of the towers were twisted to create a continuous landscape system between the ground and the building facades, establishing interrelations between landscape, building and environmental performance at different scales. This 'green carpet' system, in which the hills, slopes and disposition of the trees and lakes are distributed based on wind depression and high-pressure areas, allows wind speed and direction to be modified through the management of the double-skin system of the towers combined with the cooling effect of lake evaporation to achieve the desired comfort zones throughout the park. For example, in summer the wind flow from the south waterfront would cool down as it crossed the lake area. The air would then be forced upwards by the stack effect of the double-skin system in order to improve the thermal comfort levels of the urban area along the lakefront. In winter, the double-skin system can be turned off to reduce the stack effect, the bumps on the landscape becoming shields to block and slow down the northeastern wind.

Working as a synchronised system, the City of Breeze uses wind as a form-generator while simultaneously modifying the forces of the airstream. The stack effect of the tower skins amplifies ventilation in the central park, which in turn determines the configuration of the site topography. The wind is channelled by the behaviour of thermal effects on the urban form, passing through the vertical landscape to achieve an urban environment generated by climatic criteria. The project thus effectively aspires to the parallel aims of holistically addressing the performance of the environment while establishing a new identifiable landmark for the Shenzhen Bay Ring. ⌀

An Interview with
Jerry Ku + Philip Vernon of E-Grow, Shanghai

Tom Verebes

Technological Transitions, Industrial Innovations and the Marching Chinese Urban Revolution

How scalable are current manufacturing and production techniques? What might their application be in the mass-customised city? Specialist material fabricator E-Grow is based in Shanghai, from where it has collaborated with premier cutting-edge architects such as Gehry Partners, Zaha Hadid Architects and Morphosis on the delivery internationally of unique building parts. To find out more about the innovative work that E-Grow are undertaking in the field of computer-controlled material production, Guest-Editor **Tom Verebes** interviewed its CEO **Jerry Ku** and design engineer **Philip Vernon**.

UA Architects with MRT Interiors
Greenland Showflat
Chengdu, China, 2012

The exterior applies E-Grow's 3D metal system, maximising its capacity to be mapped onto complex three-dimensional curved surface geometries.

Jerry Ku, CEO, and Design Engineer Philip Vernon, of E-Grow, are uniquely positioned to discuss the histories, legacies and futures of industrialisation and its catalytic relationship to urbanisation in China. Founded in 1997, E-Grow is a specialist material fabricator based in Shanghai, positioned at the epicentre of producing parts of some of the most innovative and striking architecture in the last decade. E-Grow collaborates with some of the world's most experimental architects, within the most prolific and dynamic of contemporary urban environments – China. Their portfolio of work includes some pre-eminent flagship buildings in China, including the Guangzhou Opera House by Zaha Hadid Architects and Giant Group Campus by Morphosis (both 2010).

E-Grow's entrepreneurial model of specialist fabrication and construction delivery is representative of the current transitions in industrial production paradigms, and of the re-emergence of a 'workshop model'. Their innovative methods serve the delivery of custom and unique building parts, thus challenging the inflexibility of the Fordist factory and the limitations of repetitious production. Standardised architectural production has been the default mode of producing millions of buildings in China, which sets the background for E-Grow's unique products. The lingering bad habits of Modernist urban planning and a messy divorce with architecture have led to building countless 'cities without architecture', qualified by Andrea Branzi to describe Archizoom's No-Stop City in 1968, an urbanism impoverished with quality.[1] Some 30 years later, Rem Koolhaas was still celebrating what he branded The Generic City, or 'what is left when identity is stripped', a city still being rolled out all over Asia.[2] Land-use and infrastructural planning precedes architectural design initiatives in China, and, as Sanford Kwinter warns, all aspects of 'the technology of rational administration' serve only to further 'routinise life'.[3] Though China's urban revolution may be seemingly unstoppable, the blind spot of contemporary Asian urbanisation is not only obfuscated by the smog. The commonly understood failures of the modernist city – its monotony and a lack of diversity – are being repeated again and again.

Jerry Ku rightly locates China at the centre of global industry in the last three decades, and he declares: 'In China, the market decides everything and all is influenced by the market.' Iconicity is often dismissed as the commodification and politicisation of non-standard architecture, propelled by the appetite of an insatiable market for 'ever more complex and formally exotic buildings'.[4] Amidst this opportunistic landscape, there exists, for a multitude of intentions, openness by investors and politicians to experimental architecture, and a culture which evidently promotes innovation. E-Grow eschews the efficiency of familiarity, over the opportunities, challenges and rewards of experimental digital building. Little seemed to temper the techno-euphoria of our conversation with Ku and Vernon – both of whom are true believers that anything which can be imagined can in fact be materialised. E-Grow experiments foremost with, and through, matter.

'In China, the market decides everything and all is influenced by the market.'

UA Architects
with MRT Interiors
Greenland Showflat
Chengdu
China
2012

The interior demonstrates the craft of E-Grow's 3D glass-reinforced plaster to create seamless interior surfaces.

Shifts in Industrial Paradigm to the New Specialist Workshop

> 'The shift from an empirical, tradition-bound technics to an experimental mode has opened up such new realms as those of nuclear energy, supersonic transportation, cybernetic intelligence, and instantaneous distant communication.'
> – Lewis Mumford, 'The Myth of the Machine', 1971[5]

Contemporary design culture is witnessing 'an accelerated process of transformation' in the use and application of technology, representative of substantive transitions in industrial production paradigms.[6] As Thomas Kuhn, a philosopher of science, remarks in his text 'Scientific Revolutions': 'As in manufacture so in science – retooling is an extravagance to be reserved for the occasion that demands it.'[7] Taylorism emerged in the 19th century, as the scientific management of rationalised industrial work tasks into discrete, measurable, simpler segmented components. Coupled with Fordism, or Henry Ford's application of the assembly line facilitating repetitive production, routinisation and standardisation took command. Transiting from the 'batch-production' industrial workshop of the 19th century, the mechanised factory reigned supreme over the industrial workshop, with its limited capacity to produce smaller, more distinct and bespoke batches of production, despite the de-skilling of factory workers and the diminishing of craft.[8]

China is often referred to as the 'world's factory'. E-Grow has made substantive headway to narrow the paradoxical discrepancies between the most advanced material manufacturing in architectural production, and conventional, normative, low-tech building practices in China, which are rooted in cheap, unskilled manual labour. Paradoxically, E-Grow's highly specialised workshop relies on the tenacious inventiveness of their highly skilled workers, for the capacity to produce large quantities, or batches, of non-standard production, at a faster pace than any western factory can do. The new specialist workshop points towards the re-emergence of the new bespoke, articulated by dialectics such as repetition versus differentiation, or stability versus flexibility. E-Grow's portfolio of projects is indicative of the ongoing evolution of consumption patterns towards increasing variation, standing in opposition to standardisation, and economies of scale, both of which can no longer be fulfilled through mass production methods.[9] Despite the absence of an accepted universal 'theory of transition' to the 'epoch-making transformation' of the shifts away from Fordism, there are, apparently, no 'absolute turning points' in historical evolutions, but rather today's industrial culture is more evolutionary, characterised by both continuity and change.[10] If we are indeed witnessing a paradigm shift, it can be summarised succinctly, as a transition from uniformity towards variance, and the re-emergence of craft through digital making. Despite the constraints of resistant 'old-school' technologies and their prevailing epistemologies, E-Grow's flexible post-Fordist business model of the specialist workshop can easily inflect to market demands and instabilities, and to disparate geographies, through networking.[11] Contemporary processes of specialised architectural production, as championed by E-Grow, have also become increasingly decentralised and collaborative.

COLLABORATIVE WORKFLOWS AND OPEN-SOURCE CULTURE

The proliferation of specialist production workshops, such as E-Grow, has been largely facilitated by the digital communication infrastructure of the information age. In addition, the technology transfer across design disciplines, consultants and specialists has enabled greater interdisciplinarity and collaborative practices within the globalisation of architectural production. Jerry Ku is a true innovator in computer-controlled material production, and E-Grow's tenaciousness to innovate relies on the flow of electronic information, technology transfers and disciplinary integration. E-Grow pioneered glass-fibre-reinforced gypsum (GFRG) and glass-fibre-reinforced polymers (GFRP) in China, through large-scale CNC production and unique reusable wax moulding processes. Their expertise is currently expanding to innovations in glass-fibre-reinforced concrete (GFRC) and 3D-moulded metal for larger-scale structural and cladding applications. They work at a distance with architects worldwide on large-scale ambitious projects, from furniture to interiors, structures and cladding. The non-authorial, or multi-authored, collaborative cultures surrounding computational coding and numerical control machining enables an unprecedented fluid sharing of design information, hypermobility and an 'open-source' technological culture, all of which are crucial to E-Grow's global model of a specialist collaborative practice.

NEW MATERIALS, FABRICATION PROCESSES AND QUALITIES

> '[W]hoever regrets that the house of the future can no longer be constructed by building craftsmen should bear in mind that the motor-car is no longer built by the wheelwright.'
> – Mies van der Rohe, 'Industrialised Building', 1924[12]

New material behaviours and the geometric qualities of suppleness and inflection are facilitated by flexible machining methods such as those pioneered by E-Grow. Ku and Vernon described to me how E-Grow migrates across scales, to work with various composite materials, including GFRG for internal use, GFRP for furniture, and GFRC and 3D-moulded metal for cladding and external facades. A new liquefied materiality is achieved through serial modulation and flexible moulding as an approach to variation – not unlike Gilbert Simondon's theorisation of electrified material in variable moulding processes, nearly 50 years ago.[13]

Frank Gehry & Partners
National Art Museum of China competition
Beijing
China
2012

Prototype for developing the use of E-Grow's patented 3D metal system for the facade of the project, designed by Frank Gehry. (The competition was won by Jean Nouvel.)

E-Grow's tenaciousness to innovate relies on the flow of electronic information, technology transfers and disciplinary integration.

NEW ENTREPRENEURIAL MODELS TARGETING INNOVATION

Ku rightly claims to have influenced his competitors, most of whom he says have not graduated from high school, and many of whom now follow, modify or copy his model and methods of specialist design and production. More than a fabricator of material systems and components, E-Grow takes on digital design modelling for collaborating designers. Ku was not satisfied with producing and delivering standard products, so he began his own manufacturing company, E-Grow – a company which stands out in the world for making exceptionally special and unique material products and installations. Before relocating to Shanghai, Ku was supplying modular ceiling systems in Taiwan, and he was one of the first people to bring this technology to Shanghai. Ku was doing custom ceilings at Pudong Airport Terminal 1 and on the Bund, which no one else locally could manufacture at that time, but has also become readily available today. Vernon says Ku's competitors are 'always two steps behind what E-Grow is doing and that is why he's always on the lookout for new material approaches', such as 3D curved metal panelling or ultra-high-performance concrete. Initially Ku successfully worked towards building complex surfaces directly from 3D models. E-Grow has also developed thermoforming moulding methods, for glass and polycarbonates, which is ongoing R&D. The firm is beginning to work on tower facades with composites, and can produce a few thousand panels with only 10 different moulds. Innovation is often challenged by the consolidation of standards. Vernon states the conundrum as, 'on the one side we're trying to push for a unique product and on the other, there is always a drive to standardise the product and to keep the client's confidence, and keep construction managers and building inspectors contented'. E-Grow's technological workshop culture arises from the spirit of technologically driven innovation.

CITIES AND THEIR SPECIFICITIES

Ku discussed the ways in which and the extent to which the proliferation of new digital and material interests are shaping Chinese cities in the 21st century. He recounted E-Grow's evolution from products and interiors, to components and finishes, to exteriors of buildings and structures, and how E-Grow's production methods can be scaled up, from prototyping parts of unique buildings, to fabricating at the scale of the city. This big leap in scale represents far greater implications for architecture and even cities, as their products are external, much more visible and hence more influential and impactful towards urbanism. It is Ku's view that 'Architects should play the main role in influencing cities and the whole country. This is a revolution which should last over fifty years.' We mulled over the context of Chinese urbanisation, and the economic constraints of an investment culture aiming for short-term profit gains, and some of the political issues related to an emerging vernacularism and low-tech movement in China, within what is also the most globalised of playing fields in architecture.

'Architects should play the main role in influencing cities and the whole country. This is a revolution which should last over 50 years.'

Canon Design
Langzhou Aimee Skin Clinic
Langzhou
China
2014

Rippling gold GFRP facade set against a typical second-tier city streetscape.

The prevalence and subsequent normalisation of new production paradigms in China, and their increasing transition from special, unique and singular moments to more normative and conventional, marks a shift in which this work is no longer confined to extraordinary buildings, but instead has become part of everyday imagination. I asked Ku whether he imagines that the kinds of manufacturing and fabrication in which E-Grow engages will come, in the future, to be considered less as experimental and more as mainstream and conventional. His response stated how every creative business must have two parts: one which carries out work through tried and tested methods and processes, and another part which is committed to research and development. This is the new technological vernacular and the culture of innovation of the specialist fabrication workshop. In his words: 'If we compare Nokia to Apple, I always tell my staff, remember we don't want to be like Nokia. Each day we need to set targets, criticise ourselves and ask how we can improve. This is my theory: to find my faults every day and to make improvements, just to stay ahead.'

Ku reflects on the consequences of these shifts in production paradigms and these newly developed prototypical practices for the 21st-century city, asserting: 'Contemporary parametric design concepts and digital building methods will influence cities for decades to come. I see this as a revolution for architecture just as the Bauhaus was for the early 20th century.' We are currently still within the most profound revolution in industry since the Industrial Revolution – of computation and digital fabrication. The particularities of cities are already being born from the evolutionary transitions to these new production paradigms, methods, tools and business plans, in the backdrop of old habits, yet driven by motivation to initiate new customs, traditions and histories. This new type of specialist workshop, by which advanced material technologies are developed, is in effect a new kind of artisanal craft activity, generating products at the building scale for the global elite. Even if there is a growing demand for the output of specialist production workshops, what new opportunities will arise to scale up E-Grow's processes to the urban scale? A 'Distinctive Urbanism'[14] will be propelled by the specialist technological expertise of 21st-century workshops, such as E-Grow, driven by their tenacious entrepreneurial approach to innovate upon the managerial and material methods of construction delivery. ◻

This article is based on an interview by Guest-Editor Tom Verebes with Jerry Ku and Philip Vernon on 15 January 2015 at E-Grow's office, in Shanghai.

Zaha Hadid Architects
Guangzhou Opera House
Guangzhou
China
2010

opposite and above: Produced by E-Grow, the custom-moulded glass-fibre-reinforced gypsum (GFRG) units of the interior of the auditorium articulate an architectural language of fluidity and seamlessness.

Morphosis Architects
Giant Group Campus
Shanghai
China
2010

Besides cladding the structural columns, E-Grow's exterior glass-fibre-reinforced concrete cones and interior glass-fibre-reinforced gypsum cones hide air diffusers and lighting fixtures. They also serve as a spatial system throughout the project, drifting from interior to exterior as pure volume with apparently no shift in materiality.

Notes

1. Andrea Branzi, *Weak and Diffuse Modernity: The World of Projects at the Beginning of the 21st Century*, Skira (Milan), 2006, pp 68–71.
2. Rem Koolhaas, 'The Generic City', in Rem Koolhaas and Bruce Mau *S,M,L,XL*, Monacelli Press (New York), 1998, pp 1248–64.
3. Sanford Kwinter, *Requiem for the City at the end of the Millennium*, Actar (Barcelona), 2001, p 20.
4. Michael Speaks, 'Introduction', in H Kara (ed), *Design Engineering AKT*, Actar (Barcelona), 2008, p 218.
5. Lewis Mumford, 'The Myth of the Machine' [1971], in DL Millner (ed), *The Lewis Mumford Reader*, University of Georgia Press (Athens, GA and London), 1986, p 304.
6. William W Braham and Jonathan A Hale, *Rethinking Technology: A Reader in Architectural Theory*, Routledge (Abingdon, Oxfordshire), 2007, p xiii.
7. Thomas Kuhn, 'Scientific Revolutions', in Richard Boyd, Philip Gasper, and JD Trout (eds), *The Philosophy of Science*, MIT Press (Cambridge, MA), p 78.
8. Bryn Jones, 'Past Production Paradigms: The Workshop, Taylorism and Fordism', in *Forcing the Factory of the Future: Cybernation and Societal Institutions*, Cambridge University Press (Cambridge), 1997, pp 23–50.
9. Klaus Neilsen, 'Towards a Flexible Future – Theories and Politics', in Bob Jessop, Hans Kastendiek, Klaus Neilsen and Ove K Pedersen (eds), *The Politics of Flexibility*, Edward Elgar (Aldershot), 1991, p 24.
10. Ash Amin, 'Post-Fordism: Models, Fantasies and Phantoms of Transition', in Ash Amin (ed), *Post-Fordism: A Reader*, Blackwell (Oxford), 1994, p 3.
11. David Harvey and Allen J Scott, 'The Practice of Human Geography: Theory and Empirical Specificity in the Transition from Fordism to Flexible Accumulation', in WD Macmillan (ed), *Remodelling Geography*, Blackwell (Oxford), 1988–9, pp 217–29.
12. Mies van der Rohe, 'Industrialised Building' [1924], in Ulrich Conrads (ed), *Programs and Manifestoes on 20th-Century Architecture*, MIT Press (Cambridge, MA), 1971, p 82.
13. Gilbert Simondon, *On the Mode of Existence of Technical Objects* [*Du mode d'existence des objets techniques*, 1958], trans Ninian Mellamphy, University of Western Ontario (London, ON), 1980.
14. See Tom Verebes, 'The Adaptive City: Urban Change, Resilience, and the Trajectory Towards a Distinctive Urbanism', in Huang Weixin, Liu Yanchuan and Weiguo Xu (eds), *DADA2013: Digital Infiltration and Parametricism*, Tsinghua University Press (Beijing), 2013, pp 477–87.

Jan Willmann,
Fabio Gramazio and
Matthias Kohler

Gramazio Kohler Research

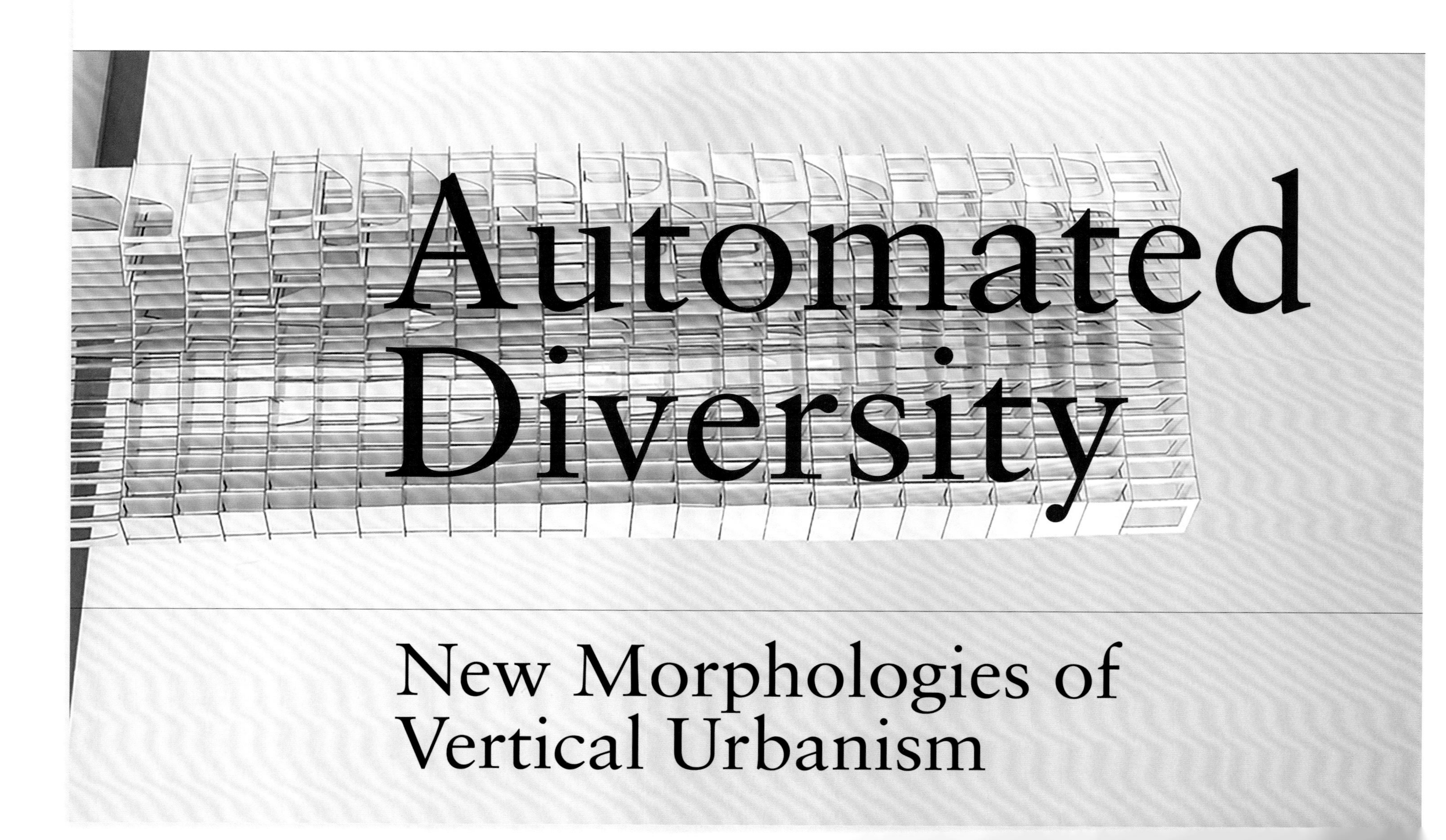

Automated Diversity

New Morphologies of Vertical Urbanism

Automated fabrication techniques are currently largely confined to the production of discrete objects or building elements. To notch up the potential of robotics for architectural design, it is necessary to start to push the limits and experiment at a larger urban scale. **Fabio Gramazio and Matthias Kohler** are pioneers in this field. Here, with **Jan Willmann**, they describe the research that they are undertaking as part of the Future Cities Laboratory (FCL) located at the Singapore-ETH Centre for Global Environmental Sustainability (SEC) and ETH Zurich, in which robotic fabrication technologies are employed to realise 1:50 physical models of mixed-use high-rise structures that are unique in their spatial layouts.

Gramazio Kohler Research, Robotic Foldings, Future Cities Laboratory (FCL), Singapore-ETH Centre for Global Environmental Sustainability (SEC), Zurich, 2014

top left: The installation – realised at the scale of 1:50 – was computationally designed and fabricated directly with the robot. This genuinely constructive and comprehensive approach turns away from the predominant representational role of the architectural model and, as such, does not content itself with formal codification. Rather, the installation negotiates spatial and tectonic criteria and brings them into a real-world architectural coherence.

Gramazio Kohler Research, Design of Robotic Fabricated High Rises, Future Cities Laboratory (FCL), Singapore-ETH Centre for Global Environmental Sustainability (SEC), Singapore, 2012

middle left: In order to investigate and develop customised robotic processes, products and planning methods for architecture at the large scale, a unique robotic laboratory was installed at the Future Cities Laboratory in Singapore that allowed the fabrication of 1:50 scaled models of up to 50-storeys high buildings.

Gramazio Kohler Research, Design of Robotic Fabricated High Rises, Future Cities Laboratory (FCL), Singapore-ETH Centre for Global Environmental Sustainability (SEC), Singapore, 2013

bottom left and detail opposite: The design research studio was one of the first attempts to explore robotic fabrication in the context of large-scale residential tower development. In this experimental approach, through hybrid digital-material methods the physical model – even in the age of computation – again gains central significance in investigations of novel building typologies in larger urban developments.

Gramazio Kohler Research, Robotic Foldings, Future Cities Laboratory (FCL), Singapore-ETH Centre for Global Environmental Sustainability (SEC), Zurich, 2014

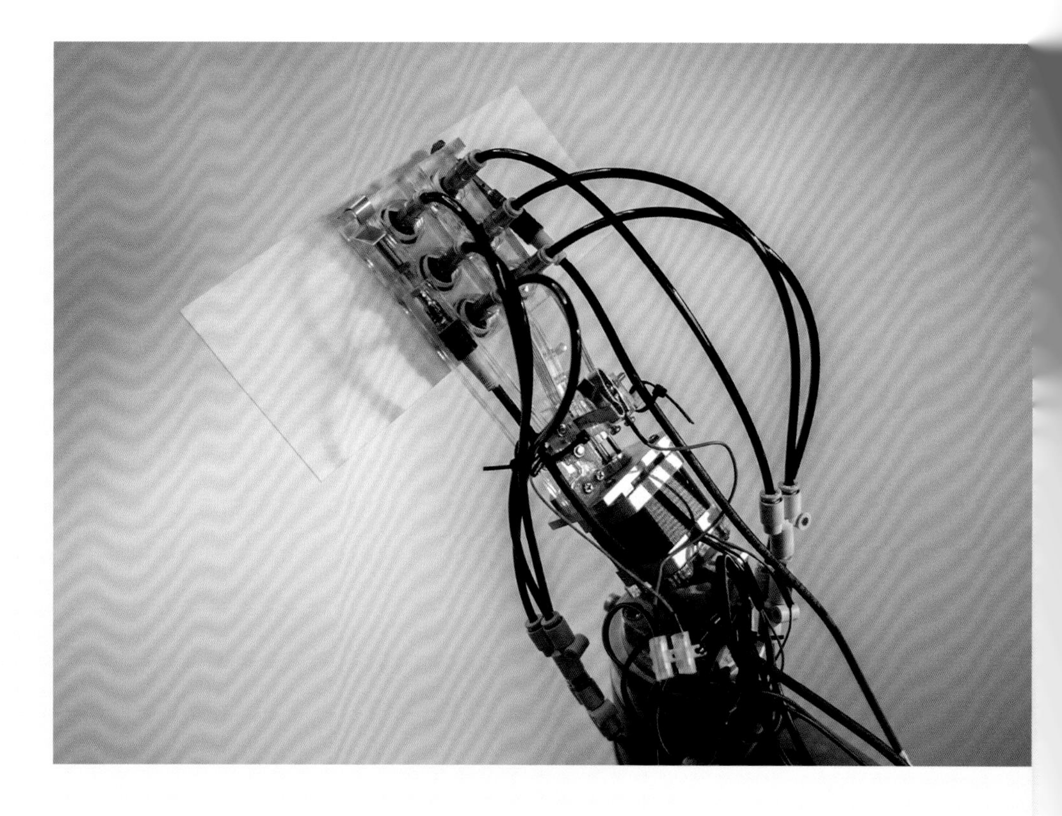

For this project a unique multifunctional end-effector was developed, allowing the robot to manipulate and position paper elements precisely in space. In this way, the integration of picking, cutting, folding and placing allowed an efficient and fully digitally controlled production process.

The project – assembled live at the 'Research, Outcomes and Prospects' SEC Future Cities Laboratory Conference at ETH Zurich – embodies a new morphology of vertical urbanism, where the robot serves as a 'door opener' to make possible an urban vision that does not need to exclude its concrete material implementation.

In the Second Digital Age,[1] the employment of robotics in architecture is opening up the prospect of entirely new material capacities that will fundamentally alter architectural design and the culture of building.[2] Architects, however, should not only focus on the technological investigation of robotic processes themselves, no matter how fascinating this might be, but also seek to establish an architectural vision through exploring the potential of robot-induced design and construction at a larger scale. Only then can the notions of the digital in architecture be significantly expanded, enabling new material dimensions to emerge, flourish and find expression.

The Robotic Foldings project, undertaken by Gramazio Kohler Research in the framework of the Future Cities Laboratory (FCL) at the Singapore-ETH Centre for Global Environmental Sustainability (SEC) and ETH Zurich, explores the architectural potential of robotic fabrication for residential tower developments. Building directly on the 2012–13 Design of Robotic Fabricated High Rises research project at FCL Singapore,[3] it proposes an experimental approach in which the robot directly links computational design to the automated fabrication of 1:50 physical models. Such hybrid digital-material explorations are central in overcoming not only the prevailing paradigm of repetition and mono-functionality in larger urban developments, but also that of purely physical computational design.[4]

As such, Robotic Foldings was conceived as a mixed-use high-rise structure created by a multitude of unique interior spatial configurations by computationally controlling the transformation and arrangements of a large number of generic elements. These were assembled through a custom robotic fabrication setup in which a multifunctional end-effector picks a paper stripe, cuts it at a predefined distance, folds it into the desired angle and then places it on the already built structure. Overall, 3,643 bespoke wall elements were amalgamated into two interwoven tectonic strands that branch and merge into a continuous overall shape in which the programmed design distributes predefined openings in sequences of shear walls to accommodate different apartment types. Each wall element specifically adjusts its folded geometry by negotiating between the required structural performance and the desired cut-out for the apartments.

The self-similarity of individual wall elements repeatedly assembled in different configurations dissolves not only the tectonic distinction between the whole and its single elements, but actually also what essentially characterises many conventional large-scale urban building typologies: the repetitive vertical addition of standard wall and floor elements. On the contrary, what remains in this project is a phenomenon that is no longer apparent in a pure object-character, but rather oscillates between the complex arrangement of elements and the resulting intermediate spaces. This 'otherness' takes on an

Central to the project is an intimate dialogue between digital and material logic that enhances its specific properties and results in a highly informed aggregation committed to the detail and its precise articulation within the overall structure. The installation can be experienced intuitively and speaks to the human cognitive capacity to recognise processual originating and highly articulated forms of material organisation, and to interpret their inherent (digital) logic.

Robotic Foldings was conceived as a parametrically designed mixed-use high-rise structure, created by a multitude of unique interior spatial configurations by algorithmically controlling 3,643 folded wall elements. These are connected through a continuous force-flow and are specifically adapted to local and global spatial and structural criteria.

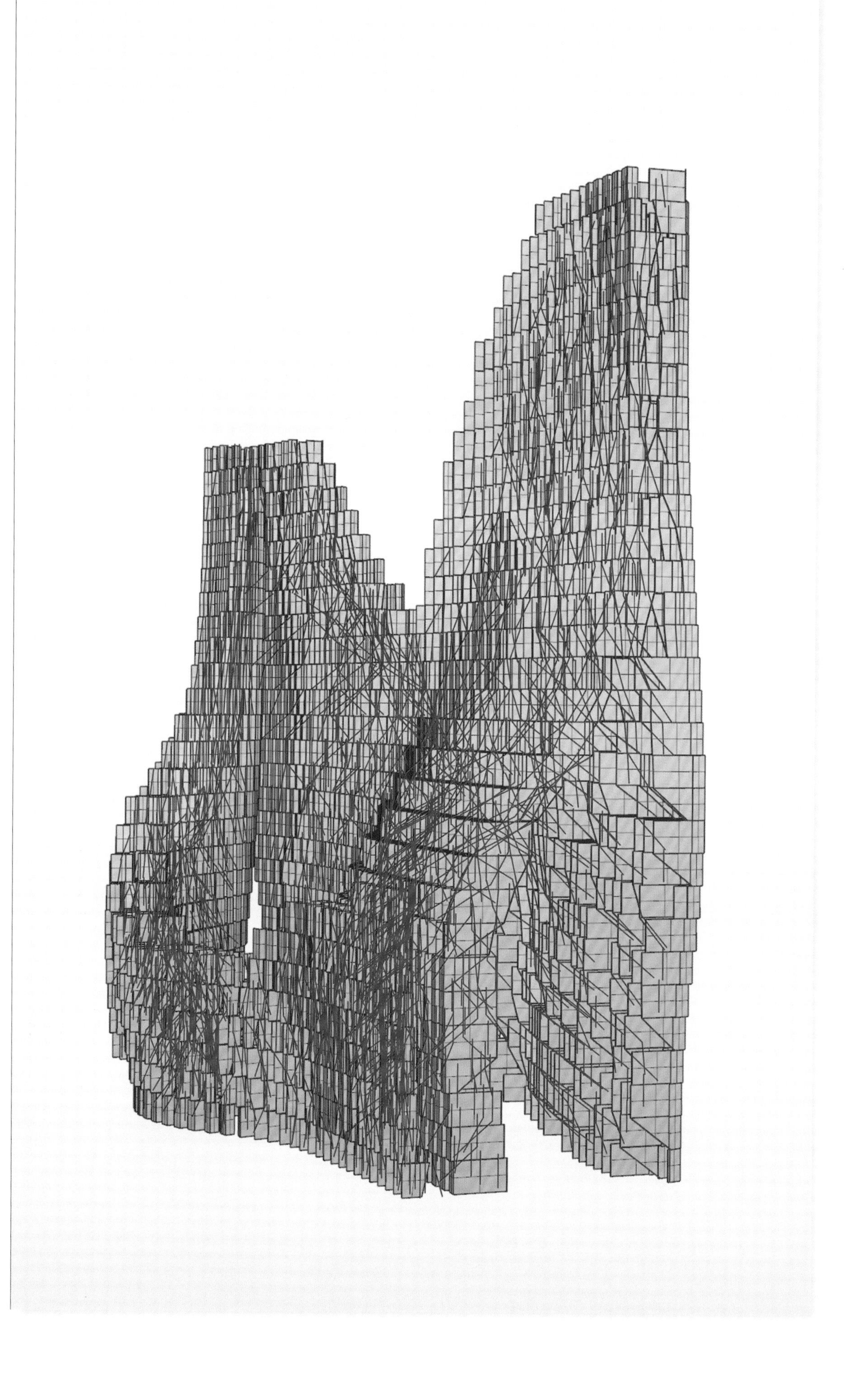

almost virtual character that stands in contrast to the scale and materiality of its constructive physis.

The Robotic Foldings project is not only exceptional in its tectonic differentiation, but also in terms of its overall development process, having been refined and physically 'versioned' over a number of design iterations. It thus turns away from the predominant representational mode of 3D-printed architecture, where the underlying constructive logic of the design is often not embedded.[5] Programmed constructive principles are pivotal in guiding the robotic fabrication of the models. This is significant in that the architectural model has to function as a physically load-bearing artefact, and bring fabrication and structural logics into a concrete architectural aggregation. Conversely, in this approach it is possible by means of computational design and robotic fabrication to anticipate the real-world building process through material experimentation, and thereby integrate its constructive nature into the programmed architectural design. The installation thus embodies, in an almost inescapable way, the knowledge of its own incremental building logic as well as that of its materiality.

Today, mass production at the urban scale has led to the global conformity of cities. The explorations at the SEC FCL and ETH Zurich, however, propose an alternative ontology where robotic fabrication catalyses a seminal change in the production conditions of the city, entering into a creative dialogue with industrial logics and paradigms, and thereby creating opportunities for automated diversity at new dimensions and intensities. Within such an approach, multiple mass-customised morphologies can evolve whereby robotic fabrication at an urban scale is no longer a magical thing that is going to fulfil a vision in the future, but rather a concrete approach with character and constraints and its own implications for the *Jetztzeit*, for the now.[6]

Ultimately, in projects such as Robotic Foldings, the Design of Robotic Fabricated High Rises and Flight Assembled Architecture[7] (which was presented in 2011 at the FRAC Centre in Orléans, France), the digitalisation of architecture not only becomes physical and tangible; these explorations also take away the forced microscopic character of the digital and imbue it with a creative and critical vision for a novel material culture of the contemporary city. AD

Notes

1. Jan Willmann, Fabio Gramazio and Matthias Kohler, *The Robotic Touch: How Robots Change Architecture*, Park Books (Zurich), 2014, pp 310–23.
2. Fabio Gramazio and Matthias Kohler, *Digital Materiality in Architecture*, Lars Müller (Baden), 2008, pp 8–11.
3. Fabio Gramazio and Matthias Kohler (eds), *AD Made by Robots: Challenging Architecture at a Larger Scale*, May/June (no 3), 2014.
4. Michael Budig, Willi Lauer, Jason Lim and Raffael Petrovic, 'The Design of Robotic Fabricated High Rises', in Wes McGee and Monica Ponce de Leon (eds), *Robotic Fabrication in Architecture, Art and Design 2014*, Springer (New York), 2014, pp 111–30.
5. Fabio Gramazio, Matthias Kohler and Michael Budig, 'The Tectonics of 3D Printed Architecture', *FCL Gazette*, 19, 2013.
6. Walter Benjamin, *Illuminations*, Schocken Books (New York), 1969, pp 261–4.
7. Jan Willmann, Fabio Gramazio and Matthias Kohler, 'The Vertical Village', in Fabio Gramazio, Matthias Kohler and Raffaello D'Andrea (eds), *Flight Assembled Architecture*, Editions HYX (Orléans), 2013, pp 13–23.

Gramazio & Kohler and Raffaello D'Andrea with ETH Zurich, Flight Assembled Architecture, FRAC Centre, Orléans, France, 2011

Flight Assembled Architecture explores future robot-induced urbanity by using an autonomous flying quadrocopter that collaboratively assembles over 1,500 modules freely in airspace to form a porous, vertical, hyperdense urban structure.

Cities on the Edge of Chaos

COUNTERPOINT
06/2015
No 238
AD

Colin Fournier

Is the mass-customised city no more than a smokescreen, a re-evocation of Modernist positivism and its problem-solving ideology? **Colin Fournier**, Emeritus Professor of Architecture and Urbanism at the Bartlett School of Architecture, University College London (UCL), and Visiting Professor at the Chinese University of Hong Kong (CUHK), questions the premise of this issue and asks if the variation required for a city's survival 'at the edge of chaos' lies beyond mass customisation.

With a few words of fire written in 1968 that became a mantra for Surrealism, the poet Comte de Lautréamont described a young boy as being as 'beautiful as the chance meeting, on a dissecting-table, of a sewing-machine and an umbrella'.[1] Few writers, challenging the prevalent conventions and homogeneity of language, have ever found words that burned as bright as these, thrusting upon us such a disconcerting juxtaposition of incompatible objects.

Return of the Repressed

The burning desire behind this issue of AD, as can be perceived through the critical theoretical questions raised by Tom Verebes and further elaborated upon by the contributors he invited to participate, is also a call for a radical reassessment of the positivistic conventions and homogeneity of another language: that of Modernist architecture and urbanism.

It is not the first time that Modernism has been held responsible for all that is monotonous, repetitive, generic, oppressive and barren in the world around us, the world we have somewhat irresponsibly constructed for ourselves and for generations to come. 'Postmodernism', as it was prematurely named, subjected its Oedipian father to repeated salvos of well-aimed intellectual contempt, moral discredit and ridicule that should have been deadly. And yet, even though Taylorism and Fordism, its fellow travellers in the heroic years following the Industrial Revolution, fell by the side, Modernism itself was clearly able not only to survive, but to proliferate more than ever under the current conditions of neoliberal global capitalism.

The virulence of the renewed attacks, as manifested in this publication, is an *a contrario* proof that the dominant ideology and praxis of Modernism are still in place, and that they are more than mere relics of the past. In fact, the staying power of Modernism is such that, even though

The customised city: Hong Kong Island

The total absence of any overall planning guidance in Hong Kong has fortunately resulted in the city being spared, at least in part, the homogenising impact of Modernist urbanism. The skyline of the island's wonderfully varied bespoke architecture, while reflecting the triumph of laissez-faire capitalism, is an almost perfect example of a city 'on the edge of chaos' – exhibiting a healthy balance between order and disorder.

they may not be fully conscious of the fact, contemporary critics are already contaminated at source and carry within them the very attributes that they have most feared and strongly rejected. In Freudian terms, this is a classic case of a 'return of the repressed'.

This criticism merits an explanation. Given that the authors are genuinely calling for more differentiation of the built environment, more variety, more identifiable specificities, in opposition to the generic, one would expect, in the texts and in the design examples that are given as illustrations of the newly emerging paradigm, convincing demonstrations of bespoke customisation, singularities that would be as striking, as creatively 'illegitimate', as the magic words used by Lautréamont, in his time, to slay the literary beast.

However, what we read and see in the pages of this issue is still largely, with a few notable exceptions, an unconscious reproduction of the positivistic language and design tropes of neo-functionalism and of its technocratic problem-solving ideological models. Similarly to their Modernist forefathers, many of the contributing authors appear, surprisingly, to retain a blind faith that advances in technological modes of industrial fabrication and, more specifically, the contemporary shift from repetitive mass production to a new culture of 'mass customisation', whether it is in the realm of product design, home marketing, architecture or urbanism, will, without even remotely challenging the capitalist mode of ownership of these modes of production, lead to a better world.

Insufficient attention is given to the fact that customisation – which is correctly identified as being a most significant contemporary trend – is nevertheless, at this stage, primarily a smokescreen to further boost consumerism, obfuscating the fact that the customised differences that are claimed to be made available to supposedly enlightened and newly empowered customers, such as the Nike shoe variations or the 'objectile' permutations proposed by Bernard Cache, are fundamentally trivial pseudo-choices. They cannot in any way be compared with the profound semantic differences inherent to the truly heterogeneous Lautréamont sentence.

Complexity and Variety

What is true difference? What are the choices that are really significant for society and for individuals, not merely in their diminished role as captive consumers, but as sentient human beings seriously concerned about the quality of their lives and aspiring to a better future? What are the choices that matter? These are, in terms of their potential impact on the long-term evolution of architecture and urbanism, the crucial existential questions that underlie this important issue of *Δ*.

The belief of the guest-editor is that the time has come to look at the implications of mass customisation, not any more at the scale of small objects, but at the scale of the city. But are we, as designers, intellectually, professionally and ethically equipped to undertake such an ambitious task? Are we ready? Verebes's key hypothesis is, optimistically, that we now finally have the means to stop the endless expansion and reproduction of 'generic city' clones.

The essential question of our time is indeed clearly the following: how is it that the city, the largest and most complex

Social complexity and mixed uses: Nathan Road, Hong Kong

above: The complexity and variety of Hong Kong's traditional urban fabric go hand in hand with the thriving socioeconomic dynamics and mixed uses that are still characteristic of the city. Like so many cities in the Far East as well as globally, the gradual homogenisation of daily life – of living, shopping, working, leisure and cultural mores – is matched by a parallel homogenisation and impoverishment of the urban environment.

The illusion of choice

below: The pseudo-choices made available through the mass customisation of consumer products are prevalent in the marketing approach of major brands within the fashion industry and in product design. Behind the apparent colourful diversity, everybody ends up dressing roughly the same and wearing the same shoes. Will such customisation strategies eventually migrate to the marketing of architecture and urbanism?

The generic city: Ma On Shan, New Territories, Hong Kong

Away from the Central District, and particularly in the New Territories, the complexity and variety of Hong Kong Island's rich urban fabric is lost: hyper-dense public housing estates and podium/tower developments are gradually taking over, imposing the same generic Modernist typologies and replicating them relentlessly, as they do all over mainland China.

of all human artefacts, the one that is the most important to our individual lives as well as the most crucial for the survival of our species as a whole, appears to be a 'meme' that got stuck, unable to evolve any further?

Of all the creations of civilisation, the city is clearly the one that needs to embody the highest level of complexity and variety in order to be able to cope with unpredictable changes in the physical and social environments. According to the 'law of requisite variety' in cybernetics, any system created by man in order to describe – and control – another system needs to have at least the same amount of variety as the system under observation: can it be claimed that we now have such a highly evolved system?

Information theory provides us with tools to measure the degree of variety required for a system to be robust, but there is no need here to go into considerations of quantitative measurement: it is sufficient to trust our qualitative intuition. We know intuitively what variety is. We know that, as far as architecture and urbanism are concerned, it is to do not only with form, with topological and typological configurations, but also with a very large set of other variables, some physical, some non-physical. With respect to form, variety hinges particularly on the unstable balance between order and disorder. Stuart Kauffman has stated that, in order to survive, complex systems have to maintain themselves 'on the edge of chaos':[2] in other

The umbrella movement: Nathan Road, Hong Kong

The choices that matter most for the future evolution of cities are the political ones. Freedom of expression and truly democratic processes of local political representation are the only way to counter the homogenising dynamics of centralised totalitarian regimes. This was the message conveyed by a significant portion of Hong Kong's population, expressing not only the desire to freely elect their own government representatives, but also questioning the materialistic values of consumerism as well as the social and urban environments that come with it.

words, the city has to have enough intrinsic order and regularity to maintain some degree of coherence, but enough disorder to be able to cope with the unknown and potentially with the advent of catastrophic events. Variety is not a question of aesthetics, it is a question of survival.

New Paradigms

I do agree with Verebes that a new paradigm has to be considered, one that can enhance the city's level of complexity and variety. But then the onus is on us to give the new paradigm a definition and configuration that do justice to the search for alternative urban models. In this respect, the various examples of design projects given in this publication are not yet fully convincing, because they do not yet possess the requisite degree of variety.

We are given, from the start, a critique of the Ville Radieuse as the archetypal example of the dreaded Modernist city (see pp 8–17), but we cannot help but notice that Le Corbusier's ghost still appears to haunt persistently the customisation experiments we are given to look at in its place. All the outcomes seem, in essence, to look the same. To be more precise: the variations tend to be concerned with relatively trivial variables, not profound ones. Permutations on facade treatments, or even on more substantial fragments of urban fabric, are not indicative of profound urbanistic transformations.

To imagine true variations from the city as we know it is not an easy undertaking. It requires taking on board not just the promising developments of more flexible and responsive manufacturing methods – and in this respect, the interview with the E-Grow practice in Shanghai (see pp 114–21) is a particularly good example – but many other experiments in the social and political realm as well as the adoption of a much more diverse set of theoretical, creative and poetic starting points.

Even in the luminous case of Italo Calvino, whose 'invisible cities'[3] opened our eyes as to how radically different cities of the mind can be conjured up by an erudite and playful imagination, the alternatives that are proposed are, on closer examination, not so very different from one another: their composition follows classic rules of contrasted opposition, antinomies and symmetry that ultimately limit the overall range of variety and strangeness of these hypothetical cities.

It is probably Colin Rowe who, starting with a similar critique of Modernism, has been the most successful so far at developing, with his 'collage city',[4] both a philosophical concept of a scope comparable to the ambitions of Modernism as well as a consistent design methodology to implement a new paradigm of fragmented differentiation in urbanism, also leading to appropriately different modes of analysis and representation.

If what we are seeking is truly a different form of urbanism, one that would no longer be based, as it is now, not only in mainland China, but universally, on a perpetuation of the status quo, perhaps what needs to be questioned first is the underlying preconception that the city is the only possible form of habitat that can ever be envisaged for the settlement of our species on planet Earth.

If urbanisation is the problem, how can continued urbanisation, whether 'customised' or not, be seen to be the solution? Surely one of the most radical antidotes would be to look into the possibility of swinging the pendulum in the opposite direction, that of the decentralisation and revitalisation of rural habitats? The exponential growth of urbanisation is taken as inevitable and this fundamental question is eluded, except for what transpires from the interview with Kenneth Frampton (see pp 24–31), whose contribution comes across as one of the most articulate dissenting theoretical positions in this issue, perhaps not surprising from the author of 'radical regionalism'.

This issue of AD addresses an extremely challenging topic. If I find fault with it, it is precisely because it is so ambitious and so well aimed that, no matter how perspicacious the search may be, one can only scratch the surface of its implications. Paradoxically, the partly unintentional oxymoron that lies within its title, with the juxtaposition of the two words 'mass' and 'customisation', reveals what might be its inherent Achilles' heel. AD

Bottom-up customisation: Street market, Central District, Hong Kong

The paradox of 'mass customisation' is that it clearly implies a top-down process of decision-making. A process of benevolent despotism, at best. It can be argued that true customisation can only emerge as the unpredictable outcome of bottom-up initiatives taken by individuals in the city. The hawker stalls and street markets in Hong Kong (as well as the illegal dwellings of informal settlements) are perfect examples of true customisation: all are inventive permutations of a basic typology and, inevitably, they are quickly being eradicated as unacceptable anomalies in the generic city.

Notes

1. Comte de Lautréamont, *Les Chants de Maldoror*, Éditions de la Baconnière, Geneva, 2012 (first published 1868).
2. Stuart Kauffman, *At Home in the Universe: The Search for the Laws of Self-Organisation and Complexity*, Oxford University Press (New York), 1995.
3. Italo Calvino, *Invisible Cities*, (*Le città invisibili*, 1972), trans William Weaver, Harcourt Brace & Company (San Diego, New York and London), 1974.
4. Colin Rowe and Fred Koetter, *Collage City*, MIT Press (Cambridge, MA), 1983.

CONTRIBUTORS

Donald Bates is the Chair of Architectural Design at the Melbourne School of Design, University of Melbourne, and is Director of LAB Architecture Studio, which he founded with Peter Davidson in 1994, and which won the competition for Federation Square, Melbourne. Through offices in Melbourne and Shanghai, LAB has built projects in Australia, Europe, the Middle East and Asia. Professor Bates has lectured and directed workshops across six continents and in more than 200 schools of architecture, and published extensively. He has been an invited juror for more than 20 international design competitions.

Michael Bell is a tenured Professor of Architecture at Columbia University, New York. He chairs the Columbia Conference on Architecture, Engineering and Materials; a School of Architecture collaboration with the Fu Foundation School of Engineering and Applied Science and the Institute for Lightweight Structures and Conceptual Design. His architectural design has been commissioned by the Museum of Modern Art (MoMA), New York, and is included in the permanent collection of the San Francisco Museum of Modern Art. His Binocular House is featured in Kenneth Frampton's *American Masterworks: Houses of the 20th and 21st Centuries* (1995).

M Christine Boyer is the William R Kenan Jr Professor at the School of Architecture, Princeton University. She is the author of *Le Corbusier: homme de lettres* (Princeton Architectural Press, 2011), *CyberCities: Visual Perception in the Age of Electronic Communication* (Princeton Architectural Press, 1996), *The City of Collective Memory: Its Historical Imagery and Architectural Entertainments* (MIT Press, 1994), *Manhattan Manners: Architecture and Style 1850–1890* (Rizzoli, 1985) and *Dreaming the Rational City: The Myth of City Planning 1890–1945* (MIT Press, 1983). She is currently preparing for publication a book entitled *Not Quiet Architecture: Writing Around Alison and Peter Smithson*. She received her PhD and Master's in City Planning from the Massachusetts Institute of Technology (MIT). She holds a Master's of Science in Computer and Information Science from the University of Pennsylvania, The Moore School of Electrical Engineering.

Martin Bressani is an architect and architectural historian, and Director of McGill University's School of Architecture in Montreal. He has published in many of the topical forums for architectural debates such as *Assemblage*, *Any Magazine* and *Log*, and contributed essays to many books and scholarly journals such as the American *Journal of the Society of Architectural Historians* and *Studies in the History of Art*, the French *Revue de l'art*, the German *Architectura: Zeitschrift für Geschichte der Baukunst*, the British *Art History* and the Canadian *Annals in the History of Canadian Art*. He is the author of a monograph on the French architect and theoretician Eugène-Emmanuel Viollet-le-Duc titled *Architecture and the Historical Imagination: Eugène-Emmanuel Viollet-le-Duc* (Ashgate, 2004).

Mark Burry is a practising architect, and has published on Antoni Gaudí, and on putting theory into practice with 'challenging' architecture. He is Senior Architect to the Sagrada Família Basilica Foundation, pioneering distant collaboration with his Barcelona colleagues. In December 2014 he joined the University of Melbourne as Professor of Urban Futures at the Faculty of Architecture, Building and Planning, where he will further develop the faculty's capacity to consolidate research in urban futures, drawing together expertise in urban visualisation, analytics and policy. Prior to this appointment, he was the Founding Director of RMIT University's Design Research Institute (DRI) and also founded the university's state-of-the-art Spatial Information Architecture Laboratory (SIAL).

Elad Eisenstein is a director at Arup and the leader for urban design and masterplanning in the UK, Middle East and Africa region. He has 15 years' international experience working on large-scale, complex urban projects with sustainability at their core and leading multidisciplinary teams globally. Combining conceptual design and city strategy skills with experience in implementation, he has won various international design competitions and advises public and private sector bodies on urban design, large-scale planning and city strategy. He lectures on sustainable urbanism and is a design tutor at the Architectural Association (AA) Graduate School in London. He further serves as an invited critic at various international universities.

David Erdman and Clover Lee are founding directors of davidclovers, which was established in 2007. They have completed over 15 projects since the practice's relocation to Hong Kong in 2009, and has won numerous international awards and lectured widely. The work of davidclovers has been exhibited in group and solo shows at various museums as well as in Asian and European biennales. Erdman is currently an Assistant Professor at the University of Hong Kong Department of Architecture where he also serves as the MArch Thesis Chair. He taught at the University of California, Los Angeles (UCLA) from 1999 to 2008, and has been a Visiting Professor at Rice University, the University of California, Berkeley and the University of Michigan. The American Academy in Rome awarded him with the prestigious Rome Prize in 2008/09. Lee was an Assistant Professor at Rice University from 2004 to 2008, where she was also the Director of the Rice School of Architecture China (RSAC). She has been a Visiting Professor at the University of Michigan and currently serves as an external examiner for the Chinese University Hong Kong School of Architecture.

Colin Fournier was educated at the AA in London. He is Emeritus Professor of Architecture and Urbanism at the Bartlett School of Architecture, University College London (UCL), where he has been Director of the Master of Architecture course in Urban Design as well as Director of Diploma Unit 18. He is currently Visiting Professor at the Chinese University of Hong Kong (CUHK) and Chairman of TETRA X, an architectural and urban design practice based in Hong Kong.

Kenneth Frampton is a renowned architectural historian, critic and the Ware Professor of Architecture at the Graduate School of Architecture, Planning and Preservation (GSAPP) at Columbia University. He has also taught at a number of leading institutions including the Royal College of Art (RCA), ETH Zurich, EPFL Lausanne, the Accademia di Architettura in Mendrisio, and the Berlage Institute in the Netherlands. His books include: *Modern Architecture: A Critical History* (Thames & Hudson, 1980; revised 1985, 1992 and 2007); *Studies in Tectonic Culture* (MIT Press, 1995); *Labour, Work and Architecture* (Phaidon, 2002); and *A Genealogy of Modern Architecture: Comparative Critical Analysis of Built Form* (Lars Müller, 2015).

Fabio Gramazio and Matthias Kohler are architects with multidisciplinary interests ranging from computational design and robotic fabrication to material innovation. In 2000 they founded the architecture practice Gramazio Kohler Architects, which has realised numerous award-wining designs. Opening also the world's first architectural robotic laboratory at ETH Zurich, Fabio Gramazio's and Matthias Kohler's research has been formative in the field of digital architecture, through the merging of advanced architectural design and additive robotic fabrication. The have been Principal Investigators at the SEC Futures Cities Laboratory (Module II) since 2011. Their work has been published in a large number of publications, and part of numerous exhibitions, including the 2008 Architectural Biennale in Venice, the Storefront Gallery for Art and Architecture, New York (2009) and 'Flight Assembled Architecture' in Orléans, France (2011).

Jeffrey Huang is a Professor and the Head of the Architecture and Sustainable Design Pillar at the Singapore University of Technology and Design (SUTD), and Director of the Media x Design Lab at the EPFL in Lausanne. His work examines the convergence of physical and digital architecture. He holds a Diploma in Architecture from ETH Zurich, and Master's and Doctoral Degrees from Harvard Graduate School of Design (GSD). In collaboration with Muriel Waldvogel, he heads the strategic design firm Convergeo, based in Switzerland.

Branko Kolarevic is a Professor and Chair in Integrated Design at the University of Calgary Faculty of Environmental Design. He has taught architecture at several universities in North America and Asia, and has lectured worldwide on the use of digital technologies in design and production. He has authored, edited or co-edited several books, including *Building Dynamics: Exploring Architecture of Change* (Routledge, 2015), *Manufacturing Material Effects* (Routledge, 2008), *Performative Architecture: Beyond Instrumentality* (Routledge, 2004) and *Architecture in the Digital Age* (Taylor & Francis, 2005). He holds doctoral and Master's degrees in design from Harvard University, and a diploma engineer in architecture degree from the University of Belgrade.

Jerry Ku studied architecture at the Chinese Culture University in Taiwan. He started an architecture firm with several classmates before founding his own building materials company in Taipei. In 1997 he moved to Shanghai to start E-Grow and gradually began to expand into custom-moulded fibre-glass composites. While working on the Guangzhou Opera House, he invented the wax mould system allowing panels to be produced with minimal mould waste. He continues to innovate to bring digital design together with high-quality materials.

Christian J Lange is a founding partner of Rocker-Lange Architects, a research and design practice based in Boston and Hong Kong. He is a registered German architect and Assistant Professor of Architecture in the Department of Architecture at the University of Hong Kong. His work and research on alternative building typologies and housing structures has been published internationally and featured in numerous exhibitions, including the Venice Biennale (2010) and the Hong Kong and Shenzhen Bi-city Biennale (2012 and 2014).

Neil Leach is Professor at the European Graduate School, Visiting Professor at Harvard GSD and Tongji University, Adjunct Professor at the University of Southern California (USC), and a NASA Innovative Advanced Concepts Fellow. He is currently working on a research project funded by NASA to develop a robotic fabrication technology to print structures on the Moon and Mars. He has published 25 books, which have been translated into six languages. His recent publications on computational design include *Machinic Processes* (CABP, 2010), *Fabricating the Future* (Tongji University Press, 2012), *Scripting the Future* (Tongji University Press, 2012), *Design Intelligence: Advanced Computational Research* (CABP, 2013) and *Swarm Intelligence* (Tongji University Press, forthcoming).

Elena Manferdini, principal and owner of Atelier Manferdini, has over 15 years of professional experience in architecture, art, design and education. She received a Professional Engineering Degree from the University of Civil Engineering (Bologna, Italy) and a Master of Architecture and Urban Design from UCLA. She currently teaches at the Southern California Institute of Architecture (SCI-Arc), where she is Graduate Programs Chair. In 2013 she received a Graham Award for architecture, the ACADIA Innovative Research Award of Excellence, and was selected as recipient for the Educator of the Year presidential award given by the AIA Los Angeles.

Rob May is an Associate Director at BuroHappold Engineering based in Beijing where he leads the structures team. He has over 10 years of experience in structural engineering across a broad range of built projects around the world. He joined BuroHappold Leeds as a Graduate Engineer, has since worked in the Leeds and New York offices, and was a founding member of the Los Angeles office. He joined the Hong Kong office in its early days in late 2009 and has since transitioned to China to help establish a presence on the mainland.

Ali Rahim and Hina Jamelle have established an award-winning profile in futuristic designs using digital techniques for the design and manufacturing of architecture. They have both been named as one of the 'Top 50 Innovators in the discipline of architecture in the 21st Century'. The evidence is in their work for their project designs commissioned by significant global brands such as Reebok, Viceroy Hotel, Samsung, Lutron, and MoMA. The resulting projects have been exhibited extensively, and their work published globally in newspapers, magazines, books and journals. They have also been awarded the Architectural Record Product of the Month (2007) for the fixture titled 'Opale' for Ivalo, as well as the Outstanding Far Eastern International Digital Design Award (FEIDAD) 2006. In 2005, their work was selected for Phaidon Press's *10x10x2* by 10 internationally prominent critics, architects and curators. Contemporary Architecture Practice also won the prestigious Architectural Design Vanguard Award (2004) as one of 11 practices worldwide 'building the future of architecture'.

Philip Vernon studied in the Bachelor of Architecture programme at Rensselaer Polytechnic Institute (RPI) from 2007 until 2012. In 2010 he designed a small chapel in Cameroon in conjunction with Method Design. He joined E-Grow as an intern in 2011, and became full-time in 2012. He currently divides his interests between composite materials and contemporary culture.

Jan Willmann is Senior Research Assistant at the Chair of Architecture and Digital Fabrication at ETH Zurich. He studied architecture in Liechtenstein, Oxford and Innsbruck where he received his PhD degree in 2010. He was previously a research assistant and lecturer at the Chair of Architectural Theory of Professor Ir Bart Lootsma, and gained professional experience in numerous architectural offices. His research focuses on digital architecture and its theoretical implications as a composed computational and material score. He has lectured and exhibited internationally, and published extensively, including *The Robotic Touch: How Robots Change Architecture* (Park Books, 2014).

Philip F Yuan is an Associate Professor in Architecture at Tongji University in Shanghai, and the director of the Digital Design Research Center (DDRC) at the College of Architecture and Urban Planning (CAUP), Tongji University. He is also the founder and director of Archi-Union Architects. As one of the founders of the Digital Architectural Design Association (DADA) of the Architectural Society of China (ASC), his research and practice focuses on digital design and fabrication methodology with the combination of Chinese traditional material and craftsmanship. His publications include *A Tectonic Reality* (China Architecture & Building Press, 2011) and *Theater Design* (Tongji University Press, 2012), and he is co-editor with Neil Leach of *Fabricating the Future and Scripting the Future (*Tongji University Press, 2012) and *Digital Workshop in China* (Tongji University Press, 2013).

What is *Architectural Design*?

Founded in 1930, *Architectural Design* (AD) is an influential and prestigious publication. It combines the currency and topicality of a newsstand journal with the rigour and production qualities of a book. With an almost unrivalled reputation worldwide, it is consistently at the forefront of cultural thought and design.

Each title of AD is edited by an invited Guest-Editor, who is an international expert in the field. Renowned for being at the leading edge of design and new technologies, AD also covers themes as diverse as architectural history, the environment, interior design, landscape architecture and urban design.

Provocative and inspirational, AD inspires theoretical, creative and technological advances. It questions the outcome of technical innovations as well as the far-reaching social, cultural and environmental challenges that present themselves today.

For further information on AD, subscriptions and purchasing single issues see:

www.architectural-design-magazine.com

Volume 84 No 6
ISBN 978 1118 663301

Volume 85 No 1
ISBN 978 1118 759066

Volume 85 No 2
ISBN 978 1118 700570

Volume 85 No 3
ISBN 978 1118 829011

Volume 85 No 4
ISBN 978 1118 914830

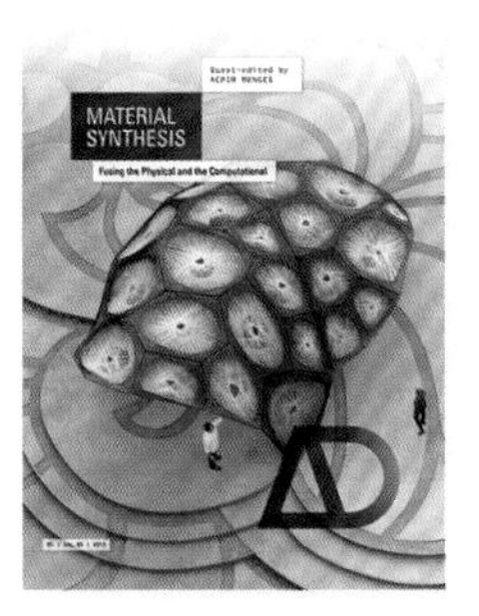

Volume 85 No 5
ISBN 978 1118 878378

Individual backlist issues of AD are available as books for purchase at £24.99 / US$39.95

www.wiley.com

How to Subscribe
With 6 issues a year, you can subscribe to AD (either print, online or through the AD App for iPad)

Institutional subscription
£212 / US$398 print or online

Institutional subscription
£244 / US$457 combined print and online

Personal-rate subscription
£120 / US$189 print and iPad access

Student-rate subscription
£75 / US$117 print only

AD App for iPad
6-issue subscription: £44.99 / US$64.99
Individual issue: £9.99 / US$13.99

To subscribe to print or online
E: cs-journals@wiley.com

Americas
E: cs-journals@wiley.com
T: +1 781 388 8598 or +1 800 835 6770 (toll free in the USA & Canada)

Europe, Middle East and Africa
E: cs-journals@wiley.com
T: +44 (0) 1865 778315

Asia Pacific
E: cs-journals@wiley.com
T: +65 6511 8000

Japan (for Japanese-speaking support)
E: cs-japan@wiley.com
T: +65 6511 8010 or 005 316 50 480 (toll-free)

Visit our Online Customer Help available in 7 languages at www.wileycustomerhelp.com/ask

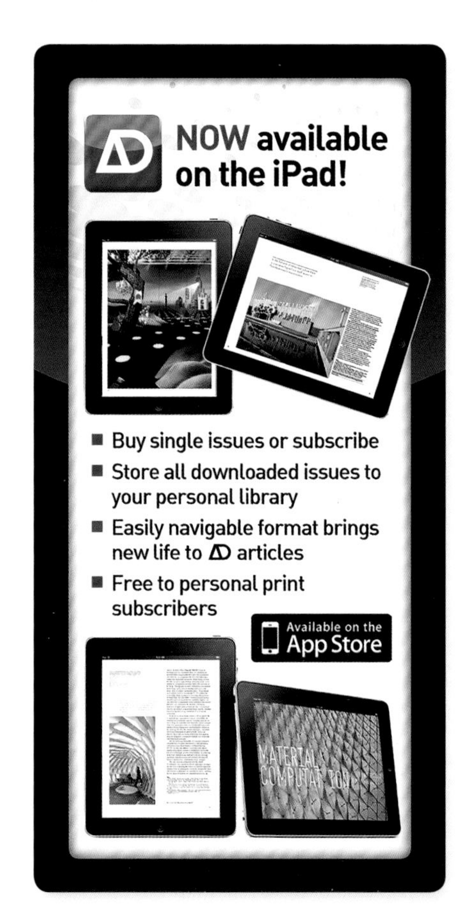